BEEN T...
DON...

Best Wishes

Steve Ludzik

Steve Ludzik
with Steve Wilson

Library and Archives Canada Cataloguing in Publication

Ludzik, Steve, 1961-
Been there, done that/Steve Ludzik; with Steve Wilson.

ISBN 978-0-9865273-0-2

1. Ludzik, Steve, 1961-. 2. Hockey players--Biography.
3. Hockey coaches--Biography. 4. National Hockey League--
Biography I. Wilson,Steve, 1958- II Title

GV848.5.L84A3 2010   796.962092   C2010-900457-4

© 2010 Steve Ludzik

ISBN 978-0-9865273-0-2

Publisher
Ludzy Inc.
www.ludzy.com

Editing and Project Management
Debbie Elicksen, Freelance Communications, Calgary, Alberta

Design and Production
Nadien Cole Advertising, Calgary, Alberta

Been There, Done That – First Edition

Printed and Bound in China
Copyright 2010

What They're Saying About Ludzy's Book

"The reason I always got along with Ludzy is because we were two of the same: a lot of fun, a lot of laughs but a lot of hard work, also. He's a straight up guy, and he pulls no punches in this book – just the way Ludzy's always been. You gotta respect that in a man. This is the funniest hockey book I've ever read."

Paul Coffey

"This is the funniest book I've ever read and it's from a man who's done it all and done it well. If Ludzy's your friend, you're a lucky person. He's the real deal. What you see is what you get. And in this book, "Been There, Done That," you get a real look inside the game from one of the greatest characters I've ever met."

Clint Malarchuk

"I have always told people the greatest part about playing this game is not the goals you score or the places it takes you, but the people you meet. Steve Ludzik is one of the greatest. I have played with a lot of people over the years, but none of them has been a better teammate and friend than Steve Ludzik. We laughed together, cried together, and fought together. In this book, Ludzy talks about many of our adventures together and many others I had not heard before. I'm sure you will laugh at all the stories as much as I did. He tells it the way it was."

Steve Larmer

"Steve Ludzik's storytelling was a big part of the Blackhawks dressing room in the 1980s. I had the great pleasure of playing with and coaching him, and believe me, he was a colorful character. The book is for sure very funny, very insightful and very refreshing. It's about time he put all his B.S. on paper."

Darryl Sutter

"What can I say about my buddy Steve Ludzik. Because he is blessed with a retentive mind and is able to recall in detail, he is uniquely able to describe the great stories and events that could only happen to him. Ludzy is a what you see is what you get guy. A man void of any agenda and has not an ounce of politician in him – a trait that is very rare in the hockey world. I'll always treasure my friendship with Ludzy."

Rick Dudley

"Ludzy is a love him or leave him type of guy. There is nothing in the middle. His fuck you-I-will-do-what-is-needed-clean-or-dirty-to-win attitude was always on display. Walking to school with my best friend every day meant you'd better be ready for action at all times. Being involved in countless tussles and scuffles along the way, I know Ludzy was never, ever going to lose for lack of effort or lack of heart.

"As his best friend for more than 46 years, I am biased. The man is a brother. We talk the same. Our mannerisms are identical. We finish each other's thoughts. We laugh at the same things. I call Ludzy my pick and shovel man. If I needed some shoveling, he would not ask questions. He would just dig in. I carry a piece of Steve Ludzik with me wherever I go."

John Kirk

Dedication

To my dad, I never got the chance to say thank you.

With love and respect to my mom, wife Mary Ann,
sons Stephen and Ryan...to my hockey brothers who tried
to climb the mountain and either made it or slipped and
tumbled along the way.

Steve Ludzik

To my beautiful wife Cathy, son Scott, and daughter
Kendyl, who endured many hours of reviewing the stories
for this book.

To my Mom and Dad (big Frank), who would have loved
the stories in this book.

Steve Wilson

1967 on Centennial Pond – that's me on the left, with my dad Ted Ludzik and my best friend John Kirk on the right

There is no doubt in my mind that the driving force behind Steve Ludzik's success in hockey was his father Ted.

Ted was a big, gruff but lovable character, who wanted only the best for his son Stephen, especially when it came to hockey. Our families have lived side by side for almost 50 years, and it is a unique friendship. We have always been there for each other, good times and bad.

My earliest memories are of Stephen and Ted on a frozen pond at Centennial Park that "Teddy" had found. Ted would spend hours and hours with his son on this frozen surface, all alone, much like Wayne Gretzky's dad Walter. Ted was no dummy. He was not going to spend hours prepping for ice when "the pond" was five minutes away.

Eventually, he told me about it and my son John would also spend hours skating on that same frozen surface.

The fact a "no trespassing" sign and a bright green "no skating" sign were clearly posted were of no consequence to Ted Ludzik. The fact he had spent the time and effort to train young Stephen paid off. He was always the most dynamic skater on every team he played for. In fact, it was largely his calling card. He had a great stride.

From the age of six, Stephen and John played on the same hockey teams. Eventually, both were drafted and played major junior A in Niagara Falls. Ted and I shared in the driving to tournaments, games, and to practices. It was usually a five or six nights a week act of love.

It was during those car rides that Ted and I formed a special friendship. I quickly admired his passion. He left nothing to chance – to say something or chance missing a small detail. He coached in a very modulated but direct way and made sure his son knew what he was expected to do. Number one was effort. I would usually have the same chat with my son when we got home. Ted made sure he got it off his chest right then and there.

The Ludziks and the Kirks have a very special bond. My wife Bette, who also did a lot of driving with Ted, passed away two years ago. She was a very special woman. Sadly, Ted died very young, but lived just long enough to see his son play in the NHL. Because of this, Steve has always looked at me as his second father for the last 25 years. I know the great friendship between the Ludziks and Kirks was forged on the pond at Centennial Park so many winters ago.

Norman Kirk

The True Grit One...with Donald S. Cherry before a game versus the
Leafs at the ACC, maybe the greatest Canadian of all time – a friend
and the ultimate foxhole guy. A what you see is what you get guy.
It gets no better than that.

Foreword

Steve Ludzik and I are kindred spirits. We both played junior hockey for the same organization. Steve: the Niagara Falls Flyers, and me: the Barrie Flyers. At the end of Steve's career, he was captain of the Rochester Americans of the American Hockey League. I was also captain of the Rochester Americans at the end of my career. We both coached in the AHL and NHL, and we both coached the same team in the Ontario Hockey League: The Mississauga Ice Dogs. We both spent many, many hours on the buses. We both played in the NHL, but we differ here. I played one game and Steve played 424. We are both on TV now, sharp dressers, and good looking. We both wrote stories on our careers, so I am qualified to write a foreword for his book!

When you coach the great Gordie Howe in his last professional game, you know you got something going for you. I love the stories on Mike Keenan, Denis Savard, Behn Wilson, and Tom Lysiak, to name a few.

Steve has done and seen it all. He has paid his dues, as has Mary Ann, his beautiful wife, who packed the car and made all those stops along the way. This is a book about two people who "stuck it out," as they say.

I know you're going to love it; I couldn't put it down.

Don Cherry

Introduction

Let's Giddy Up

As my name was called out over the public address system, I smiled like a bulldog in a butcher shop. I was escorted to the podium at the front of the Hilton Ballroom in Niagara Falls. Amongst family, friends, fans, and even a couple of foes, the gala event was held to name the greatest Niagara Falls Flyers of all time. As I stood and acknowledged the applause, my mind quickly went into rewind mode – the draft that brought me to Niagara Falls, my first National Hockey League goal, the Turner Cup we won in the International Hockey League, my hiring and firing as head coach of the Tampa Bay Lightning, and the television show on The Score, which is seen coast to coast.

Then, as if hit by a lightning bolt, a sobering thought streaked across my mind, "Man, I almost didn't make it here."

This is my story, which includes the good, the bad, and the ugly – the highs and lows while living the Canadian dream. You'll meet the famous and the infamous, plain and simple. You will laugh your ass off, scratch your head in disbelief, and I know you will find inspiration on these pages.

I want you to come down to my den, grab a beer, and spend a few hours with me as I weave you through a plethora of my favorite hockey tales: stories of success and triumph, failure and tragedy, and you will find fact stranger than fiction in the hit or be hit world of hockey.

To those people who have often told me I should write a book, here it is – warts and all – the way I want to write it. Remember that I will never get into the NHL Hall of Fame without a ticket, but hopefully some of these gems will.

Oh yeah, by the way, the other Niagara Falls Flyers on that All Time Team included Bernie Parent in goal, Rick Ley, Bryan Fogarty on defense, and up front, there was Derek Sanderson, Steve Larmer, and yours truly. I now know what a mule feels like in a thoroughbred race.

Okay, let's giddy up…

Steve Ludzik

Table of Contents

Nightmare and a Vow

It almost never happened. In the spring of 1978, at 16 years old, I was allowed to go home for the weekend, and my mom drove south on Bathurst Street from the Wellesley Hospital and turned right along Lakeshore Boulevard. I distinctly remember it was a dark, dreary, rainy night, very appropriate for the situation I now faced. It had been three short months since I was diagnosed with Crohn's disease and colitis.

Having gone from a muscular 160 pounds to a gaunt 130 pounds, I was extremely weak, had no energy, and was at my wit's end. I went from a kid who could not stand still to a young man who could barely get up a flight of stairs. I was depressed and could not understand why this was happening to me. I had never touched drugs or even had a sip of a beer – and cigarettes – they were for bums that weren't going to be athletes. I even made homemade weights in my basement, which included old paint cans filled with rocks and concrete cement attached to an old broken hockey stick that I used like a French curl barbell. I read a book penned by a man named Lloyd Percival, who talked about conditioning and the positive effects of off-ice training. The street I lived on was, in actuality, a large circle that was exactly 2.2 miles around. I ran around it in the dead of night so no one would see me and think "that boy is nuts." I never neglected my health but had probably taken it for granted, like most kids. Not knowing what else to do or to think, I was worried that my hockey career might be over before it even started.

I remember telling my mom, "This is the darkest day in my life."

To this day, I can barely stand to look at pictures from that Christmas. When I do, I squirm, shift, and fidget, and eventually look away, for I do not recognize the young man in the photographs. I was smiling but not a natural grin. I was in pain, both physically and mentally. I knew even then the next eight months would no doubt have a great bearing on the direction my life would take; it would shape my resolve, toughen me up, make me realize what was important and what was not, teach me to read people, and make me realize that no matter how tough things got, it could never get this bad again. It would take a great deal of luck, too. Looking back, I had a will to survive, which held me in good stead for the different directions my life would go in.

Barb Ludzik (Mom): Lots of people knew he was sick, but I don't think anyone knew how ill he really was. He was literally fighting for his life, never mind hockey. I remember going to see him at the Wellesley, and Stephen lifted his undershirt up and said, 'Who would believe this, Mom?'

I went home and told my husband that he'd better forget any thought of him playing hockey again, ever. My husband's response was that he didn't want to hear it. That year, he was so deathly ill. I could not have cared less if he ever played hockey again. I just wanted him to have a normal life and thought at the time, it was going to be next to impossible. When he got out of the hospital, he wrote a note to himself. I still have that note dated Saturday, February 11, 1978. He tucked it in his old Christmas sock and it read:

My wish is that next year at this time, I will be in excellent health or back on the track.

Wishes do come true. By the next Christmas, he was flying high in Niagara Falls.

I vividly remember lying in my hospital bed late at night listening to my old transistor radio and coming across a show about the Ontario Hockey League, which back then was called the Ontario Hockey Association. I got addicted to this fascinating voice that sounded like it was emanating from a basement apartment. None of the patients in my room shared my enthusiasm for the show.

"Hey kid, can you turn that thing off; I'm sick ya know," they would plead.

I would answer, "Yeah, well, so am I, Pops!"

I would tuck it under my pillow and try to muffle the sound, but at exactly 11:15 pm every night, I would hear that magical voice. A gentleman named Tommy Garriock from radio station CKTB in St. Catharines would take his time and seemed to be able to talk as long as he wanted. He took me on a magical carpet ride throughout the OHA, from Windsor to Ottawa, Kingston to Sudbury. No destination was ever out of his reach. Describing the heroics of Bobby Smith, or the goal scoring of Mike Gartner, no name was too big or too small for this man's radio show. The legendary Garriock delivered the most extensive, in depth coverage of junior A hockey I had ever heard. A typical broadcast would start out something like this:

"There were six games on the schedule tonight. Let's go to Sudbury where the Wolves, led by Mike Foligno, defeat the visiting Toronto Marlies by a score of 7-6."

Many times the transistor would fade in and out for a micro second like an extraterrestrial lost in orbit, but this would only add to the mystique of the program. Mr. Garriock would, in the same order, tell you the score, a short headline of the game, and then proceed to run down all the scoring plays and finish off with the three stars, and even the attendance.

I made a deal with myself one night while listening to that larger than life show. On that night, I think Tommy McCarthy had scored a hat trick for the Generals in Oshawa versus the London Knights. Tommy was a great player who was a year older than me, so I knew exactly who he was. Today, they would call it visualization, but after that broadcast, I made a mental image of a three-rung ladder that I was going to climb in order to escape from this nightmare I was living.

The first step was priority number one. I had to get my health back. The second rung involved rebuilding my body, making it stronger, and gaining back the almost 30 pounds I had lost. But I had to make sure it was only muscle I was gaining. And the third rung was hearing Steve Ludzik's name being announced across the air waves on Tommy Garriock's radio show. Just as I had heard Tom McCarthy's name barked out, I would know I was back when my name was included in that great broadcast.

It would turn out to be the first of many obstacles and hurdles that I would have to overcome to make a career out of hockey, and it began to shape my life.

The Early Years

My early start in hockey mirrored millions of youngsters across Canada in that it began at a young age. I was three when my parents propped me up on an outdoor rink in New Toronto in the dead of winter. Although no one has asked recently to see that footage, I still have it on eight-millemeter tape.

Ludzy with best friend John Kirk at age six

Many folks believe I am originally from Niagara Falls. Stephen Paul Ludzik was born and raised in Etobicoke. My mother and father were both from the rough and tumble area of the "Lakeshore," a fact they were both very proud of. I was signed up to play in the famous Faustina Hockey League in 1965. There was one small problem. You had to be at least five years old to join the six-team league, and I was only four. Much to my mother's dismay, my father "forgot" to inform the league of my age, so I got in.

"He's the next Frank Mahovlich," my dad would joke at the tryouts to anyone listening. Tryouts? Talk about a cattle call. There must have been 60 kids, all with numbers pinned to their shoulders, zooming around the Lakeshore Arena ice. Some were skating clockwise, some counterclockwise, some crying, and some doing snow angels in front of less than impressed coaches who sat in the stands and tried to pick a team from this mish mash of talent. Talk about little lambs at auction.

I did not score a goal my first two seasons. I don't even recall touching the puck very often in my house league apprenticeship. My dad tried to teach me the basics.

Remember those old table hockey games with the tin hockey players that all looked like funeral directors and "skated" up and down the board on a track? With the PlayStation games of today's generation, any goal dispute will go to instant replay. Back in the 1960s, any disputed calls would usually result in the 10-pound rink being tossed to the ground and 12 metal midgets scattering across the floor.

My dad would say, "Stephen, bring that board up here. I want to show you something."

After examining the dents and fresh divots on the game and giving me a sideways glance, he would go over a few things. Now, rest assured, he was not breaking down the trap or explaining a neutral zone counter, but he would impart basic knowledge on me that made sense even then.

"Why the hell, when seven guys are all around the puck like flies on cow shit, do you always come into the scrum! Anticipate where the puck is going to come out. Jeeeesssssuuuusssss."

I believe it was the same oratory that Walter Gretzky was giving to his son, Wayne, down the highway in Brantford. Either Walter had a better way of explaining the basic skills and anticipation, or the Great One was just born that way. I have always said that great hockey players are born and not made.

I then graduated to the old Metropolitan Toronto Hockey League, better known as the MTHL. I played for a number of teams in that league, including the Toronto Olympics and the Don Valley Jacks Pack, which was owned by the late John F. Bassett of Toronto Telegram fame.

The Don Valley Jacks Pack - that's me front row left.

From the age of 10, when I was captain of the Toronto Olympics and scored 50 plus goals, I never wavered from my belief that I would one day play in the NHL. My confidence was bolstered when, a couple of days after one season, a package came to our home addressed to Steve

Ludzik. I opened the box and saw the most beautiful trophy I had seen in my life. It read: "Presented to Stephen Ludzik, Captain, Toronto Olympics, 51 Goals, 16 Assists."

The trophy solidified my belief in myself. Any doubt to whether I was good enough was washed away. I knew I could play. I might have to work on my playmaking ability, however, as 16 assists was pitiful. For several years after that, I always led the MTHL in scoring but found it odd that I never again received a trophy from the league. I always thought that was kind of strange, and cheap. Years later, when I was playing in junior in Niagara Falls, my father fessed up that he was the one who had purchased the trophy, had it engraved, and sent to the house.

I joined the Toronto Marlie organization in minor bantam, and one of my teammates was Paul Coffey. I'm not sure why we quickly became such good friends, but he often came to my house to play ball hockey, and generally goof around with me and my other buddies. To this day, Coffey and I call each other by the weird nickname of "Baldy Hawn."

Paul Coffey: We all had names for each other back then. I have no idea where 'Baldy Hawn' came from.

My minor hockey development was helped by the fact I would spend countless hours skating on Centennial Park pond, a frozen body of water near our home.

Paul Coffey: Ludz was a lot of fun. I remember the year we played together, he and I organized a massive shinny game on Centennial pond with our whole Marlie team. As we're getting our skates on to get ready to play, it began to rain, wind started to blow, and it was freezing cold. Everyone left except for me and Ludzy. There was

no way we were leaving. In hindsight, I think we formed a special bond that day, as we both realized we were equally committed to getting better.

After playing my first year of midget hockey with the Toronto Marlies at 16, I opted to go directly to Tier II Provincial Junior A hockey with the respected Markham Waxers. They were a feeder to the Toronto Marlies OHL club. There were very few 16 year olds in the loop. The league demanded a high level of physical and mental maturity. The time commitment was huge, not to mention what a road trip to North Bay and back did to your scholastic endeavors. To top it all off, the maximum age limit of the league was 20. The point is a lot of players were old. Paul Coffey and Tom McCarthy, to name but two, also elected to take the same route. The allure of being just one step away from the OHL was the tonic that made the decision easy.

Coff and I always had a lot of laughs together. He was a gifted boy who worked very hard to get to the top of the mountain. We worked hockey camps in the summer together. We would work all day, skate from four to six pm with a gang of guys, then "Baldy Hawn" and I would hit the weights for an hour afterwards.

One evening, we were driving home at maybe eight o'clock; Coff in his beat up Chevy and me in a brown beat up Mustang. Oh yeah, we're on the 401 going west, a route that's usually packed with angry drivers. Coffey's gas pedal got stuck and the car was going faster and faster. I could barely catch up to him and when I did, he waved frantically at me from the front seat. He hit the brake and his foot went through the floor board, now travelling at 80 miles an hour. Paul Coffey might as well have used the Fred Flintstone method of braking: his feet. As I watched in complete horror, the rambling relic slowed down, hit the guard rail at, say 40 miles an hour. The back end started literally bouncing, and the car careened backwards across the 401 and crashed against the other guard rail. The white, black, and blue smoke that poured out of the death machine made you feel like a Stelco foundry worker. My buddy had cooly slammed the car into reverse.

"Ludz, you would have been the last person to see me alive," a visibly shaken Coffey crowed.

Paul Coffey: Ludzy and I pushed the car off the highway, then got pulled over by the cops.

Baldy (Coffey) would pedal his bike an hour and a half to play ball hockey in my area with my pals. One afternoon, we had a beautiful game all set up: five guys on each team. We were excited but something happened before the ball dropped, and Coff and I got into a feverish tussle. He had a broken beak that was on the mend, so every time I wheeled back to throw a shot, he'd scream 'not my nose, Ludz!' And I'd hit him on the shoulder. This was a great friend I was battling here; you gotta fight fair, eh?

This went on for 30 minutes, like rams with their horns locked, Coff punching me in the head, and stupid me hitting him in the chest, to preserve his fractured proboscis. The guys, finally fed up with our churlish display and the inability to start the game, picked up the nets, sticks, and goalie equipment and quit. They just went home. They were thoroughly disgusted at both of us.

"Do us a favor and kill each other," yelled one guy, as another shouted "assholes." The two of us continued our grappling for another 10 minutes and then both of us, realizing at the same time that we had caused the cancelation of the much anticipated tilt, started laughing like two looney birds. Everyone had left the game site.

We actually had a "disagreement" in the Stanley Cup playoffs one year. I threw a punch and Coff grabbed me   in a cobra hold of some kind. I felt like a fucking calf having his hoofs tied up by a cowboy on the prairie plains. No damage done, but the old Chicago Stadium crowd was going crazy, as we sat in the penalty box with 20,000 maniacs of Madison Avenue screaming themselves hoarse. Coffey yelled over to me and I tried my best not to look. I knew what was coming, but eventually curiosity got the best of me. I had to look at my pal, who was in the sin bin giggling and laughing. I could only chuckle and think it was almost a flashback to that ball hockey game, played long ago when we were 13 years old. Hey, you can't make this up.

The Natural...that's me on the right and Paul Coffey on the left, my good friend. He was a quick skater with a quick wit, quick sense of humor, and a quick temper. We had a lot of fun along the way, and a few tussles, too.

Those who have seen me on The Score know I care little about statistics. Stats can lie and often camouflage weaknesses. When I was coaching, I did not have to look at the scoring summary to tell if a player had performed to his max that night. I could feel it. I know myself that I could sometimes score a couple of goals on a given night and not feel that I had played particularly well. And on another night, I would come up bagels on the score sheet and know I had played one hell of a game. The key is to not kid yourself.

Skating in Mud

In today's world of statistics where stats can easily be confirmed or denied via the Internet, athletes often equate their age to where they were in their hockey career in a particular year. In 1971, I wasn't 10 years old; I was in minor atom with the Jacks Pack. In 1979, oh yeah, I was in my first year of junior hockey. In 1985, I was in Chicago with the Blackhawks. In 1998, my team won the Turner Cup. And so on.

My 1977-78 season had a dark and dreadful feel to it. Statistics will simply read: Steve Ludzik, Markham Waxers, Provincial Junior A, 30 games played, 30 goals, 20 assists, 50 points. But during the last 15 games, because my illness was starting to rear its ugly head, I felt like I was skating in mud and shooting marshmallows. I had always been a lean kid, but my weight dropped 30 pounds. I was fighting a losing battle with Crohn's disease, which as most know, is an inflammation on the bowel. Any food I ate would shoot right through me.

<u>Karen Ludzik (sister)</u>: It was so bad that at the end, before he was treated properly, drinking even a glass of water would make him vomit. I would hear my brother come home at one am from a game or practice and hear him vomit for an hour. His disease was so rampant, his entire digestive tract was affected; any food could not even get to his colon. The inflammation had really spread. Mom was a nurse for 30 years, and I've been one for 25 years. Never saw as violent a case as this.

I was always a very good, solid skater, but now, with my strength sapped, I tipped over with the slightest bump and every hit shook me to the core. I would barrel up the ice, and after six or seven strides, I would be out of petrol with no gas station in sight.

The coach of the team, Bruce Wallace, pulled what was left of his hair out. Mr. Wallace coached the Young Nats the year before, and his prized pupil was a fellow from Brantford named Wayne Gretzky. One evening during my decline, Coach Bruce came over to me before a game, intending to instill a bit of confidence in me.

"You know, you remind me a lot of Wayne. You are both blonde, you both skate the same, you're both skinny, you have big noses, and you both carry the puck all over the place," he lamented.

And then Wallace adds, "And the other thing that you both do is fall down all the time!"

Nice morale boosting! I was both sour and embarrassed, and had a rage in me so strong, I remember trembling inside. I did the only thing I could do. I stood up for myself.

I quickly retorted, "First of all, Coach, no one is Gretzky."

Even then, I realized Wayne Gretzky was going to be something special. "And second of all," I barked to Wallace, "I don't have a big nose."

Sam McMaster: Steve Ludzik was the closest thing Toronto had to Wayne Gretzky. People didn't want to believe he's good. Let me tell you, he was good.

That was said by the man who tried to bring Wayne Gretzky to the Toronto area in the mid 1970s when Gretzky was a bantam. Gretzky was supposed to play for the Young Nats but, as usual, people got their nostril hairs flared up, and he was ruled ineligible due to residency rules. He was forced to play junior B hockey instead, where he simply dominated. I was really pissed off because I really wanted to play against him that season. The comment about me by Sam McMaster is flattering, but I was not even in the same area code as Wayne and knew it. It didn't bother me one iota. He was simply the best even then.

In 1972, there was a distinct buzz and rumor swirling through the hockey grapevine about a skinny kid from Brantford, Ontario. He was not yet known as the "The Great One," but simply as the "Brantford Tornado." He was described by breathless fans who crammed smoky hockey arenas as a ghost with skates on. He was quite simply, untouchable. His scoring feats were unheard of. He would routinely score 10 or 12 goals in a game. Due to the fact that Brantford is a small locale in southern Ontario, I had only heard of him but never saw him play or played against him. In my opinion, most people were green with envy and jealousy. To me, it sounded like a kid who was born to play hockey. In the 1972 season, Wayne Gretzky scored 350 plus goals for the Nadrofsky Steelers. He was just coming into prominence and his name was mispronounced and misspelled more than anybody's, including mine. Gresky, Gretsky, Gretski were but a few of the Polish jaw breakers he was called.

Back when I went to tournaments as a youngster, all the players were billeted out to homes, a practice long gone now. My first recollection of seeing Gretzky was in the Brockville Arena. We all waited for our billet people to take us back to their homes. That was when I was playing for that dynamo of a club called the Don Valley Jacks Pack, coached by Boris Tipoff, and like I mentioned, was sponsored by the late John F. Bassett, media mogul, sports tycoon, and debonair millionaire.

"The Pack," as we were known by friend and foe, was a hockey machine gobbling up teams on the way to two city titles and a Silver Stick championship. We may have been the best team at that age group in Canada. I was the big scorer on the team with 75 goals, a rather miniscule total compared to Gretzky. Gretzky always had his critics, even back then, and he always had to perform. In the Brockville Silver Stick tournament, which included a collection of the best players in North America, the fans flocked to the rink and stood five deep to see this scoring phenom take on "the Pack" from Toronto in the semi-final. What I witnessed that day is but a blur to me 38 years later, but this is what I do remember. The arena was jam-packed with excitement. Danny Gallivan would probably have called it "scintillating." Gretzky wore white gloves and used a Koho stick with the blade taped at the end with white tape. He never came off the ice; he literally played the whole game. He was as game as they came. When he got tired, he simply went back and played defense. History shows that "the Pack" won that game 4-3. As the future Great One left the ice surface, he did so with great difficulty as hordes of fans, young and old, were leaning over the chicken wire fence to see, touch, and pull on this phenom. It was surreal; it was as if the messiah had arrived. He was 11 years old. I distinctly recall that Gretzky wept uncontrollably leaving the ice, all the pressure pouring out of him. Wayne Gretzky learned that day that one great player cannot beat a great team – a lesson taught to us by our coach and mentor Boris Tipoff.

His picture appeared about one month later in the Toronto Star. I cut it out and taped it into my scrapbook. Interesting enough, he was labeled a defenseman in that photo.

The Great One...that's a 12-year-old Gretzky, the greatest player of my generation, the year he scored some 350 goals. He was just number nine then, and interestingly, this is out of a scrap book of mine! My admiration for him as the best player I ever saw did little to curb my goal to irritate him. Note he is listed as a defenseman in this photo. He had the Four G's: gameness, guts, gumption, and greatness, and he had 'em in spades.

DEFENCE WAYNE GRETZKY

But back to Tier II Junior A. When I was playing with the Markham Waxers, we used to have to weigh in every few weeks. I would hide my weight loss by wearing heavy sweaters (and usually several of them). When I weighed in, I would always wear heavy work boots. In my mind, I just figured my illness would somehow cure itself.

I underwent a battery of medical tests with our family doctor, and when he had done all he could do, he sent me to the Wellesley Hospital in Toronto. I caught a huge break at this old relic of a hospital when I was assigned to a young doctor by the name of Dr. Norm Marcon. He has gone on to serve as the Director of the Therapeutic Endoscopy Training Program at St. Michael's Hospital, which is one of the largest in North America. For the past 17 years, he and his colleagues have run a successful annual International Course of Therapeutic Endoscopy, which attracts faculty and attendees from around the world. Dr. Marcon thought mine was an interesting case. In the 1970s, the most common procedure was to remove all the inflamed and scarred tissue. If that had been done, almost all of my upper and lower colon would have been removed. The good doctor was of the opinion that, despite the severity of my condition, he would treat it with prednisone (steroids) and sulfa drugs. No one rides for free.

Comeback and Redemption

In my last year before the OHL draft, during the 1977-78 season, the Toronto Marlies promised me they would choose me for the club. I was projected to go very high. All was perfect. I could live at home and finish high school at Silverthorn Collegiate Institute and play hockey in the OHA. All that changed when I was stricken with Crohn's disease and hospitalized for two months.

All the OHA teams that had spoken to me no longer wanted to talk, as they did not think I would be able to play in the near future. After getting 50 points in 30 games as an under ager in Junior A Tier II hockey, I was no longer a desirable commodity in the hockey cattle call. Scouts, who had been touting my praises for several years, refused to take a chance on me. The hockey brain trust did not think I would be able to handle the speed of play in the OHL after my illness.

Sam McMaster (GM of Niagara Falls Flyers at the time): No one thought he would be able to handle the pace of the OHL.

I was especially hurt by the management of the Markham Waxers, whose manager was associated with the Toronto Marlies. He did not even once come to visit me in the hospital when I got sick. Even a phone call would have been nice. I was no use to him anymore, so he was not interested. I was treated like the red-headed stepchild.

The only general manager that would speak to me was Sam McMaster, the newly appointed GM of the Niagara Falls Flyers. He asked me if I was going to be able to play hockey the next year, and I told him if there was any physical way that I could, I would. Hockey was my life. McMaster told me that the Flyers thought I would be playing, too, but admitted that many of those he had spoken to in junior hockey circles thought there was no way I could bounce back that fast. He also told me that it might be a blow to my ego, but they were not going to take me until the seventh or eighth round, and they did not expect any other teams to take me.

Marty York (Globe and Mail sportswriter) wrote: The Toronto Marlies, unwisely playing the role of doctor, did not believe Ludzik could come back.

Reg Quinn (new owner of the Flyers at the time): If Ludzik had not gotten sick, he would have been one of the top three players of the draft. He was that good.

And so, that is how it came to pass. That is how I ended up playing junior hockey in Niagara Falls, of all places. In the end, it turned out pretty good. I had a great three years there, met my future wife, Mary Ann, and I still have a permanent home there, where we have raised our two sons, Stephen and Ryan.

Mark Osborne (Flyer teammate): Most of us were from Toronto and the school A.N. Myer was abuzz with 'Flyer Fever,' as they called it then. We were two weeks late attending classes and knew absolutely no one. We were eating lunch in our eight man 'Flyer' group in the cafeteria on the first day we got there, when in walks a beautiful blonde girl. Ludz leaned back to ask a guy

sitting at another table, 'Who is that girl'? 'Mary Ann Czaplicki,' the guy answers, 'but she's dating another guy.' Ludz turns to us and says matter of fact, 'That's the girl I'm going to marry.' They've been together over 25 years.

The Gorgeous One...that's me and my future wife Mary Ann and we're 17 years old here on one of our first dates. We've been married 25 years.

The Tempestuous One...
Bert Templeton cared little if you liked him or not. In fact, he spent his entire coaching career pissing off people. Tough as any marine sergeant. When he told you to jump, you did not ask how high, you just started bounding towards the stars. He taught you "When push comes to shove, shove back harder." Easily, no question, the greatest coach that lived.

Hello Niagara Falls and Thank You

Years later, in retrospect, I came to realize that coming to Niagara Falls was one of the best things that ever happened to me. The Niagara Falls Flyers were coached by the legendary OHL coach, the late Bert Templeton. I was determined to prove the critics wrong, and at the same time, make the people that took a chance on me look good.

My first Flyer camp, in 1978, was memorable. My best friend John Kirk, who coincidentally had also been drafted by Niagara Falls, and I marched into camp with total confidence, figuring we would rule the roost. The Flyer camp, like most junior camps, had 80 players looking for 20 spots. As you can imagine, the competition for the valued positions was fierce. The team was a laughing stock the year before, so many of the jobs were open. It was first come, first served.

I proudly entered the Niagara Falls Memorial Arena, which looks the same today as it did in 1978 – old and worn down. The sweet smell of the Nabisco plant beside the old arena quickly gave way to the smell of the fresh paint, body odor, and stale farts of the dressing room. Your stall had a piece of white tape haphazardly slapped above it with your name written on it in magic marker. Imagine my reality check when I noticed my name was spelled incorrectly: 'LUDZIG.'

The 80 players were spliced into four teams, and Bert Templeton ran the camp in military like fashion. There were two games a day, two workouts a day, a weight workout, and a run. Bert was *everywhere.* He saw everything. Nothing got by his scowling face. He walked around with his arms crossed and looked like a hawk stalking his prey.

Much is made of the carnage that occurs on the ice during training camps: brawls, beatings, and debauchery. The stories I heard from those who had previously gone to junior A camps and lived to tell about it would leave an army trooper with a head full of nightmares. From the first day, Steve Larmer, John Kirk, and I were on the same line. Fortunately for the three of us, the line would stick, and we would eventually be called the "Kid Line."

That first morning, Kirky and I were scheduled to play in the second game. As we sat in the dressing room getting ready, in stumbled a player supported by two trainers. Both of his eyes were already closed with matching four- to five-inch slits, and his face looked like it had lost a battle with a chain saw. I was doing my skates up and just leaning down to pull the laces snug and glanced over at Kirky, who was doing the same. We both just gulped and elected to not view the spectacle again. No words needed to be spoken among friends, just a tap on the pads, and a "Let's go pal." It was showtime.

James "The Mobes" Mundy (trainer): Paul Thomas caught the guy with two or three bombs, and the victim was a local guy named Larry Boscoe. He was out cold. Thomas was the hardest body checker, but was not a real fighter. That was just the first scrimmage game, and this guy's head looked like someone had used it as a punching bag.

Paul Thomas: I felt bad for the guy and heard he was in danger of losing his eye, so I went down to the hospital. The guy understood perfectly, but his mom and dad were hostile towards me.

It took the rink attendants extra time to flood the ice before our game. Scrapers and shovels feverishly chiseled at the blood puddle near center ice, and after they were finished, the circumference of the puddle looked like a chalk line outlining the area where a homicide had occurred. Before the Zamboni driver was on his last turn, a monster with a full beard pounced on the ice, roared like a gorilla, and made a rink length dash down the ice, and then propelled himself into the glass. He bounced off the glass and raced in the other direction, and proceeded to duplicate his madness at the other end of the rink. His name was Bob Phillips, an over ager, who was six-foot four inches and tipped the scales at 222 pounds. His nickname was Bionic Bob or Battleship Bob, depending on how he felt that day. Unfortunately for Kirky and me, Bionic Bob was on the other team. He was not finished with his antics. Just to show Coach Bert that his cardio was in peak shape, he raced down the ice yet again and crushed the end boards with such power, it was like mortar shells had been detonated. His performance was obviously intended to intimidate the other players, like a dog marking his territory. It worked.

James Mundy: Ludzy weighed in at our first camp at 159 pounds. He was actually very shy, which might surprise a lot of people today. He dominated his first scrimmage, scored three or four goals, set up five or six more, and even fought our resident tough guy, Bionic Bob Phillips. Ludzy was a guy possessed – literally.

Wayne Crawford (teammate): Our first camp in the Falls was tough. A guy named Battleship Bob Phillips tried to intimidate all the rookies who were trying to make the club. He was a complete sideshow. He had a full beard, which made him even tougher looking, and he would skate around with a big grin on his face. I have red hair and maybe three whiskers on my face, and here's this full-bearded guy. First practice, I thought my boy Ludzy had lost his mind when he and Battleship Bob fought in the third period.

On a side note, Bob turned out to be a good guy. A number of years ago, we invited him to an alumni game. It was a charity game between the 1978 Flyers and the Niagara Falls Thunder Alumni, who had Keith Primeau, Paul Laus, and Dennis Vial on the team, among others. There was a good crowd of around 2,500 on hand, and the old Flyers were all introduced one by one with a spotlight beaming on them. When "Number 20, Bob Phillips" was announced, Battleship Bob must have had a flashback to that 1978 training camp. As soon as he stepped on the ice, he skated full bore towards the end boards and launched himself towards the Plexiglas. However, with the advancement of age, 'The Battleship' was now a 'Cruise Liner.' As he rebounded off the glass, he ripped his groin muscle, which rendered him useless for the game. He never played a shift.

Even though it was a charity game, the juices started to flow. To illustrate how good that 1978 team was, we won the game 7-6.

Niagara Falls Flyers' Kid Line: Steve Larmer, Steve Ludzik, and John Kirk

Dirty Bert and Crew

If I was forced to name the best coach I've ever had, I would have to say Bert Templeton. He was often referred to as "Dirty Bert" for reasons that will become obvious.

<u>Reg Quinn (the owner who hired him)</u>: Bert Templeton probably understood the game more than any coach I ever met in my whole life.

He was 37 years old when I joined the Flyers in 1978, and he already had the reputation of being a career killer to those who really weren't prepared to pay the price to get to the next level. In fact, he would break anyone who was not prepared to work hard enough to stay in the OHA. I learned things from Bert that would hold me in good stead in my early coaching years. I have often told people that I would gladly have paid Bert's salary for one year, if both my sons had been given the opportunity to play for him. Because after playing for Bert for just one year, you would definitely know whether or not you were destined to be a hockey player. You would know if you were going to be able to make the grade.

Bert Templeton was an impressive figure of a man, a shade under six feet, immaculate, hair perfectly combed, and was obviously in top physical condition. He moved with an air of confidence and chewed on a toothpick that he would lodge into one of his teeth. Surely this could not be the legendary tough man, whose rap sheet, even at that early stage of his career, was long and colorful. He had already garnered hefty fines and suspensions. As with most legends, it is hard to separate the fact from the fiction. The only giveaway to the fire that burned inside were those steely eyes that shot laser beams and were tucked under an explosive patch of eyebrows. As I stood in my running gear about to run the required two miles, the general approached, "You Ludzik?" He sized me up as though reading a Chinese food menu. "Good luck kid." He was not smiling.

Reg Quinn: I told Bert to take a look at this kid Ludzik. He's pretty good. Bert watched him at the first skate and asked me 'why did it take you so long to take this kid'?

So six months after wondering if I was ever going to play hockey again, I had climbed up two rungs of that ladder. My health was back and I was back up to 160 pounds, not exactly an Adonis but very strong and ready. I was about to play in my first regular season home game: the Niagara Falls Flyers versus the London Knights. I am not ashamed to admit that immediately after the game, I showered and dried my hair quickly, put on the only suit I owned, and went directly home to my billet's house. I ate a peanut butter sandwich and three bananas, and waited patiently for 11:15 pm to strike. As I laid in bed staring at the ceiling, all of a sudden, there it was blaring across the airwaves. A much anticipated and familiar voice came booming across the crackling night air. I leaned in towards the transistor to make sure I caught every utterance from Mr. Garriock.

"In Niagara Falls tonight, the Flyers defeat the London Knights seven to three, and rookie Steve Ludzik had a goal and three assists… Here's the run down…"

I had reached the top rung and later found out, coincidently, that the radio show was done just 10 minutes from Niagara

Falls. Justifiably, for me at least, Mr. Garriock was inducted into the St. Catharines Sports Hall of Fame in 1992.

Bert Templeton was a man who danced to his own drummer. He was a fighter who was unafraid to pick a fight with upper management, lower management, the commissioner of the league, his players, opponent players and coaches, and even fans. Bert was way ahead of his time, especially in the way of off-ice conditioning.

In 1977, even after the 1972 Canada-Russia Series made us realize what off-ice conditioning could do for a team, it was still considered an afterthought with most organizations. I saved all of the conditioning programs that every team has ever given me, and Bert was definitely the forerunner to all great conditioning programs, even though by today's standards, they seem rudimentary. I never felt Bert got the credit he deserved for this innovation. Like a great 16th century painter, he would not be appreciated until he was gone from this earth.

David Branch (Commissioner of the OHA/OHL since 1977): Bert Templeton? The first thing that comes to mind is brilliant. He had an incredible mind. Bert was as good or better as any lawyer in the court room. He changed with the times. During his lengthy career, all he wanted was respect.

Bert Templeton was just a tough man. For several coaches I played for, such as Orval Tessier, and to a certain extent, Mike Keenan, you could tell deep down they were good men who thought they had to put on a gruff exterior to be effective. With Templeton, I was never sure. He would threaten players with a fury in his eyes that would scare the fur off a bear. His steely eyes could look right through you. I remember a young 15-year-old player with the Flyers, Brian Rorabeck, had a shy habit of not looking you in the eye when you spoke to him. Templeton told him if he didn't look him in the eye when he was speaking, he would break a chair over the youngster's head.

At one point, he simply said to Rorabeck, "Ah shit, Rorabeck. It's not your fault, it's ours. We bloody drafted you."

Bert was the tempestuous one. Bert Templeton cared little if you liked him or not. In fact, he spent his entire coaching career pissing off people. Tough as any marine sergeant. When he told you to jump, you did not ask how high, you just started bounding towards the stars. He taught you "When push comes to shove, shove back harder." Easily, no question, the greatest coach that ever lived.

Bert was severe when applying punishment. On a road trip to Sault Ste. Marie, he caught two players entertaining two chambermaids. The chambermaids were doing more than turning down the bed sheets and dropping a mint on the pillow. The two young athletes were caught red handed by the enraged Templeton. Both were booted out of the hotel immediately at midnight into -20 degree weather. They were banned from the bus trip home to Niagara Falls. Both were also suspended immediately and eventually traded. That would just not happen in today's game.

Bill Root was a powerful, dependable, and reliable stay-at-home defenseman whose honest play never garnered fanfare, headlines, or three star selections. Root was in his final year of junior eligibility and apparently had never been tapped as one of the three stars. That changed in November of 1978 in Brantford. Unfortunately for Billy Root, we lost that evening to the Alexanders, who were extremely high on our coach's hate list, as he had been released from the organization previously. Walking towards our dressing room after his quick spin on the ice as the third star, the smiling "Rooter" could hear the distinctive sound of sticks breaking, garbage cans being tossed, and the hostile vocabulary of a frustrated Bert.

"Ya think you bastards could fucking suck it up for one night."

He then continued to demolish the stick rack. Sherwoods, Canadians, Titans, and even my poor Louisville were reduced to firewood. With the scene set and the actors all in place, the final act was about to unfold. In walked Root, smiling like a Cheshire cat to all the guys, proudly holding his Brute Faberge shaving kit, the award for receiving an all star selection. Templeton pounced on him like a wounded puma.

"Rrrrroooooottttttt, what the fuck is that in your hands...give me that thing!"

He snatched the Brute bag from the befuddled Root, and Bert let 'er fly against the wall. Aftershave, cologne, soap, and shampoo exploded against the wall and sent fractured Faberge fragments flying about the room like shrapnel.

I had early success with Bert Templeton from a playing perspective.

<u>Bert Templeton was quoted:</u> The fact Ludzik made the team and is leading the league is a credit to him. No one else.

However, I could not escape his wrath. It was early in my first season with the Flyers, and we had only been together as a team for a month or so. We were in Windsor playing against the Spitfires, and late in the game with the score tied, I was out killing a penalty. I wasn't used to that role to begin with and went out to block a shot from the point. My legs came apart ever so slightly, and the defenseman, Claude Julien, let a howitzer go. It went between my legs, past our goalie, and bulged the twine in the back of the net. Bert was fuming as we came in the dressing room after the game.

One by one, he paraded around the room, telling each player how brutal he had played, and when he came to me, he yelled, "And Ludzik…"

"I know, I know, I should have kept my legs together," I responded quickly to show my new coach that I knew what I had done wrong.

Bert paused for a moment and screamed right in my face, "NO, YOUR MOTHER SHOULD HAVE!"

If you were in Bert's doghouse, you could forget about getting out for a while.

James Mundy (trainer): Templeton was a SOB – period. Great coach, bad guy. He would always scream, 'You guys want, want, want, but you don't want to give, give, give.' He would make you feel guilty about something as simple as deodorant. Really! If we lost a game, he would rant, 'You fucking bastards, you want soap… shampoo…aftershave…deodorant…fucking hairdryers, and you give nothing!'

We were playing the Toronto Marlies in Maple Leaf Gardens. As many Torontonians and Leaf fans know, Harold Ballard used to park his dark blue Lincoln Town Car on the north side of the building, near the Zamboni entrance. In those days, that was where the visiting team's dressing room was. After losing a game to the Marlies, which we should have won, Bert grabbed a stick and took a two-handed slash right into the side of Ballard's car. The thud could be heard throughout the arena. I never figured out how he got out of that one unscathed.

Bert had an incredible way of getting the best out of his players. He was able to push and push them until they did things that did not seem physically possible.

<u>Daryl Evans (teammate)</u>: He was a great coach who pushed and pushed, and heaven help the poor soul that Bert didn't think was tough enough. I remember he didn't think a fellow named Wayne Crawford was tough enough, and he fired a puck at him during practice.

<u>Wayne Crawford</u>: He took a puck one afternoon in practice and fired it at me, actually shot a puck at me in practice; it was crazy, man. After that practice, I asked Bert to just take me out by the Zamboni doors and shoot me. Please, get it over with. This was killing me.

He trained us in a Spartan like way. No stone was left unturned. Even in the dead of winter, we would run five miles two times a week at five o'clock in the morning. Niagara Falls is beautiful at that time of the morning! Many of us wore work boots or snow boots because the snow was so deep. And Bert would run with us. He was a physically imposing man and a great physical specimen. Heaven help the poor soul who finished behind him in the run. When we went to school after our runs, the teachers would comment on our rosy cheeks. Little did they know it was most likely frostbite.

Steve Larmer: He pushed you hard, but he was fair about it. He brought in a weight machine, and we did a lot of running, circuit training. I had never done off-ice training like that before.

If you looked at Larmer's first-year statistics in the Falls, he missed only two games. He was always a durable player. He missed one tilt because Bert thought Larms had a sloth like practice. Halfway through the practice in question, the explosive coach bolted to the players' bench and screamed, "Remind me not to have Larmer dress tomorrow night. He sits!"

Looking back, I find this funny because it's still hard to believe Bert would have needed to be reminded.

I also met many lifelong friends on that team. Little did I know I would be on the same team as Steve Larmer for many years after my stint in Niagara Falls. We quickly became close. As I would later realize, your best friends are the ones you meet when you are young.

Steve Larmer: We both got drafted by Niagara Falls, had just met, and were in training camp. We went to eat at some Italian restaurant on Main Street. Ludzy got up to go to the washroom, and you know those red hot chili pepper shakers that are on the tables? Well, I put half a jar into his pasta and mixed it all in. He came back and took a couple of mouthfuls and his mouth was on fire. I

had no idea he had gone through a tough summer with his colitis. We always kept an eye out for one another.

I remember meeting Larmer for the first time. All I knew was he was a hot shot sniper from Peterborough. He played as an under ager for the Petes the previous year. The first time I laid eyes on him, I was somewhat surprised. Here was this out of shape, or so it looked to me, guy who appeared to be a chain smoker, who could barely run the two miles expected of him. He was friendly enough but had a grumpy, dour personality about him that made me instantly nickname him "Grampa." I call him that to this day.

We got along well from the outset because our personalities were quite different. I liked to have fun and, by nature, was a more extroverted person. I would initiate bedlam. Larmer would be the calming influence. I would play more pranks on him than he would on me.

We would be on a road trip, and if he got up in the night to go to the washroom and I woke up, too, I would rush and put peanut butter and grapes on his pillow. He would jump back into bed and get peanut butter all over himself. He would jump up and curse, "You son of a bitch." Then he would have to take a shower to clean off. If the sides were reversed, I don't think I would have been as understanding, but it didn't bother Larmer. He always went along with it. The odd time he would put grapes in my bed, and when I got back into bed, I would just lie there pretending I didn't feel anything. That would piss him off. We shared a lot of miles, many laughs, crappy food, long bus rides, and plane trips – great memories that will last a lifetime.

I'm not sure why but a sports writer in Niagara Falls, Doug Austin, named Larmer and me the "Gold Dust Twins" for the years we were with the Flyers. I guess Austin was somewhat of a fortune teller when he gave us that nickname because when we got to the NHL, Larms got the gold, and I got the dust.

That first fall in Niagara Falls, I still had to watch what I ate because of my sickness the winter and spring before. One fruit I started to eat was bananas. Other foods simply were not going through my system properly. I ate them primarily to gain weight.

Jim Mundy (billet): Ludz used to eat, and this is hard to believe, 12 to 15 bananas a day. The reason was he was so sick that year with a stomach ailment. Bananas were about the only food he could digest. It became an unusual story that was picked up by the Globe and Mail and The Sault Star of Sault Ste. Marie. Some fans called him 'The Banana Man' for a while.

I figured I would keep eating massive amounts of bananas until I gained the desired amount of weight, and then I would cut back.

Alex Mitchell (of The Sault Star) wrote: …which is good news for his landlady and parents, his supplier of fruit. Ludzik says his landlady goes to the supermarket nearly every day for a fresh banana supply.

Larry Anstett of the Kitchener-Waterloo Record took the story one step further. He actually calculated that I had eaten 1,824 bananas over a few short months. I can't even stand the look of bananas today – I don't care how much potassium they have in them.

We had some great tough guys on that team. John Gibson, a native of St. Catharines, was the toughest player I had seen up to that time. I was in my first year; he was in his last. He had the quickest temper, biggest hands, and longest reach of any player I had ever played with or against. And he could turn that mean streak and toughness on in an instant. He did not have muscle strength; he was just strong. I would call it tendon strength.

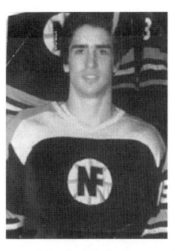

The Dangerous One...a young and very restless John Gibson, a talented and raw hide tough customer, who in either skates or cowboy boots, was the toughest SOB in the house. You don't believe me, just read on.

<u>John Gibson</u>: The first year guys like Daryl Evans could bench press 300 pounds. Really, I could not get 130 pounds up on the old universal gyms if my life depended on it. But those grip calipers with the red needle that would measure and register your hand strength, I would blow the needle past the last mark.

Behn Wilson would later tell me that the one player that really clipped him in junior was Gibby. During one altercation, Behn said he could see Gibson start to loosen his glove off his hand, but by the time he realized, it was too late, and the barrage of punches that followed felt like the arena roof was falling on his head. Gibby had mittens on him like Sonny Liston. And he knew how to use them.

John was in constant battles with the coaching staff about the way he was going to play. He could be a mad man. During my first year in Niagara Falls, he had a fight with a Windsor Spitfire. The other player obviously knew he was outmatched, so as soon as the fisticuffs started, the Spitfire player went to his knees, put his hands over his head, and began to turtle. Gibby was infuriated by this and viciously pulled the player up out of his turtle position and kicked him right in the face.

Paul Thomas (Niagara Falls Flyer teammate): Actually, the guy's name was Dave Hurst, who was a stick man extraordinaire who tried to really hurt you. John Gibson totally flipped out, and Hurst turtled on him. Gibby pulled Hurst's helmet off, and for a second or two, I thought he'd pulled Hurst's head off. Really! Then John just booted this guy in the head.

John Gibson: I got a three-game suspension from the league. The player was a pain in the ass. I was trying to knee him in the face, but if you talk to anybody who was in attendance, be it fan or teammate, they'll say I kicked him.

Even Templeton, the toughest of coaches, had a hard time swallowing that one. Bert told Gibby that if the league didn't suspend him for that act, he would suspend him. Templeton preached and encouraged tough hockey. His line was pretty high, but he understood where that line was. Bert always said if you have to pick one of "the good," "the bad," or "the ugly," be the "bad." However, even this act of violence was too much for the normally impervious Templeton.

John Gibson: Everyone knew Bert was a great coach, but he treated us not like kids but like toddlers. I walked off the team because I could not take his crap anymore. To this day that decision still haunts me. We should have won the Memorial Cup.

Even though I don't understand why he short circuited sometimes, I enjoyed John very much and got along well with him, thank God. I can still clearly see him walking out the back door the day he quit.

A year later, in 1978, John Gibson played for the Saginaw Gears of the old IHL. Gibby played that year with a fellow named Mel Hewitt. For some reason, Mel's wife was always getting Mel into altercations. She made Don King look like an amateur fight promoter. Late in the season, Mel challenged Gibby to a fight in the dressing room. Let it be said that Mel did not need much encouragement to fight man or beast, but his wife wanted to let the fur fly to see who was the toughest hombre in that toddling town of Saginaw, Michigan.

John Gibson: His wife did start a lot of crap and no doubt pushed him to do this. Mel was not as stupid as people thought. He was going to lose, no question about it. In my prime, if I hit ya square and you didn't go down, I would walk behind you and see what was holding you up.

If Mel wanted to go, Gibby laid down the ground rules, "I'll tell you what I'm going to do, Mel. I'm going to put my hands behind my back, and you can do whatever you want to do with one shot. You got one punch to my face. When I get up, and I will get up, you have to put your hands behind your back and give me one punch."

Mel Hewitt, surprisingly showing immense intelligence after observing the size of Gibson's hands, decided to pass. In a life full of tough decisions, in this case, Mel made the right one.

John Gibson: Mel and I became friends after that set to. He was a good guy.

Gibson had a brief stop in Los Angeles to start his professional career and brought his toughness with him. His reputation quickly spread like a California forest fire.

John Gibson: I was 20 years old in maybe my second or third game in the NHL with the Kings. I dropped Paul Holmgren from the Flyers with a sucker shot. The owner of Los Angeles, Dr. Jerry Buss, came over to me after the game and presented me with a huge TV set for my handiwork.

He also had a pit stop in Toronto with the Leafs, but only if you are a true hockey fanatic would you recognize his name. But for a few years, John Gibson walked it large. John now lives in St. Catharines, Ontario. I saw him at the Flyer reunion that was held a few years ago. He looked good and tranquil. Even at 50, he still had that vice like grip. He still was truly the toughest son of a bitch in the house.

Bert also taught me something else very important about coaching. In my first year in Niagara Falls, in 1978, we were up three games to one against the Peterborough Petes. One more win and our Cinderella team would be off to the Memorial Cup. We had it in the bag. Then Bert boasted to a reporter that there was no way a team could beat us three games straight like Peterborough needed to do, "because we were the best conditioned athletes in Canadian junior hockey."

Reg Quinn, the owner, had also been quoted as saying, "One thing's for sure. We have the best conditioned team in the whole OHA. No, make that the whole of Canada."

Years later, when playing with Billy Gardner in Chicago, who was on that Peterborough team, I found out that the Petes had smartly enlarged that quote, laminated it, put it up in the dressing room, and used it as a calling card for the next three games. They beat us three games in a row to go on to the Memorial Cup. I learned then to not speak ill of the dead, or near dead, as they can always come back and haunt you. For that reason, when I began coaching, I was always careful when speaking about a team we were about to play, especially in the playoffs, where no cannon fodder is needed.

Bert also taught me a new vocabulary.

"Holy fiddlers fuck, you guys are awful," was one of his favorites.

One evening he quipped, "You guys are playing like the Sisters of St. Mary's." And he used the same genre when he used to lambaste, "Are you guys nervous out there? Because you are playing like virgins on the verge!"

Bert would yell at John Kirk and me, "Ludzik! Kirk! You stupid bastards have played on the same fucking line since you were in the sand box together. You'd think you'd know by now that those drop passes don't work. Fuck off! The both of ya."

If you were not so frightened of him, you would have realized he was quite funny.

"Kirk," he screamed one night, "disco here, disco there, fuck off. The only time I see your name on the score sheet is when I write it on the line-up card. Ya really think these broads would have anything to do with you if you were digging ditches?"

When I went to Niagara Falls, I had heard about Bert's drinking binges and his fiery temper, which apparently increased to a different level when under the influence. But to be honest, I was never a witness to any of that – the drinking part I mean. I was just witness to his fiery temper, almost every day. What I saw was a very dedicated man to his profession, who took losing like a personal slap in the face and expected all of his players to react in the same way.

He could not stand it when people were late. If practice was slated at 4:00 pm, you'd better be on the ice by 10 minutes to four with a bit of a lather on or there would be hell to pay. Everyone was so respectful of Bert, we were always on the ice at 3:50 pm sharp. Bert ran his teams with military precision and demanded cohesion among the ranks. He had some tough rules: it was a $1/minute if you missed curfew. So, one hour cost you 60 dollars and a night in the press box. Back in the 1970s, that was a lot of money. But everyone was too afraid to be late anyways. I took a page out of Bert's book when I began coaching. If I called a meeting for 10 am, I would always start talking at 9:55 am. Players would walk in around 10 am and think, "Holy crap, I'm late." You only have to do that once or twice, and after that, everyone will be ready to go at 9:55 am. Guaranteed.

An unfortunate defining moment in Bert's career came during the World Junior Championships in Piestany in 1987. As many Canadian hockey fans remember, Canada was playing for a medal against a Russian team that was out of medal contention. Many fans will not remember that Bert Templeton was the head coach of that team. This was before the World Juniors adopted the playoff style format. During the hotly contested game, Russian player Pavel Kostichkin took a two-handed slash on a young Theoren Fleury, which ultimately resulted in a bench clearing brawl. The idiotic officials actually turned out the lights of the arena in an effort to restore calm, and in the resulting aftermath, Canada was disqualified from the tournament and thus deprived of the opportunity to garner a medal. I felt, as did many others, that unfortunate occurrence may have cost Bert a chance at a NHL coaching position. I am undecided, however, if Bert would have been effective in the NHL. However, it scarred his reputation – unjustly so, in my opinion. He was forever tarred and feathered. Templeton, for the rest of his life, would never comment on this incident. He offered no apology, and in my opinion, none was needed.

Reg Quinn: Bert's style really didn't work with the older players. It worked better with the younger players. 'Give me 100 percent all the time' idea didn't work with everyone. Same reason why Brian Kilrea was not given a head coaching job in the NHL. It just wouldn't work with the professionals.

Somewhat ironically, that incident was one that propelled Don Cherry's prominence to new heights as he fervently defended Canadian patriotism. On a side note, an assistant coach on that team was Pat Burns, who did have a very successful NHL coaching career.

Near the end of his career and, in fact, his life, Bert became an extremely bitter man and was very unhappy with how hockey had evolved. He remained a hard ass all the way through. Two small incidents come to mind that make that clear.

Like I mentioned, growing up in my neighborhood my best friend was John Kirk. He still is. "Kirky," like most players, never saw eye to eye with Bert. In the 1990s, they were both at the same sports banquet, and at one point, Kirky noticed his old coach Templeton standing alone at the bar. He figured he would go over and say hello to his old general. Kirky had not seen Dirty Bert for at least 15 years and Kirky's appearance had changed dramatically. His hair, which was once his calling card when it flowed well past his shoulders, was now completely gone. As they say, he now combs his hair with a washcloth. Or, as Kirky, who is always the friendliest and funniest guy in the house often says, "I still have a lot of hair but it's on my back now!"

As he approached Bert, Kirky stuck out his hand, which was meekly accepted by the old coach. Surely, after the passage of time, the fires within Bert would have subsided somewhat. Bert had visibly changed, too, having gone completely gray.

After about five minutes of trying to carry the conversation, and Bert giving one-syllable answers, Kirky said to Bert, "You don't remember me, do you?"

The crusty mentor looked him dead in the eye and quickly responded, "Yah, I know who you are. You're John Kirk, and you're a fucking loser."

Like a cow choking on its cud, Bert was still seething about our playoff collapse some 15 years later.

Unbelievable. My best friend just nodded and told Bert to "have a nice life."

Best pals and next door neighbors. Me and John Kirk alive and well after our first training camp in Niagara Falls. Our first day of camp was almost our last.

When I coached the Mississauga Ice Dogs and he was coaching the Sudbury Wolves, we would sit and talk after the game, and he would say, "You know, Ludzy, this is shit, eh?"

"What?" I didn't quite understand him, as I figured he had the perfect job for him, coaching youngsters and having a profound influence on their lives. But he went on.

"At least half these kids couldn't have played 25 years ago. Now, we have to kiss their ass to have them come and play. I know everybody's parents, everybody's agent. When you were playing, I didn't even know who your parents were. And I don't like the changes in the game."

I would have to say that I don't agree with my old mentor. Today's players are bigger, faster, better conditioned, and more skilled than in the 1970s. To me, under the guidance of David Branch, the junior scene is the greatest league in hockey; it runs like clockwork.

An ironic and really useless tidbit of hockey knowledge is this: Bert Templeton coached 1,828 regular season games in the Ontario Hockey League. The very last game that he ever coached was against me and my Mississauga Ice Dogs. It was an afternoon game, and it was a must win for us. A win ensured us a playoff spot for the first time in franchise history. We destroyed the Wolves 7-2. Although I was extremely proud of my group, I could only stare across the ice at my former coach and feel a touch of sadness. His club did not reach the playoffs – a first for the proud, and yes, egotistical bench boss. My heart sank as I noticed huge blue signs around the corridor of the Sudbury arena. The 10 or 12 signs posted all over the arena read the same. They contained a personal apology from Bert Templeton, criticizing his poor performance that year. It was an apology from the most unapologetic man I knew.

As I boarded the team bus for our return to Mississauga, a familiar voice called out, "Stevie, hey Ludz." It was the cantankerous Templeton. I thought 'ohh, shit, he wants to play another game, right now.' He knew deep down he was going to walk the plank for an underachieving season, and he was indeed subsequently fired. As I said goodbye, he said, "Good luck, kid, in the playoffs." It was almost a mirror statement of what he said the first time I met him in 1978.

I never saw Dirty Bert again. He died nine months later, a victim of a ravenous cancer that attacked his kidneys and liver. A fall left him paralyzed from the neck down the last week of his life. I read all the obituaries written by men who could not possibly understand, and more importantly, could not hope to explain to the reader, the man who was Bert Templeton.

To Bert, life was like a cowboy movie, you know, the old black and white ones. In these movies, the good guy in the white hat always beats the bad guy in the black hat. Bert Templeton relished wearing the black hat, but in his movie, the guy in the black hat won. He was 63 years old.

Look Back and Laugh

Back to my old Flyer team. After our great run to the Ontario finals against Peterborough during my rookie year in 1979, the players on the team were given the choice to get $250 cash in our pockets or a seven-day all expenses paid trip to the Bahamas. The majority of the guys took the offer of the Bahamas, which today seems like a no brainer. But I remember the best part was I was going to get a week off of school.

A funny incident occurred on that trip. In retrospect, we were actually a really good bunch of kids. Almost all the trouble we got into was good honest fun, nothing hurtful, and we didn't get into fights or anything like that. I think that was a big change for Templeton. He had previously coached the Hamilton Fin Cups, which got into all sorts of havoc and trouble. One of our goalies on the Flyers was Nick Ricci. His family was in the hotel business in a big way in the Niagara Region. Perhaps for that reason, Nick was always paranoid about where to put his wallet in hotel rooms at night. He was always concerned about break-ins. While on the Bahamas trip, Nick would meticulously build a pyramid of empty pop cans, which he had collected off the beach, and place them against the base of the hotel room door. If the door ever opened up, the cans would fall all over the place and wake him up.

Unfortunately, I was the lucky person to room with him on this trip. As an added security feature, Ricci placed a tennis racket between our two beds. We figured his paranoia could not go unpunished. Some players decided to plan a "break-in" in the middle of the night. I left the key over the door for them and was trying to stay awake until they came, but I must have dozed off. The next thing I knew, the guys were coming in the room with panty hose masks on and yelling and screaming.

Ricci jumped out of bed and yelled, "Ludz, they're here."

Nick grabbed the racket and started swinging it wildly, imploring me to get out of the room. He then jumped over the bed and out the patio door and headed off toward the beach. Everyone had a great laugh except for Ricci. I don't think he appreciated the humor. Actually, Ricci had displayed a lot of guts and valor.

After my first year in Niagara Falls, Bert Templeton moved on to coach in the AHL in Nova Scotia, the farm team of the Montreal Canadiens. His successor was an old Niagara Falls Flyer and veteran Boston Bruin, Fred Stanfield. Patty Graham got traded from the Toronto Marlies to the Flyers at the beginning of my second year. In appearance, Patty looked like a handsome Mick Jagger. I remember he wore purple cowboy boots. He was promptly put on the line with me and Larmer. Patty was a gritty player who fit in nicely on our line.

Pat Graham: I got traded from the Marlies to the Niagara Falls Flyers in my second year of junior. I arrived at the Niagara Falls Memorial Arena, and the coach told me I'm with Ludzik and Larmer that night. I thought I'd just won the lottery. I only knew them from playing against them but knew they were magic together. I couldn't wait. First game, first shift, I came back to the bench and Larmer was smacking his lips with a wad of gum

that could choke an elephant. He turned to me and says, 'What the fuck can't you pass?...don't dump it in...go to the fucking net...did you not see me?' All of this after one 40-second shift. I was shocked and looked at Ludz, whose eyes remained glued to the action on the ice. He pretended he didn't even hear it. Then as we jumped on the ice for our second shift of the game, I looked over at Ludzy who just shrugged, then leaned into me, and snapped, 'Just tell Larmer to shut his yap.'

The Wild Man...my pal Patrick Graham, teammate and left winger for two seasons in junior. He wore black leather pants and purple cowboy boots and looked like a muscular Mick Jagger. He played 103 NHL games with the Leafs and Penguins then became one of Canada's best chiropractors.

Even though I was from Toronto and had been spurned by the Marlies, I don't think I put any extra emphasis on my games in Toronto. I got up for all games as much as I could. Larmer was not like that. He prepared for all games thoroughly, but when we were playing in Peterborough, his hometown, he started to get fired up a week before. He wanted to play his best game of the season in Peterborough. One time in Peterborough, Larms was all geared up as he, Patty, and I went out for our first shift.

Pat Graham: We got a three-on-two going, and as I carried it over the blue line, Larmer dropped back slightly and starting screaming in his raspy voice, 'PATTY...PATTY... THREE-ON-TWO...PATTY...'

The puck was on end, and I couldn't get proper control of it but tried to throw it back to Larmer anyway. I fanned on the pass a bit, and the puck rolled end over end slowly towards him. Two Peterborough defensemen: Greg Therberge and Stuart Smith converged on him. One went high and the other went low. Larmer did a full cartwheel in the air. As soon as he was hit and as he was still flying in the air, you could hear Larmer bellow, 'N-i-c-e f-u-c-k-i-n-g p-a-s-s!'

I know it's hard to believe, but Grampa Larmer seemed to be suspended in mid air as he yelled that line. Patty and I both had tears in our eyes.

A weird, comical, incident occurred in Sudbury while playing against the Sudbury Wolves. The Sudbury mascot harassed Pat Graham and me in the penalty box.

Howard Berger wrote: In a widely publicized incident, Ludzik took exception to the taunting tactics of one Steve Lindsay, who dresses up in a wolf costume as the Sudbury team mascot for each home game. Steve recalls, 'We were leaning back with our heads against a pane of glass when that wolf started banging on it from the other side.' After some minutes of razzing in the penalty box, Lindsay was awarded a swift conk on the head via the player's hockey stick. Ludzik says the wolf's reaction scared him slightly. 'He went down like a Coke bottle.'

The problem was that the game had gotten a little out of hand. Back in the 1970s, the games up north were often refereed by locals and not OHA referees, so the calls were often biased, as the officials did not want to receive the wrath of family and friends after the game. That night, the Sudbury area had been hit with a horrific storm, so the normal refs could not make it in. Local officials were called in on an emergency basis. The "officials" that were assigned to the game may as well have grabbed a green Sudbury Wolves' sweater and put it on. Anyway, that's my story, and I'm sticking to it.

They were actually going to arrest Patty and me. While the police were trying to get into our dressing room to get me, Moby held the door shut as long as he could. Sudbury's finest finally rammed the door down and put me in handcuffs, even though I was still half dressed, and took me upstairs.

Patty Graham stepped out from the shower naked. "Don't worry Ludzy, I'll be right there."

Patty Graham: I was lathering my hair with shampoo as they handcuffed Ludzy and took him to the paddy wagon.

But they only wanted me.

James "The Mobes" Mundy: The Sudbury police actually arrested him. The cops lined up in front of our dressing room. We got Ludzy in the dressing room and barricaded the door, but it was no use. After a 10-minute standoff, they came in and cuffed Brother Ludz. The wolf didn't want to press charges but the general manager, Joe Drago, threatened to. Eventually we got Ludz outta

Dodge that night. Sudbury had the last laugh, however. One of our last games that year was in Sudbury, and Ludzy was in line to win an OHA award for the most all star selections during the season. I recall he had a pretty good game and should have been in line for at least a third star, but there was no way the Sudbury selector was putting him on the ice at the end of the game.

I think I missed the award by one overall selection. Payback is a bitch. I got a lot of negative publicity concerning this incident. To my astonishment, the TV Guide rated me as the second worst sportsman in North America for my churlish display of behavior. John McEnroe was named number one. Pretty good company!

<u>Jim "Chief" Mundy (my billet for three years)</u>: Ludz got back to the hotel at around three o'clock and the first person he called was his father, because he didn't want him hearing it in the morning from another source.

My sons went to the same high school that I went to in Niagara Falls and had some of the same teachers. They used to come home and tell me that what some of the teachers remembered about me was that I used to come to school all the time with cuts, scrapes, and bruises all over my face. There was a time when I kept track of all my stitches, a la Gerry Cheevers. I had one of those porcelain little hockey men, so when I got five or six stitches in my face, I would mark it with a red marking pen. When I was putting on what seemed like the 200th mark, the head shattered into smithereens. Now my face is no oil painting to begin with, but it has been high sticked, punched, clawed, cut, and kicked, among other things.

I got a particularly bad laceration in Kingston one night when I was hit from behind by Shawn Babcock, a big bulky guy. I was about five feet from the boards, the most vulnerable place to be, and he hit me full tilt. I went into the boards chin first. The weird thing was that my chin wasn't really cut; there was more like a three-inch divot gauged out of it right down to the jawbone. I was more stunned than anything else. One of my teammates, Patty Graham, was the first to arrive, and I think he almost gagged on the ice.

"Oh Ludzy, get to the bench quick!" Patty implored.

<u>Patty Graham</u>: Easily the worst cut I'd ever seen. Just awful. He had two mouths. You could actually see the jawbone. It was just disgusting. I'm not sure how many stitches he got, 40, 50, but he came back and scored a goal late in the game.

I'm not sure if he was saying that for my own good, or the fact that he wouldn't have to look at it anymore. The trainer, "Mobes," took a look at it and I saw him turn white.

"Mobes, just put some tape on it; we got a five-minute power play coming up!" I calmly told him.

That was my gravy train, a five-minute power play. All the players couldn't bear to look at it. Moby made me go to the dressing room to see the doctor.

I told the doctor, "Listen, don't bother freezing it. We got a five-minute power play; I'd like to get out there."

But the doctor was more interested in shooting the breeze, joking with the assistant nurse, and was in no rush to attend to it. To make matters worse, he did a piss poor job of sewing it up. When the final count was rendered, I had 45 sutures. And that is why to this day I have that huge scar on my chin. For about a year and half, it looked like I had been sewn up with rope rather than a needle and thread. I was in that rink about 10 years later, and I swear I could still see the mark on the boards where I had been hit.

I have also had some close calls with respect to my eyes.

Pat Graham: He was a courageous guy. One night in London, he took a slap shot, bang right in the eye. Ludz got back to the bench under his own steam and they took him right to the dressing room. We got word he'd lost his eye. I just completely lost it after the game. He played two nights later. He looked like the elephant man, but he played.

In junior, I was known more as a point getter than anything else. But I grew up having more than my fair share of scraps. I boxed a bit and really loved that sport. I could handle myself but was not a real good fighter on the pond. I know that according to NHLFights. com, I had a grand total of 34 fights during my pro career, but I don't recall hurting anyone or ever being hurt.

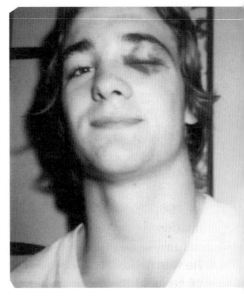

Patty Graham: When push came to shove, the 'Baby Boy' Ludzik could fight. We had a classic bench clearer in Oshawa when they were coached by that nut Bill Laforge. They had this guy, Barry 'Hawk' Tabobondung, who was from the Wasausking First Nation area near Parry Sound. He used to wear a headdress in warm up, and one night he chased Larmer all over the ice every shift, hacking at him, slashing him, in short, he was just looking for a fight. It was Larmer's worst nightmare. The next night we played them again, this time in Oshawa, and a bench clearing brawl started because the 'Hawk' came by our bench and challenged the whole team. It was 10 seconds into the game. We all look at each other and Ludzy jumped over the boards first and took on the 'Hawk.' I ended up having a bird's eye view, as I was on my back being held down. It was a beauty and Ludz had more trouble trying to keep his pants up than with fighting Tabobondung. He kept his pants up with a long skate lace instead of suspenders and the lace busted during the fight. What a brawl.

Tabobondung was a really tough kid and they nicknamed him "the Hawk." I knew I could handle myself, but I had my hands full with him. I held my own and came out of that encounter unscathed. Hey, I thought fighting, especially in junior, was a waste of time. I was there to score goals and carry the puck. In fact, one night in Brantford, I was involved in an ugly incident and got slapped with a three-game 'sabbatical.' Anyway, Barry was a powerful, scary dude. In 1981, Tabobondung was involved in an embarrassing incident at the draft. It was the first year that a lot of players actually went to the draft. Tabobondung was so happy when he was picked in the third round that he jumped over a row of seats at the Montreal Forum and got his foot caught in one of the folding chairs. An arena maintenance man had to actually unscrew a portion of the seat for him to get free. Tragically, Barry Tabobondung died in 2000 in a farming equipment accident in his hometown. Heroically, however, he was able to save his son in the same accident.

For some reason, I also liked to push the envelope during warm up. Back in the day, the officials did not come on the ice for warm up so the supervision was somewhat lapse.

Mark Osborne: There was an unwritten rule that when in warm up, if your puck bounced into the opposition's half of center, you just let it go, as you had 20 more pucks on your side. Not Ludzy. He would saunter into enemy territory to get the puck and return with it. Gosh, when I think about it, that was pretty stupid. I can't believe he left some buildings alive by some of the things he did.

Daryl Evans is one of the funniest guys I know and if you don't think the game has changed for the better, let Big "D" bring one tale out of the vault to tell ya. People often said Daryl and I talked alike. Maybe that was why I enjoyed his stories so much.

Daryl Evans: When I was 15 and playing junior B for the Young Nats, I got called up to play one game for the Marlies Junior A Club. The game was in Hamilton against the Fin Cups. I felt lucky to get a look-see at the OHL and was ready to go. I walked into the dressing room and didn't know a soul. For some reason, everyone was scared shitless; some guys didn't even want to go out for the warm up, which should have sent up some warning flares. The Hamilton Fin Cups had a very scary squad that included Al Secord and Tim Coulis. It would

have been nice if someone had told me about them before the warm up. Usually, when you warm up, each club has half the ice up to the red line. But on this night, I could not figure out why the Marlies only used the area up to their own blue line. It seemed kinda cramped and a little unusual. I went to get a puck in what should still have been our warm up area between our blue line and center, and that's the last thing I remember. I got laid out cold. I didn't even know my own phone number, and even if I did, I would have had to call home to find out what my name was. They carried me off on a stretcher. I was asleep, not even a twitch. The trainers got me in the dressing room and hit me with water, face slaps, smelling salts, and ammonia tablets. I think one guy even put the boots to me to stand me up, but I was like a Weeble Wobble. I was literally hallucinating on the rubbing table and then the idiot trainer asked me, 'You all right to go?' I felt like hitting this guy with a flying forearm!

The Fin Cups, coached by none other than Bert Templeton, were the most feared team in the nation. What his teammates neglected to tell Daryl was that the Fin Cups would attempt to maim anyone coming near the red line in warm up. That was simply the way it was back in the late 1970s and early 1980s in junior hockey. You can eat or be eaten.

During a playoff battle with the Kitchener Rangers in 1978, the year Bert coached me, their head coach resigned immediately after Game Four, citing the barbaric play and hooliganism displayed by our team. Our fiendish coach Bert would simply smile and roll a toothpick around his lips. He thought it was a compliment.

During that second season in 1979-80, Larmer broke his scaphoid bone, a major bone in his wrist. The team doctors and trainers said he was done for three months and insisted he would be lucky to be back by the playoffs. That would obviously be a large blow to our team. Fortunately for us, Larms did not take much credence in what the doctors had to say. Our very next game was in Windsor against the Spitfires. Larmer declared he was fit enough to play that night. With the help of a rasp, the "Mobes" was able to shave down the palm of Larmer's cast so he could hold his stick. And with a good supply of 222 painkillers, Larms was ready to roll. During the entire four-hour bus trip to Windsor, Larms kept going over his game plan.

"I can't shoot. I can't stickhandle. I have no power in my top hand...I'll just stay to the side of the net for the empty netters," he repeated to anyone that would listen.

On the second shift of the game, I carried the puck over Windsor's blue line and, by instinct, I guess, dropped the puck to Larms, who let go a rocket and top cheese, top shelf, whatever you want to call it, it bulged the twine at the back of the net. Rollie Melanson barely moved. We went back to the bench and the whole team was in a state of bedlam.

As we nestled the cheeks of our asses on the bench, Larms turned to me and stated matter of fact, "Ludzy, I thought I told you not to pass to me. I can't shoot." Classic Larms.

To me, Larms was the perfect example of toughness personified. For me, fighting was the last step on the toughness ladder. I would rather have had a guy who played hurt, played through pain, took a hit to make a play, and was mentally tough than a guy who could just fight. Steve Larmer was tough.

All junior A players look forward with great anticipation to the NHL draft that normally takes place in June. I was no exception. I had what I considered were two very strong years with the Niagara Falls Flyers. My junior career produced 125 goals, 233 assists, and 358 points, but I knew it was going to be a deep draft, as two age groups were to be available that year.

The extravaganza the draft is today is much different than it was back then. In 1980, it was held at the old Montreal Forum. There were no fans or fanfare. There was no television, no team baseball hats, no sweaters, and no interviews. The only people in attendance were players, players' agents, a few girlfriends, and a spattering of parents. After going through the draft myself and witnessing subsequent drafts, I strongly agree with Don Cherry that unless you are certain you will be drafted in the first few rounds, it is better not to attend. Obviously, with the allure and spotlight, it is difficult for young players to stay away. They do not want to miss it if they are drafted. I personally have witnessed disappointment and despair.

Back in those days, there were five rounds, a break for lunch, and then you came back for the other five rounds. The first pick in the 1980 draft was the late Doug Wickenheiser, who was selected by the Montreal Canadiens from the Regina Pats of the Western Hockey League. Dave Babych was selected second overall, and then Denis Savard from the Montreal Juniors was picked third by the Chicago Blackhawks. I obviously didn't realize it at the time, but that pick would impact me.

You just sat there and waited. I had spoken with several teams but a lot of different things can happen at the draft. Players can move up or down in the draft order depending on various circumstances, and sometimes players get unexpectedly drafted earlier than anticipated so team lists get changed. It is a stressful day to say the least. I ended up getting picked in the second round, 28th overall, by the Chicago Blackhawks. I remember just being stunned at the time. There wasn't an abundance of fanfare. In fact, when I met General Manager Bob Pulford a little later that day, he did not even know who I was.

Daryl Evans and I sat together at the draft. He was my teammate on the Niagara Falls Flyers and had become a good friend. He could bench press 300 pounds six or seven times. I don't care what his official stats said, he could not have been taller the 5'6." He was, bar none, the greatest eater I have ever seen. Coming back on the bus from Maple Leaf Gardens one day, everyone bet that Daryl could not finish over a dozen Harvey's hamburgers. He finished them easily and gobbled down some fries to boot.

Wayne Crawford (teammate): I sat beside Daryl on almost every road trip. We bet him he could not finish 15 Harvey's hamburgers, a pack of fries, and a chocolate milkshake by the time we went from Toronto to Niagara Falls, roughly one hour and 15 minutes. By Hamilton, the food was gone. Completely demolished. Forget about the Miracle on Manchester, how about the eating display on the Flyer bus? During another performance, he downed six 12-inch subs. Now that was child's play.

You knew you were in the presence of a true professional eater when he took two Harvey's hamburgers, slapped them together, buns and all, and bang they were gone. It was like watching a python gobble up a cow. We would cheer him on and stupidly forgo our food just to watch him eat. I saw him eat 12 hot dogs as a snack on a fishing trip once with Mark Osborne and me. He actually brought a Hibachi on the small boat to cook the said hot dogs on the French River. He never came up for air. And he was never full. The only problem with Daryl in Niagara Falls was that he did not like to go to school and therefore always struggled to keep his marks up. He was actually a very bright guy.

Daryl Evans: My mom and dad came down for the weekend, and we had just received our report cards. Dad said, 'Let's take a look at those marks, son.' He took a look at them and commented they were not too bad. Thank God he was looking at my 'Days Absent' and not my marks! I mean 60, 59, 62 were my days absent. The real marks looked like a low scoring football game: 12, 22, 15!

But back to the draft. Evans fully expected to go in the first five rounds. He was a prolific scorer in junior, having tallied 43 goals and 38 goals respectively in the two seasons prior to the draft. Daryl and I were still sitting together after I was drafted, and it started to become well beyond the time where Daryl had expected to be drafted. He visibly became more and more frustrated. Like I mentioned, after the first five rounds, there was a break for lunch. Daryl left the Forum in a huff, and I couldn't believe it when he went across the street and bought several sheets of neon yellow Bristol board and the thickest colored magic markers he could find. He marched back into the Montreal Forum and started to write on them:

"EVANS STILL AVAILABLE," "EVANS STILL NOT TAKEN."

He actually held them up while the draft was going on. It was something to see. He looked like a sandwich board advertising a pastrami on rye. At the time, it was not funny, and I felt bad for him. Our agent, Gus Badali, actually had the nerve to ask Daryl to keep track of Gus's players who were getting drafted in the last five rounds. At one point, I remember Gus coming up to us and asking if we wanted to meet Gordie Howe.

Daryl looked at Gus and snorted, "I would probably sucker punch him right now the way I feel!"

As each player got drafted ahead of him, Daryl got madder and madder. If he knew the drafted player wasn't half the player he was, he would take the pad that Gus had given him and throw it down in disgust. Loose sheets would fly out and scatter all over the Forum. Daryl was finally drafted in the ninth round, 178th overall to the Los Angeles Kings.

When Daryl's name was finally announced, he was in such a funk he didn't even hear the call. I had to give him a shot on the arm and yell, "Hey pal, I think you just got picked by the Los Angeles Kings." He was stunned.

Daryl simply said, "Now that is a fine place to go!"

In retrospect for Daryl, it actually was a fine place to go. He still lives there and never moved back. For the past decade, he has also been the color man for the Kings on their radio broadcasts. And he is, of course, the player that scored that famous overtime goal against the Oilers, which is often referred to as the Miracle on Manchester. I will always remember him as one of the funniest players I ever met, and was by far, the biggest eater I have ever met.

Several other fellow teammates on the Niagara Falls Flyers got drafted in that draft. Mark Osborne was drafted 46th overall to Detroit; Kevin McClelland was taken in the fourth round, 71st overall, to the Hartford Whalers; Pat Graham, 114th overall to Pittsburgh; Mike Braun 130th to Detroit; and Brian Rorabeck 193rd overall. Most surprisingly, in hindsight, Steve Larmer wasn't selected until the sixth round, 120th overall, by the Chicago Blackhawks. I was thrilled I would be going to my first NHL camp with a familiar and friendly face.

Pat Graham, Daryl Evans, and I took the train back from Montreal to Toronto. My dad picked us up at the train station. There was no big celebratory dinner or anything like that. On the way home, after dropping Pat and Daryl off, Dad stopped at Kentucky Fried Chicken, got a bucket of chicken, and we ate it at our kitchen table. There was no champagne or Chateaubriand. My best friend, John Kirk, came running over with an old Blackhawks pennant. It was a sign of his class, as it must have devastated him to see hockey players drafted on that day that could not have carried his skates. As my best friend and Dad enjoyed a drink together, I could only sit and stare at a Chicago lineup card and the glut of centermen: Terry Ruskowski, Tom Lysiak, Troy Murray, Billy Gardner, and this little guy by the name of Denis Savard. My work had just begun.

Shortly after, I went to visit Steve Larmer in Peterborough, where we went camping with our girlfriends. One of the Chicago scouts told Larmer shortly after the draft that he didn't know why they drafted him because they already had enough right wingers. Larmer was really discouraged and thought he might be better off getting a job digging pools than going to camp. Larms was a great player. Grampa had the playing style that made it look like he was just out there sauntering around, as if he were being interrupted from a game of scrabble. But he was a very smart man. He really knew how to find the holes and come late on the play. I told him he had to be joking; he had to go to camp. Thankfully, that unsure feeling soon passed and he opted to go.

To the Show

Derek (Turk) Sanderson was a riddle to anyone that knew him, especially when he was young. He was born and raised in Niagara Falls and was a great guy. Unfortunately, he had some big demons inside him that eventually got the best of him. He had a fierce temper and was a great competitor. Legend has it that during a game in junior, when he was about to play against Bobby Orr, his father told him that the scouts would remember two people in the game: Bobby Orr, and the player who hurts Bobby Orr. So he better hurt Bobby Orr.

I got to know Derek quite well in Niagara Falls. He was a star for the Flyers in the 1960s and came back to be an assistant coach when I was there. He was supposedly cleaned up by then, but years later, at a Niagara Falls reunion, he told me he was still drinking on the side during the time he coached me. He had a way of talking that was difficult to follow until you got to know him. He spoke quickly and seemed to mumble his words. If you didn't listen closely enough, you would have no idea what he was talking about. When I was 11, I got his book, "I Got to Be Me" for my birthday. I'm pretty sure it is the first sports book I ever read. Little did I know at the time that a lot of the people mentioned in his book were from Niagara Falls, and I would get to know a lot of them years later.

Sanderson's battles against alcohol are well documented. He was once so downtrodden, he had to sleep on a New York City park bench.

When Sanderson was rebuffed by a Central Park bum who refused Turk a gulp of his vino, Sanderson said incredulously, "Don't you know who I am?"

The hobo quickly quipped back, "Yeah, you're a bum like me."

But when Steve Larmer and I were going to Chicago for the first time, Derek took us aside and said, "Com'on boys, I know a great cowboy shop in Welland. We can get a good deal on cowboy boots and a hat. You two can't look like riff raff when you go to the Blackhawks. You have to look good!"

So the three of us go into this cowboy shop, Turk with a cigarette hanging out of his mouth and his hair flowing, although it was beginning to gray at the temples.

The guy obviously recognized Sanderson and he was gushing all over him, "Turk, you're the greatest."

Turk said, "We're looking for cowboy boots for these two young men, and I want good ones."

The fellow showed us these light brown suede cowboy boots. Turk thought they would be perfect for us. Then he told the guy he wanted us to get hats. So we were shown some nice, big, white cowboy hats, which Turk deemed to be appropriate. Turk thought we needed to add a feather to each of the hats, so we did.

The gentleman started tallying up the bill and Turk asked, "What kind of deal can you give me on the boots?"

The fellow replied, "No, I'm sorry Turk. I can't give you anything on the boots."

"Com'on, you gotta give us some discount on the boots," Turk pleaded.

Turk's bartering skills were obviously not on display this evening. This was the guy whose agent had negotiated a two million dollar deal in the early 1970s, making the Niagara Falls native the highest paid athlete on the globe.

The salesman responded again that he could not discount the boots. Turk then proceeded to ask if we could get a deal on the hats, as we were buying two pairs of boots, two hats, and two feathers. The guy said he could not give us a deal on *any* of it. The guy obviously threw his nickels around like manhole covers.

The bill came to about $350 for all the stuff, and Turk told us, totally unexpectedly, "Okay, I'm paying for all this; this is my gift to you boys going to Chicago!"

As we were leaving, the guy that tabulated the bill, who was obviously the owner of the store, asked Sanderson to sign a huge piece of paper to go on the front of a poster he had at home. He said he would hang the poster in the front of the store. He brought out the paper and asked Sanderson to sign it to him "in big writing."

Derek looked at the picture, sized it up, looked at the guy who owned the shop, took a big drag of his cigarette, blew it right in the man's face and calmly stated, "I charge $300 per autograph," and simply turned and walked out of the store, leaving Larmer and me standing in the shop with the hat and boots in hand. It was kind of uncomfortable. Sanderson was pissed off the guy didn't want to play ball.

Steve Larmer: I remember Sanderson walking out and telling us we could pay him back later. Great, like I needed a pair of cowboy boots – suede, nonetheless.

But Larmer and I really appreciated Turk's kindness and the hat and boots. Unfortunately, about six months later the hat blew off my head when I was driving on the QEW (Queen Elizabeth Way, a freeway linking Buffalo and the Niagara Peninsula with Toronto), and the boots were an unattractive beige suede, so I was too embarrassed to wear them very much.

Turk also taught me and Larmer something important about making a team. He told us that when you went to a pro camp, you could tell how good of a chance you had to make the team by the number they gave you at the start of camp. I was a little bit skeptical, but he turned out to be absolutely correct. At my first pro training camp in Chicago, Steve Larmer and I were given 67 and 68 respectively. The next year, we were given 47 and 48, and the year that we both finally made the big club, we were 28 and 29. So the veteran was absolutely correct on that count.

The last time I saw Sanderson was at a Flyer gala in 2009. He was gray haired and reformed. He had come a long way. What he disclosed to me at that time chilled me to the core. Turk revealed that during the season he was our assistant coach in Niagara Falls, he found himself bare naked in a Lundy's Lane field. He said he looked skyward and yelled out, "Either heal me or take me. I can't take this."

Thank goodness, the Lord listened that night, and with the help of a physician in St. Catharines and friends like Bobby Orr, he made a complete recovery. The man who squandered millions of dollars now teaches young athletes how to save and invest their money. If you asked me to describe Turk, I would need only one adjective: survivor.

The Feather Ruffler...shown here with a slight smile, and without his ever present purple beaver pelt chapeaux. My personal favorite coach Orval Tessier could administer a volatile lathering that would peel the paint off the dressing room walls. When he finished chewing your ass out on a Friday night, he forgot about it Saturday morning.

Orval Tessier

I had a strange introduction to the coach who would turn out to be my favorite coach of all time: Orval Tessier. In my junior career, as well as being an offensive threat, I also had the reputation, and quite frankly, one that I relished, of being a disturber of sorts. During my last year of major junior A with the Flyers, the coach of the Kitchener Rangers was none other than Orval Tessier. For some unknown reason, he rubbed me the wrong way and had a way about him that always got under my skin.

<u>Mark Osborne</u>: Ludz was a guy who could really antagonize the enemy, especially in junior. He had a real rivalry with Orval Tessier and the Rangers. They both hated each other's guts for some reason. Ludz would scoop up a pile of ice shavings on his blade as he was skating back to the bench after a whistle and launch it at Tessier's bald head.

This obviously rattled Tessier to no end, but I didn't care. He always tried to irritate me, and the chances of running into this junior coach again was slim. Well, that little snow prank came back to bite me in the ass quite quickly. After being drafted in the 1980 draft, I felt I had a good first camp in Chicago but was sent back from the Blackhawks to play one more year in junior. After that last year in Niagara Falls, I was home for the summer in my parents' Etobicoke house, where I grew up.

I was in my room when my dad came in and said, "Well son, you'd better make the Chicago Blackhawks at training camp because I just read in the Toronto Star that they just named Orval Tessier as the head coach of the Moncton Hawks."

Lesson #49: Be careful in life, because you never know who you will run into again.

The Hawks were the AHL affiliate of both the Chicago Blackhawks and Toronto Maple Leafs. The AHL was, and is, a place for three different levels of players. First, it is a place for the young and restless – young guys that will probably go somewhere. Tessier put Larmer and me in that category. Second, there is a group you could call the leaders and bleeders – really tough guys who can pound you game in and game out. And finally, there is the group that is done like dinner – either they will never make it, or they are on their way down and will never make it back to the NHL. Even in the early 1980s, it was unusual for two NHL teams to be associated with one AHL team.

I felt I had an extremely good second camp in Chicago, but with the good young team they already had, and the fact that they had drafted another pretty good center third overall the previous year in Denis Savard, I was eventually reassigned, along with Steve Larmer, to the Moncton Blackhawks. It was 1981. I really didn't mind playing in Moncton. I was still only 20 but was a little anxious at the prospect of playing for Orval Tessier. Would he give me a fair shot, or relish me to the pine? Larmer and I stayed at Moncton's "Canadian Inn," which was nicknamed the "Shady Rest Motel" by the hockey players who inhabited it.

A couple of funny things happened even before the season began, a foreshadowing of the next nine months. The Toronto Maple Leafs had sent a goaltender by the name of Curt Ridley, a good enough guy from Manitoba, to Moncton. He was playing out the string. "Ridds" had seen the NHL with Toronto and Vancouver but knew only a plane crash or a bout of influenza to the Leafs would have him ever called back up to the show. The night before camp opened, the grizzled veteran toddled over to a small watering hole and sat down by himself. He cared little that the curfew was at 11:00 pm and ordered a beer. There were 10 patrons in the place, and he got to chit chatting with a couple of them. Ridley, enjoying the company of the Monctonians and their small talk, bought a couple of rounds, as did the kindly older gentleman at the bar. The word hockey was not even spoken, as Ridley felt no need to explain his plight. This went on for a couple of hours before the gentleman, who had had his fill, said, "Good night, it's 2:00 am." At 8:00 am the next day, as Curt Ridley pulled his mask over his somewhat aching head, his eyeballs almost popped from their sockets as a short portly, bald man took to the ice with a whistle firmly entrenched in his bulldog like jaw. Ridley, despite having only four hours of sleep, was sharp enough to realize that the kindly old gent from the night before was, in fact, the not so kindly Orval Tessier. "Rids" got really hurt that camp, and I don't believe he ever played another game.

Bill Riley (Moncton Captain): Yes sir, Orval was quite a man, enjoyed his beer, and liked a certain type of player. Curt Ridley? He got hurt a couple of days later...he still hadn't let Orval see his face up until then.

To this day, I remember Larmer sitting at night in our hotel room, chain smoking, worried sick that a fellow by the name of Bruno Baseotto was going to take over his spot on the team. I had the coach to worry about. I figured Tessier and I would not be bosom buddies but was still surprised that for the first two weeks of camp, my worst fears were realized. I was like a mirage to the man.

Tessier did not utter one word to me, not even a passing "hello." I told Larmer I was in big trouble with this guy. He would not even acknowledge my presence. Tessier was described by many as a short, fat, sweaty, bald guy that reminded them of Friar Tuck, who took from the rich and gave to the poor. I don't know if I agree with the Friar Tuck comparison with regard to his character, but he was a coach who was a motivator, effectively utilizing both actions and words.

As often happens when you think nothing good can come from a situation, the experience in Moncton turned out to be good for me and my career. Gradually, Orval took a liking to the two young upstarts: me and Steve Larmer. And over the next few years, he became my favorite coach ever. Not the best, but my favorite.

Steve Larmer: He was a great coach that I enjoyed playing for. He was fair and honest and he let you play the game. I think of him a lot.

We had a good team in Moncton and would go on to win the Calder Cup in my first year there.

Orval Tessier: We had a lot of rookies mixed in with some good veterans. To start the year, we had seven players (before the cuts came back from the NHL teams) and

two of them were industrial leaguers. And our backup goalie was a beer salesman.

That beer salesman was loving life, just backing up Bobby Janecek, until one night in Fredericton – a bench clearing brawl erupted. He told us after the game, "Fuck this shit, I gotta go to work tomorrow." He didn't have to fight, but I think John Wensink accosted him on the bench. Hey, it's tough to make a living selling beer if your face looks like pizza.

Tessier was French Canadian. So in Moncton, New Brunswick, which had a large French Canadian population, Orval was in big demand for community appearances and speaking engagements. I was unexpectedly introduced to public speaking one evening with Orval. He asked, or, I should say, ordered Larmer and me to drive one and a half hours to a small French Canadian community to accompany him for a dinner and a speech. Orval was greeted with thunderous applause and Larmer and I just stood in the background and watched as Orval was treated like royalty. He was treated like a balding King Tut. Everyone kept putting drinks in his hand, and not one to let a good ice cube go to waste, in short order, Orval was clearly going to have difficulty navigating to the microphone, let alone give a short oratory.

Just before he was scheduled to speak, he sauntered over to us and declared, "Okay, one of you two arseholes is going to have to speak to this crowd because I am in no shape to talk!"

"Arseholes" was his affectionate name for the two us on numerous occasions. Unfortunately for me, Larmer was not an option. Larmer's response to Tessier's request to speak for him was "hubeda, hubeda," a la Jackie Gleason. So it was up to me. I apprehensively got on the podium, said a few words and answered a few questions. I do not believe my talk that evening got me a standing ovation, but it was my satisfactory introduction to public speaking at hockey functions. I grew to rather enjoy telling stories in public, and giving dinner crowds insights into the life of a professional hockey player.

Tessier did some inventive things to motivate his troops in Moncton. He once brought our contracts into the dressing room and exclaimed that we were getting paid "tousands and tousands of dollars" and were an embarrassment. It could not have been Larms and me, as we were only making $25,000 at the time.

We lived in a run down duplex that was about 300 square feet, if that. The electrical outlets had to be chiseled free of ice before you plugged anything in. One bedroom, one couch. Larms and me took turns getting the bed; two weeks for Larms, then two weeks for me. That fucking couch. If you were not perfectly in the middle of it, it would topple over. You had to have the balance of a circus juggler.

Steve Larmer: Ludzy had to sleep with the blow dryer to keep warm.

Tessier used to mangle the English language constantly. When he had an idea, he would always say he had an "ID." Another one of his classics was to say that if we were to ever succeed as a team, we had to get off of our "padesstalls," meaning pedestals. I always had a vision of Orval sitting at home at night, with a cold beer in hand and wearing nothing but an undershirt and boxers, thinking up ideas or ways to motivate his teams, or how to get under someone's skin. Orval preached from a strange bible but he always got the congregation to listen.

In a championship season, there are usually several incidents that occur, which one can point to as turning points. One such incident occurred early in the year in Moncton. We had lost several games in a row at the start of the season, and Tessier had decided to put down the hammer. We practiced hard from nine to 11 on a Monday morning. Orval came in immediately after practice and stated we were to be back by one o'clock. We were going to have the dreaded 'two-a-day' practices for a while. He was bound and determined to get his pound of flesh.

Jack O'Callahan (teammate in Moncton and Chicago and member of the 1980 US Olympic team): Our captain, Bill Riley, stood up and told our trainer to get 'that fat son of a bitch' back in the room. A lot of the older players vented their frustrations at being treated like junior players, like Orval was used to handling. We had about a two-hour meeting and Orval ended up agreeing with the veterans. He then said he wanted to take us all out for lunch and the whole team bonded like never before. The alcohol flowed at that lunch. I think we lost six or seven games the rest of the season. That's the way Orval was. He was a great manager of people, not just hockey players.

Jack O'Callahan was a real solid player and an even better guy. He was from Charleston, Massachusetts, the toughest area around, he was proud to say. Jack had that great *Boston* accent and when ordering a beer would say, "I'll take a Budweiser, King of *Beeeerrrssss*."

A year later in Chicago, Jack was going through a bad spell of taking penalties right at the end of a period. It seemed like for five or six games in a row, he would have the puck jump over the thin blade of his stick, which would force him to put the grab on the enemy and result in a penalty.

Finally, Tessier could take it no more. His patience was always thin, but now it was non existent. With his lava flowing, he yelled at Jack, "JACK, the gentleman from Sherwood will be here tomorrow, and we will sit down with him and design you a hockey stick that you *will* use...or... you will not play."

After meeting the Sherwood guy, poor Jack had a blade as wide as any goalie stick and it looked like a shovel.

Under Orval, we had to have a weekly weigh-in session to make sure we were staying in tip top shape.

Jack O'Callahan: I remember having a weigh-in one morning in Moncton and Larmer weighed in at 210 pounds. When we looked at the chart that Orval always put on the wall for everyone to see, in big bold letters beside Larmer's name and his 210 pounds, Orval simply wrote, 'VERY DISTURBING.'

During a home game in Moncton, we had not played particularly well in the first period. Orval actually locked the entire team out of the dressing room during the first intermission. With the way the arena was laid out, we had to stand in the hallway where the fans were walking to and from the concession stands. Believe it or not, in the early 1980s, players not only smoked, but often smoked inside of the dressing room between periods. It was quite a sight to see some of our players asking the patrons walking by for a cigarette during intermission. One guy actually walked up to the concession stand, in full gear, and ordered a drink. With about three minutes left in the intermission, Orval unlocked the door with a perplexed look on his face and exclaimed that the Moncton Hawks that he knew had not made an appearance in the first period and he was now going out to the bench. If the real Hawks wanted to join him, he told us that would be just fine.

After one particularly poor performance, we knew it was going to be a long day when, before practice, the volatile Tessier snapped at our trainer Randy Lacy, "Here are the line colors for practice: fuchsia, powder blue, pink, mauve. Playing like pussies."

During my year in Moncton in 1981, I got called up for some games with the Blackhawks. In Chicago, I didn't expect to play very much and realized I might not even dress for a lot of games. Like all players who have been fortunate enough to score a goal in the NHL, I remember my first goal vividly. It was in my first NHL game. It had been an eventful 24 hours. The night before I was summoned from the minors, Steve Larmer and I had a pretty bad fire in our duplex. We were cooking French fries and the pot exploded. A serious fire resulted. Funny now, but not at the time.

Steve Larmer: *We* did not include me. Mary Ann and Ludz had almost burned the place down cooking those French fries. I had been out and when I got back around 3:00 am, half cut, Ludz stopped me outside the door and asked, 'Can you take bad news sitting down or standing up.' I thought something bad had happened at home. So I walked inside to sit down, and there was smoke damage everywhere. I'm sure if it wasn't for Mary Ann, the whole place would have burned down. Mary Ann was trying to get the smoke out, and Ludz was in the bedroom packing! I can still see Ludz leaving

**for Quebec and me stuck in a burnt out kitchen, which I
had to fix. All I could say to him as he was leaving was,
'You SOB.'**

*The Gold Dust Twins...Moncton – that's long time pal, teammate, and roomy
Steve Larmer posing proudly in our 300-square foot dungeon, which had one
miniscule bedroom, a half-assed kitchen, telephone booth-sized bathroom, and
less insulation than a tent. The couch doubled as the second bed and looked and
felt like it was purchased at the Sanford and Son junkyard.*

So the next morning, I had to travel to Quebec City to join
the Blackhawks for a game that night against the Quebec
Nordiques. We were down five or six nothing in the second
period, and I hadn't played yet. I got a couple of shifts in
the second period, and in the third, I got a chance on the
left side and let go a long slap shot, which was rare for
me, and caught Dan Bouchard napping. It went past him.
Luckily for me, Terry Ruskowski retrieved the puck and told
me he was going to get it mounted. Well, I hope Terry kept
the receipt from the trophy shop because I still don't have
it. Actually, Terry is probably a better man than I. He came

to me a couple of days later and apologized profusely and admitted that he actually lost the puck. I probably would have just taken a puck out of the practice bucket and put it on a plaque and given it to the guy.

The one thing that struck me funny in that game was Tony Esposito. I saw and faced him in training camp but had not been with him and the team during a regular season game. I began to notice that on every shot on Esposito from *outside* the blue line, the whole bench would start to rise as one in anticipation. It was really strange. I couldn't figure it out. I said to myself, "Geez, this team is really edgy."

I turned to Billy Gardner, who sat beside me on the bench and asked, "Hey, what's the big deal? They're just shooting pucks in from the red line."

Billy responded with a straight face, "Ludzy, Tony can't see! He can not see the shots coming in from near the red line."

That just stuck with me. It was kind of strange because growing up in Markland Woods in Etobicoke, I was always the goalie during our ball hockey games, and more often than not, when everyone was saying who they were going to pretend to be that day, I would declare, "I'm Tony Esposito." I had no idea he was half blind!

It was hilarious to see "Tony O" go through a physical in training camp, especially the eye exam portion. It was conducted in a portable outside of old Chicago Stadium. They would ask him to read the bottom line on the eye chart, and he would ask something like, "Can you give me a hint what the letters are?" Mr. Magoo would have had a better chance to pass that eye exam.

Another thing about Tony was the Red Hot he would put all over his body. There are varying degrees of heat rubs you can use to help with pain, but Tony applied the hottest, vilest stuff I've ever seen. It literally burned your skin red. Lava would not have been as hot. He put it on to loosen all his muscles and alleviate some of his pain. And he would put it *all over* himself.

I'll give this to Tony. He was 40 years old and really worked hard. He was already a legend, a sure Hall of Famer. During games, he would yell, "Work, work, work," in a rhythmic voice. I heard stories about Tony's histrionics when a shooter in practice unleashed a bomb that got away from him and would hit him in the mask. That would cause Tony to exit the practice as soon as possible with his stick flying like a helicopter blade. That was the legend, but I never saw it. In fact, he would get laid out once a week by Keith Brown or later on by a non-thinking Kenny Yaremchuk. He would hit the ice like he was Tasered. Let's face it, he was 40, and I was 20. Really didn't have much in common.

Near the end of the season, after I had been in Chicago about a month and a half and played in several games, Bob Pulford pulled me aside one day and asked me if I wanted to stay with the Blackhawks and maybe not get much ice time – or go back with the Moncton Hawks and try to help them win a Calder Cup. I was 20 and wanted to play. I knew if I went back, I would get a ton of ice time, play on the power play, and kill penalties. Another reason I wanted to go back was the fact there was a great group of guys there. I didn't really feel like I was a Blackhawk yet when I was only getting spot duty. So I went back.

I was determined to have a great game my first game back so Orval wouldn't think I had turned off the gas a bit after being up with the big club. I didn't want him to think I had a swollen head. If there ever was a guy who could act as a pin to burst your balloon of pomposity, it was Orval. I just knew how he would react, and I was right.

Larmer picked me up from the airport around 1:00 pm. I had a meal and a little nap and then told Larms, "I'm going to go out there in the first period and run everybody, carry the puck, set up plays, and be the best player on the ice, because Tessier is going to trim my sails one way or another."

Larmer didn't think Orval would do that. He figured Tessier would be glad to have me back. I almost played too hard in the first period, knocking guys over, passing, shooting and I think I got a goal. I even played the point on the power play, which I almost never did.

Sure enough, Tessier came storming in after the first period and started ranting and raving about this guy and that guy, and then calmly turned to me and said, "And Ludzik, I don't know where you got that style of hockey, but this is the Moncton Hawks, not the Chicago Blackhawks. You're going to play the way I want you to play."

Orval just couldn't resist putting me back in line after being up with the big club. As Orval stomped out of the room, I could only smirk at my buddy Larms with that "I told you so" look.

I was definitely not the only one who was subject to the wrath of Orval Tessier. He was an equal opportunity employer. One night Warren Skorodenski, the goalie with the famous skull and cross bones goalie mask, was in net for us. In the first intermission, Orval tried to give us a pep talk, but he kept getting distracted by Skorodenski doing his gyrations in the corner, trying to stay loose between periods.

Orval finally had enough and yelled at him, "Hey, Skoro, stop jumping around over there! AND, by the way, that last goal…I could've stopped it with the end of my dick."

When Tessier yelled, the paint would peel off the walls. He would scream at the top of his lungs. No one was safe from his attack when his quills were at attention.

Orval once told us the league wanted to step in and give us some players because they thought we were going to get beat so badly. Believing him, I remember Larms and I were very upset by the comment but, again, it was Orval's strange way of getting us going.

The great guys on that team included Dave Farrish, Dave Feamster, Jack O'Callahan, Bill Riley, and Mike Kaszycki. Kaszycki was a short, stocky, prematurely balding man, who had a lazy lisp to his voice. Everyone to him was "buddy" or "pal." I thought I was pretty good at face offs until I met Kaszycki. He was unbelievable. So after almost every practice, I would bug him to take 20 or 30 face offs with me, and he would kick my ass. At least for about a month. With everything I was learning from him, I started beating him more and more.

After about two weeks of beating him pretty regularly, one day he said, "Bugger off, I'm not doing this anymore. You're throwing my timing off." But he was a great veteran and a great mentor to me.

Dave Farrish lived in a trailer home in Moncton and his prized possession was a Night Hawk motorcycle. He parked it beside his trailer. One night, at about two or three o'clock, Steve Larmer, Mike Kaszycki, Bill Riley (our captain), and I went and got a flat bed truck. We went to his trailer and stole his motor bike right from under his nostrils as he slept. The next morning, we took the bike and put it in the shower in our dressing room. Fortunately, he also had a car that allowed him to get to the rink for practice. He marched in the dressing room and proceeded to give us an exaggerated story of how he beat up some thugs who were trying to steal his beloved motorcycle, but it was eventually stolen. He even said he hit one guy over the head with a two by four. Bill Riley led the laughter as we directed him to the shower and his bike. A good laugh was had by all, except Farrish.

<u>Billy Riley</u>: That was one of the greatest pranks of all time. Farrish was a great guy but prone to exaggeration on occasion.

We also had John Gibson's friend Mel Hewitt on that team. All the young rookies thought he was a madman, and the veterans used to take advantage of the fact the youngsters were scared stiff of Hewitt. On our first bus trip, Larmer and I got on the bus and Dave Farrish pointed to two seats and said, "Those are your seats right there."

We dutifully sat down. Hewitt got on the bus and went ape. He started yelling at us for disrespecting him and how dare we sit in his seat. Who the hell did we think we were? We were pretty scared of this guy but it was all a set up. One day soon after, Farrish told me if I wanted to get in Mel's good books, I should ask Hewitt about his sister, who was apparently in the National Ballet of Canada.

So, of course, I took the bait and asked Mel, "Hey Mel, I heard your sister's in the National Ballet of Canada."

He looked at me angrily and replied, "You trying to be a funny guy?"

I just kind of stood there speechless and he continued, "Thanks, my sister has no fucking legs!"

You had to be careful when engaging sweet Mel in conversation of any type. During a poker game in the basement of some god-forsaken Moncton pub, Hewitt joined the frolicking and shenanigans. It was rare for him to have anyone to play with, as he was banned from most watering holes within a 50 square mile radius. Six of us were playing cards and Larmer was getting a little smart with some of his comments towards Mel. About an hour into the game, street smart Mike Kaszycki leaned towards me and whispered, "Hey buddy, tell Larms to shut up!" I relayed the message to Grampa Larmer who digested the thought, butted out his cigarette, and gave me a wink. About 10 minutes later, like a flash, Hewitt reached across the table and applied a boa constrictor hold to my pal's neck. It took four or five guys to release Larms from Hewitt's grasp. If Mel imagined any slight against him, look out. He was never going to be captain of the debating team.

I just stayed away from Mel after that. I was always afraid to ask if it was true or not.

Mel had a history of mayhem both on and off the ice. I heard many stories about him as soon as I got to Moncton. The most famous is best told by Bill Riley.

Bill Riley: One of the great showdowns in a bar room involved Mel Hewitt and Bill Goldthorpe, who was the inspiration for Ogie Ogilthorpe, the nut case in the movie 'Slap Shot.' Yes, there really was a guy like that, and he was just as feared as the movie demonstrated. I was driving into Moncton with my wife and kids after a day off and heard over Radio 103.9 that Bill Goldthorpe was involved in a serious altercation with a Moncton Hawk at the Cosmo Bar. I floored the accelerator to get to the rink, but deep down, I knew it was Hewy.

Goldthorpe was in the Cosmo Bar, which was jam-packed, and everyone knew the two wing nuts were eyeing each other up and down. If I had been there, I would have grabbed Mel and got him outta there. I think Mel's wife said something to Goldthorpe as she and Mel walked to the dance floor. The next thing you knew, Hewitt and Goldthorpe were nose to nose. Apparently, Goldthorpe recently had a bullet taken out of his stomach, but he had enough strength to take what I think was a bottle of 16-ounce Schooner beer and smashed it into Mel's face. The force of the blow almost severed Mel's nose in half. Blood shot all over the place and people were screaming. I'll give it to Mel. He was tough. He shook it off and battled on. But this Goldthorpe made a huge mistake. This bar was 'our' watering hole and all our players, led by Miles Zaharko, put a licking on this SOB. Mel carries a real doozy of a scar on his nose from that one.

You could say Mel's nose for trouble almost got ripped off in that encounter.

Bill Goldthorpe: I have never had the opportunity to comment on that brawl. Never had a chance to tell my side of the story. Thanks Ludzy, for letting me tell my side of the story. This is the true version. Forget about the lies the others tell. A little background may help. I had just had a bullet taken out of my stomach – had been shot in the gut with the bullet piercing my colon and kidney. I was on a colostomy bag and had to bury my father, who had just passed away. All the stress and physical anxiety left me very weak. I didn't know who this Mel Hewitt guy was. Never heard of him. Never saw him 'til that night. Yeah, we were in the Cosmo that night with about 500 other people. It was a real popular night spot, packed to the rafters. Outta nowhere this broad claims I stepped on her toe. This set her husband off and the next thing I knew is this Mel Hewitt guy was nose to nose, eyeball to eyeball with me and the entire bar was now looking at us. No one does that to me, no one. So I gave him a backhanded belt and had on a huge gold ring that took a chunk out of his face. But it wasn't a beer bottle. And yeah, then the boys on Mel's team got brave because there's 10 or 12 of 'em. And they just piled in and I only got one guy as backup: Gordie Gallant, thank God. We held our own but I'll never forget this one guy named 'Benny' who kept sucker punching me all through the battle. Benny something or other. As the cops arrested me and I'm leaving the bar, I yelled over to Benny, 'Hey you, if I forget, remind me to beat the living shit out of you the next time we meet.' I gotta thank my backup man Gordie Gallant, who stiffened a couple of guys, and it really was like an old western movie, except there were no stuntmen. Thanks for letting me tell my side of the story…that's the real story.

Billy Riley: The guy Goldthorpe is referring to is none other than Benoit Laporte, a French Canadian kid who was a draft pick of the Toronto Maple Leafs. We called

him Benny. You would have to be out of your mind to start it up with Billy Goldthorpe and Machine Gun Gallant – so Mel bit off a little more than he could chew.

Goldthorpe's back up, Gordie Gallant, was a 5' 9," 170-pound dynamo who wreaked havoc on and off the ice in the mid 1970s. It was no coincidence that this human powder keg was at the scene. He was born and raised in the Moncton area. Gallant's legend was almost as large as Goldthorpe's. His appetite for finding fresh faces to feed his love of mayhem was insatiable. He had a lust for combat. He was nicknamed the "Machine Gun" for good reason because when he was provoked or on any day ending in a "y," he would deliver a colossal amount of punches to unsuspecting victims. His punches would never stop coming, and he gave little consideration to who would be receiving his chin music.

Infamous...not just another pretty face. There really was a Ogie Ogilthorpe of "Slap Shot" fame, who was involved in one of the greatest barroom showdowns of all time. His real name was Billy Goldthorpe, and on a freezing cold evening in Moncton's famed "Cosmo" bar, not even a bullet lodged in his belly could stop this Maestro of Mayhem. The true story is better than the bullshit one! goldie@goldiegoldthorpe.com

In 1975, while terrorizing the World Hockey Association, he was involved in an ugly incident on a road trip. Gallant, playing for the Minnesota Fighting Saints, an appropriate team name for this pugilist, was late for curfew one night and was about to receive, as per team rules, a $100 fine. Machine Gun did not appreciate the extradition of $100 from his wallet, so he set out at 2:00 am to address the situation with Harry Neale, the head coach and "fine" master. Coach Neale had only moments before received a call from Gallant's nervous roommate warning him of the incoming Gallant, who was known to punch first and ask questions later. Neale, after answering the door clad only in a pair of boxer shorts, was bombarded with a flurry of punches by the obviously deranged Gallant, who quickly bounced the chubby coach into the hallway. He then entered the bedroom, shut the door, and saw a nervous assistant coach Jack McCartan, curled up on the bed. He figured he would get his hundred dollars worth. He slapped the assistant coach around for a few minutes with Neale helplessly standing outside the room listening to the goings on. The machine guns finally ceased firing. Finally, some logic must have penetrated Gallant's head and he realized his displeasure had been sufficiently registered. Gallant, fully satisfied with his handiwork, which included the demolished bedroom, a dazed head coach, and a shaken Jack McCartan, simply surveyed the scorched landscape and opened the door.

As he exited, he said to his mystified coaches, "Good night. See you tomorrow." Like the escapade was no big deal. Gallant, to no one's shock, was booted off the club immediately.

To me, Gordie Gallant was a very nice guy. I met him numerous times during my year in Moncton, and after all the hype I had heard about him, I assumed he would have a label on his head in big lettering saying "Highly Explosive." This was not really the case. Later, Gordie became a hero when he saved his girlfriend and young daughter in a fire, but in doing so, received burns to 80 percent of his body.

As always, I judge people by how they treat me, and Mr. Gallant was always cordial to Mr. Ludzik. Then again, I didn't fine him a C note and get tossed in the hallway by him.

But back to Mel Hewitt. The thing I remember about him was that he was always late for practice. Our captain Bill Riley was the one that handed out the fines.

Mel would come in at five after nine every day and Riley would pounce, "Aha, another $25 bucks, Mel. You gotta pay it."

We would all laugh. No one made much money, but Mel was not going anywhere either. I actually started feeling a little sorry for him. He would constantly say he was chasing his dogs that got out. He seemed to always have something going on.

Mel and his wife had two Afghan dogs, and unfortunately, one of them got killed – I think by a car. Mel's wife was away at the time and he panicked. His team was going on a road trip, and not knowing what to do, Mel tossed the dog into the freezer. His wife was not scheduled to return until after Mel's road trip, so he figured he had plenty of time. Well, sure enough, she unexpectedly came home early, and of course, went down to the freezer to prepare a meal for her sweet Mel and found the dog in the deep freeze. I have always been a little leery of that story but…

Orval Tessier: Certainly, it's a true story. I talked to his wife about it. Mel was a different sort.

Jack O'Callahan: That's a true story for sure. But I'm pretty sure it happened in Maine.

Bill Riley: That dog story is true, 100 percent. But it happened in Maine.

Funny thing about strange stories like that. You hear it from a couple of different guys, so you know it is probably true. Over time, the legend grows.

Even though he enjoyed his beer as much as anyone, Tessier seemed to enjoy minimizing the player's drinking time after a game. We were coming in from Fredericton, which was affectionately called Freddy Beach on the circuit. In order to get an extra 15 minutes at the infamous Moncton bar, the Cosmos, the older players, namely Farrish and Kaszycki, made Larmer and me take their equipment from the bus and hang it in the dressing room so they could scamper over to the bar to have a few extra pops and beat last call. It was just a mild form of initiation. Orval, heading to his office, saw us with the extra bags and made us zip them up and leave them unopened, so the veterans would have stinky sweaty equipment to put on in the morning. All hockey players know what wet and gooey equipment feels like to put on.

Kaszycki and Farrish taught Larmer and me several important lessons. They asked us if we wanted to go eat with them one night early in the season. We jumped at the invitation to go out with the two veterans. Well, Kaszycki and Farrish ordered shrimp cocktails, New York steaks, and bottles of expensive wine. We were trying to watch our nickels somewhat so Larms and I ordered something like ham steak, beans, and a beer. The bill came and the total was around $300, a lot of money back then.

"Okay boys, $85 each should cover it with tip," says Kaszycki.

"Hey, all we had was ham steak," we pleaded.

Rule #132: When you go out with the boys, the bill is divided equally, so always be the last to order so you know what the standards are.

I saw a much worse "beating of the bill" when I was coaching in Tampa Bay. It was in training camp, and we had just played the Senators in Ottawa. About seven of us went out to dinner: Rick Dudley, John Torchetti, me, and a few scouts. Bottles of wine were flowing like there was no tomorrow. Steaks, prime rib, and surf and turf were all around the table. But as everyone knows, the real expense is the alcohol. Now Torchetti did not drink alcohol. Not a drop. I will have a drink but giving me a $200 bottle of wine is like putting pearls on a pig, a waste of time. So the bill came and was lying there in the middle of the table. No one was going near it, just as if it were covered in toxic waste. Dudley finally squeezed a glance at it like a blackjack player surveying his hand. He did the math and told everyone they had to throw in $180 each. Torchetti, always a classy guy, did not really want to speak up but held his hands out as if he was being held captive in a Tijuana jail cell.

I noticed his plight, which was not his fault, and stepped up to the plate for my assistant coach, "Hey Duds, Torch only had a salad and a diet coke."

Without missing a beat, and adhering to Rule #132, Dudley quickly quipped, "There was chicken on that salad!"

With all those veterans and good young players, we were able to win the Calder Cup that year in Moncton. Bill Riley, who by the way, was the third black player to play in the

NHL, taught me an important thing about leadership. He was a great captain and was on his way down at 32 years of age.

The Teacher...Bill Riley, the third black man to play in the NHL, was at the end of the trail when Steve Larmer and I played our first year pro. He distributed advice like an old sage, and taught all those who bore witness that a championship cannot be won without an act of courage.

We were playing the Adirondack Red Wings and Dennis Polonich in the second round of the playoffs. He was probably the worst stick man I have ever seen. He would wield his stick with a blatant lack of respect for the consequences. I knew I was a little cautious around him after all the stories I heard about him. In an earlier well publicized incident, Wilf Paiement, a good friend of mine, took all he could from the stick wielding Detroit Red Wing. On October 25, 1978 "Wilfy," not a shrinking violet in his own right, had his fill of the pint sized Polonich's high jinx and trash talking and went berserk – Paiement used his Sherwood hockey stick like an axe, while Polonich's head acted as a Redwood tree. Polonich, whose face was not worthy of a modeling career to begin with, had Doctor Paiement reconstruct his with a lift with no anesthetic and Paiement didn't charge him a dime. Polonich eventually sued Wilfy for $850,000 and won. He claimed his breathing was hindered from the onslaught he incurred, but when I ran into him with the Adirondack Wings, he seemed to be snorting just fine.

At the end of the second period in Game Four in Adirondack, Riley could sense even the threat of what Polonich could do was throwing us off our game. We were a young team in a tough spot. I never forgot it. I can see it to this day.

Riley stood up, threw a Gatorade cup he had in his hand against the wall and yelled, "If that guy is throwing us off our game so bad, I'm going to take this mother fucker out... myself. Right now. He will not play the rest of the series the same way."

Sure enough, Riley went out and beat Polonich to a bloody pulp. The grizzled vet Riley knew just when to step forward. It was like a showdown at the OK Corral and the sheriff was not going to lose. That was why we won the Calder Cup.

To me, Bill Riley always seemed to be the forgotten man. He was a muscular guy with a high pitched laugh and taught the younger players the price you had to pay to be successful. Bill had the unique ability to pass on knowledge like those old boxing trainers. You know, the ones chomping on a two-inch cigar expounding the road to greatness.

"Ludzy, start sleeping with the window open. Larms, cut back on the carbos, you can sweat out beer but the whisky hurts the legs," Riley would advise.

During that season, Larms went and bought an eight-year-old car with standard transmission. We couldn't wait to take it to Riley's place to show it off. We were stunned at Riley's reaction. He was pissed that we hadn't taken him with us to buy it.

"You got Riles here and you don't use him to wheel and deal."

Riley said he wanted a ride in it, so Larmer started down the road shifting gears like a Formula One race car driver, laughing hysterically. Riley was in the back and his massive frame completely filled the back seat like 10 pounds of baloney in a five-pound bag.

"This thing is the size of a robin's egg," Riley lamented. "I outta give the both of you some education slaps on the head."

We're no more than five minutes down the road and Riley starts sniffing the air like a Bloodhound and says, "Aaaaaahhhhaaaaaa, smell that boys. That's your transmission."

Tears were running down his face from laughter as the "robin's egg" started to sputter and Larmer frantically shifting gears to no avail. It was amazing Riley could even discern a smoldering clutch and transmission with all the cigarette smoke emanating from the car's cockpit.

Bill Riley: That car! No question about it. It was absolutely the worst car sold to anybody. It was puke yellow and the transmission went on it right away. Served them right for not taking me with them to purchase it. Hey, Larmer was a great hockey player, 500 goals in the NHL, but that

was the worst car I ever saw. I laughed like hell when the two of them showed up at my door. Larms acted like he had just bought a Ferrari off the showroom floor.

I did learn my lesson, however. I did take Riley with me when I bought my car: a beautiful blue and white T-Bird that I bought for $3,000 and sold for $5,000 a year later.

Bill Riley touched many men's lives along his journey, which was long and hard because of his color. He was a giver, not a taker, but unfortunately his post hockey life has not been great. In fact, it has been a struggle. He was hockey's forgotten man. But I shall never forget him.

Mike Gartner told me he often told the following story on the banquet circuit and it was embarrassingly true. When we first moved to Moncton, Larmer and I always mixed up our clothes when we did our laundry. Underwear and socks, especially, would end up in the wrong drawer. To stop the mix up, we thought we would simply put our initials on our socks and underwear so we could easily distinguish them after they were washed. So one night, we diligently put our initials on all our clothes. It wasn't until we went to separate our laundry the next time that we realized what we had done. Initials SL.

Orval was up to his old antics during the playoff run, too. At a banquet before we played the Nova Scotia Voyageurs, Tessier got rambling in a speech and when analyzing the two young guns the Voyageurs had made the comment, "Any team would like to have two centermen like Guy Charbonneau and Dan Daoust."

They were the offensive weapons for Nova Scotia and in their second year of pro. Well, Mike Kaszycki and I took that as an insult. We looked at each other and said, "Hey, they're not any better than us!"

So the next day at practice, we took some hockey tape and put it on the back of our sweaters. Mine spelled out the name "Charbonneau" and Kaszycki wore "Daoust." Orval thought it was very funny.

"We will see," Tessier said. "We will see."

History shows we won that series. Orval knew how to motivate.

Orval always sat in the front of the bus, which is a long standing tradition for coaches. He used to loudly tap his foot on the floor if the bus driver, Lionel, was driving too fast. The players always believed it was an attempt to prevent us from getting back for last call. If we drove fast enough, we could just make it. He didn't like us making last call. Or so we always thought.

Orval Tessier (coached the Chicoutimi Sagueneens of the QMJHL in 1978-79): We were going home back through the mountains. About 10 miles out of Chicoutimi, there's a hill called the Three Mile Hill and a big ravine on one side. This was October and we were coming back from Verdun. Almost everyone was sleeping. We starting going down this hill, and just as we were about to get to the bottom, a transport was very slowly coming up the hill the other way. It jackknifed right in front of us, and we hit the tractor trailer broadside. Now, the Lord was with us because if we had veered off to the right, we would have gone down the embankment. Instead, we veered off to the left and into a cement wall. Our bus

turned over on its side. The tractor trailer was wedged in front of us and we couldn't get out the door, so the guys started pushing out the windows. I was sitting behind the bus driver, as I normally did, and when the crash happened, I bent the pipes that were behind the driver's seat in two with my back. So I was just kind of laying there. They had to push me out through the window. I had no shoes on or anything, and it was freezing rain. We were there for maybe 30 minutes before even one vehicle came by. All of the guys were standing back from the bus because fuel was leaking. We were worried the bus would catch fire. The first car that came along, the guy got so excited, he didn't stop. He just kept going. Another car came by shortly after and stopped. We had one player whose ear was hanging by a thread, and one goaltender whose knee was on the side of his leg. So we put those injured players in the car. It took about an hour for them to be taken the last 10 to 12 miles and then have the police and ambulances come back for the rest of us. They sent another bus. About half of us ended up in the hospital. I was in for about four or five days. After that, I'd sit in the bus, and I was worried all the time.

Orval Tessier would be proud of the fact that I refer to him as a "feather ruffler." Orval was an expert at getting under a player's skin at the appropriate time. He was also a great quote master and sometimes came out with expressions that would make you wonder how that could motivate a team.

He told the press in Moncton one night that, "This club throws more body checks trying to make last call in the bar than it does on the ice!"

When we were struggling at the beginning of the year, he told one reporter, "We are not a hockey club; we are a winter club."

He was not really a great X's and O's hockey genius, but knew how to get the best out of his teams and players. I really enjoyed Orval; there was never a dull moment.

Orval Tessier: The type of style I coached...Ludzik fit right in. I demanded a lot from the players, and I think I gave a lot, too. Sometimes, I would just stay away from the rink. I would tell Captain Bill Riley to run practice the next day as I wouldn't be coming. Ludzik could handle that independence. Ludzy was one of my favorite players ever. What I loved about him was his skating speed, his hockey sense, his toughness; he played the same way every night. Great face off guy...now you want to know the negatives. I always had to have a little chit chat with Ludzy, a one-way chat about his temper and silly penalties, especially in the playoffs versus the Nova Scotia Voyageurs, against Daoust and Charbonneau. He was really irritated.

With Orval, the chit wasn't too bad, but the chat used to take a chunk out of your ass.

Fortunately for me, after one year coaching in Moncton and winning a Calder Cup, Orval Tessier was hired by Bob Pulford to replace Keith Magnuson as the Chicago Blackhawks head coach.

Steve Larmer: Orval was very instrumental in the development of Ludz and me. He allowed us to play and grow. We were really lucky he was named coach

of Chicago the next year and decided to take a few of us with him from Moncton. You need someone that believes in you and will put you in different situations, and he was great at doing that.

<u>Orval Tessier</u>: I knew that Ludzik and Larmer would probably make it quickest to the NHL because of their willingness to work and to learn.

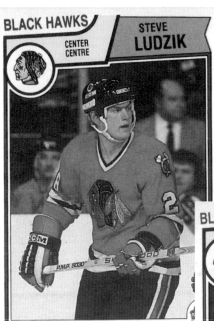

BLACK HAWKS — CENTER / CENTRE — STEVE **LUDZIK**

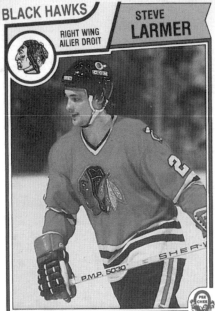

BLACK HAWKS — RIGHT WING / AILIER DROIT — STEVE **LARMER**

Someone screwed up here... if you look close enough at our rookie cards with the Chicago Blackhawks, your discerning eyes will detect that my name is on Larmer's body, and his name is on my picture – a fact that we both found funny. A mistake card... somebody lost their job.

Making the Big League

I had a pretty good training camp and realized I was about to become a full time National Hockey League player.

During training camp and the exhibition season in Chicago, Larmer and I shared a room at the Bismarck, a historic hotel opened in 1926 by German brothers Emil and Karl Eitel. It was purchased by the Wirtz family in 1956 and they installed air conditioning, automatic elevators, and telephones. Obviously impressed by their innovations, they apparently did no other upgrades before Larms and I got there. It is now known as the Hotel Allegro. The beds were like surf boards and used to move all over the place. You would go to sleep in one place and the bed would move throughout the night and end up in the corner, or so it seemed.

Knowing Larms from junior and living with him the year before in Moncton, I knew he was very much a creature of habit. He would have his pre-game meal at 12:30 pm; he would then have a cigarette after he ate; he would go up at 1:00 pm and get ready for a pre-game nap; he would get up at 4:00 pm, have a cigarette, and go downstairs for another cigarette and coffee, and then head to the rink. He was Mr. Routine. I do not know why I picked the last exhibition game, perhaps the most important game in our young professional careers, to screw up his routine, but I did. It was against the St. Louis Blues. I was lying in bed around 3:30 pm and decided I needed to get this guy's blood going a bit. So I quietly got up and set the two clocks in the room to 7:00 pm. I took his wristwatch, which was lying on the table beside him and set it for 7:00 pm. I stretched the phone cord, went into the bathroom, and called downstairs to the receptionist and asked her to call up to room 721 and say, "This is your 7:00 pm wake up call." After I explained it was just a joke, she agreed to do it. I quickly jumped back into bed.

The phone rang shortly thereafter, and Larmer struggled to wake up and answer it. I could hear the lady on the other end say, "Hello, this is your 7:00 pm wake up call."

"What? 7:00 pm?" Larmer bellowed.

Larmer panicked and jumped out of bed quickly. He was not so panicked however that he didn't have time to light up a cigarette and have it dangling out of his mouth as he tried to get his pants on. He ran around the room and screamed, "It's seven fucking o'clock. We were on the ice at seven o'clock tonight. How the hell did I sleep from 1:00 pm to 7:00 pm!"

I tried to pretend I was rushing around as well, but tears were starting to come down my face. Larms continued to rush around with the cigarette still hanging out of his mouth and had the presence of mind to start singing.

"Springfielddd, herrreee weee commme." That was the Blackhawks affiliate in the AHL. I had to walk into the bathroom as I couldn't contain myself. He thought I was just in there going to the washroom and he yelled, "Ludzy, let's go. I'm not waiting for you. Let's go! We gotta go! I'll go get a cab."

And then, rather perturbed, he added, "Hey, you think someone would have called us when we missed the team meeting at six pm!"

I finally couldn't take it anymore and opened the bathroom door and deadpanned, "Larms, it's only four o'clock."

"You cocksucker!" was all he could say.

It's your worst nightmare to sleep through your alarm and miss anything to do with the team. We obviously made the game that night and both made the team. Larmer ended up being Rookie of the Year in the NHL that year, so I guess it did stimulate him a bit.

<u>Steve Larmer</u>: Ludz set all the clocks ahead. I think we had played four games in four nights. We were exhausted. I remember looking at the clock and saying, 'Holy shit, Ludzy, it's seven o'clock. The guys are out for warm up!' I started scrambling around and singing about going to Springfield. He got me good on that one. We were always doing stuff like that to one another.

Tired of the cigarette smoke in our 'palatial mansion' in Moncton, I would implant exploding seeds into the tips of his du Maurier Lights. Once the dart was lit, it activated the seed, which would explode when he took a drag. This is not recommended therapy to help a person stop smoking. Although the explosions were funny the results were not effective.

I met Chicago's assistant general manager, Jack Davison, at that camp. He was a classy guy, and we hit it off well. I think he took a liking to me after a small incident at the first day of training camp. We were paid a per diem for meals and Davison doled out the per diem in cash. He would give us a few days' worth at a time. He counted out my money, and I thought he had made a mistake, so I told him.

"Mr. Davison, I think you gave me too much. You'd better count it again."

He counted it again and agreed, "Geez, I gave you a hundred dollars too much." And he took the extra hundred back thanking me over and over.

He liked me ever since that day, and always told me I was such an honest man. I never had the heart to tell him that the real reason I told him he had given me too much was that I thought he was setting me up. I figured it was a sting operation. I thought he *knew* he was giving me too much and was checking my honesty. I'd like to think I would have mentioned it even if I had known it was just a mistake, but I was quite young and poor at the time.

I thought I had a great training camp that year. There was no way I wasn't going to make the team. Before the last exhibition game, I had just eaten and was sitting in the lobby of the Bismarck Hotel for a few minutes.

Tessier was quoted in the Chicago Tribune, "Of all the centers on the team, Ludzik had the best camp." I was very confident I had worked my ass off to get a job.

Jack came up to me and said, "Ludzy, we have to make some decisions after this game tonight, and you're probably not going to like some of those decisions. I'm just telling you so you know."

I was stunned, "Jack, what are you talking about?"

He simply responded, "Oh, you played great, but we have to make really hard decisions and you're probably not going to like them."

I went to my room and smoldered. How the hell can he say that after the camp I've had! I was absolutely fuming. I decided that if I was going out, I was going to go out in a blaze of glory. I went out that night and played my heart out. I'm pretty sure I got a goal and two assists against Mike Liut.

I made the team.

I was happy for a whole host of reasons. Like they say, the difference between the pros and the minors are the runways. In the minors, the runways are longer.

Two years later, Davison came up to me and said, "Remember the exhibition game a couple of years ago and our discussion before the game. I just wanted to push you a little bit more because I wanted you to have an unbelievable game. I didn't want there to be any doubt in anyone's mind."

He knew that by getting me really pissed off, I would play my best. I had a lot of respect for Jack Davison; he was a class man whose word was his bond.

Just as training camp was ending, General Manager Bob Pulford went around the room with the trainer, Randy Lacey, nicknamed "Grinder," and said this guy and that guy were to be sent down to Springfield. When they got to Steve

Larmer's stall, Pulford said "Larmer is going down." Tessier stepped in and said he thought Larmer would do well playing with Denis Savard. Savard was adept at playmaking and Larmer could come in a little later in the play and use his rapier like hands to finish off Savard's playmaking.

Tessier also mentioned that he thought he was going to have carte blanche in the selection of his team, so Pulford agreed. When I heard that story a little later, it was the first time I had heard the expression "carte blanche." As most astute hockey fans are aware, Larmer went on that year to score 43 goals and won the Calder Trophy. As Steve was not the swiftest of foot, he may never have gotten a chance in the NHL if not for Tessier seeing his goal scoring ability in Moncton for one year.

<u>Steve Larmer</u>: Orval was the reason it all happened for me.

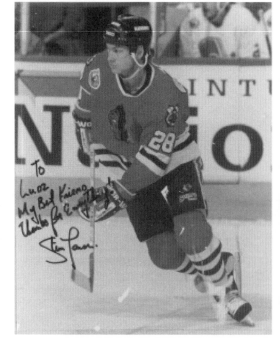

The Underrated One... Stephen Donald Larmer – as reliable as a Rolex, as a player and a friend, durable, smart, and excellent on the defensive side of the biscuit. Always accused of sauntering on the ice by his coaches, few could catch "Grampa," If he got a step on the enemy, no one went top shelf better than Larms.

Veterans were not always open to young bucks trying to nudge them from their NHL trough. During my second pro training camp, Captain Terry Ruskowski introduced Steve Larmer, Louis Begin, and me to veteran left winger Ted Bulley, a native of Windsor, Ontario. Bulley was a pretty tough cookie and sported a John L. Sullivan moustache that made him look like a turn of the century strong man. As we stood in the lobby, Ted Bulley eyeballed the youngster Begin. Louis, a nice kid, could only look down at the expensive marble floors of the Bismarck. We were all trying to crack the line up. I was a center, so I was no real threat to Bulley. Larmer was a right winger and no threat either. But Begin, he was a different story. Being a left winger, he might just be that threat. Mr. Bulley, as we called him, reached out his big paw to shake Larmer's hand and mine, and then he abruptly jerked it back from Begin, as if Louis had an electric buzzer concealed in his hand. The words were gruff and concise.

"You Begin?" he leered, knowing the answer. "Keep your fucking head up kid!"

Louis Begin never played a game in the NHL. Ted Bulley won his job at camp before being traded away. He was a survivor.

Training camps are always tough, and the exhibition games often decide who will be on the third and fourth lines to start the year. Most general managers start every training camp with the mantra of "all spots are open." That is simply not the case. A guy that has no contract, was undrafted, and is simply a "free agent," as we say, has a snowball's chance in hell of cracking the NHL lineup. I really don't think Denis

Savard was worried about Steve Ludzik taking his job, no matter how quick I did the 5.5 mile run or how many sit-ups or chin-ups I did, or even how well I played in camp.

One guy I remember well was a fellow named Victor Posa, a Toronto boy, who had played with the Marlies and came to camp with ideas of making the big club right away. I thought Vic was having a pretty good camp and he earned a spot in the lineup for the first exhibition game against the St. Louis Blues in Peoria. He had the privilege of playing with me that night. I'm sure Savard, Lysiak, and Troy Murray did not dress.

About 20 minutes before we were about to hit the ice, Victor asked to see me in the hall and his color was ashen. He stammered, "Ludzy, I was looking in the trainer's trunk for tape and saw four tickets to Saginaw (the Blackhawks farm team), and one ticket had my name on it posted to leave tomorrow!"

I was incredulous for a few reasons. First, the trainer Randy Lacey should have hidden the damn tickets. Second, I figured that Posa would now be like a poodle meeting a pit bull, his determination to do well in this game all but gone, knowing his inevitable fate. Third, I did not need a guy playing on my line that was not mentally ready to play. Quite frankly, a couple of average exhibition games by yours truly and my job was in jeopardy. I must have had a good nap that day and slept with the window open because, like a good trial lawyer, I twisted the facts around a bit.

"Victor, you're not going to fall for that old trick, are you? Every year, they test the mental toughness of a rookie and allow him to find those tickets just to see if he's got the gonads to perform."

Victor's face went from inflamed to quizzical to enraged. He crinkled his face and said, "I'll show these bastards. I'm taking all the big boys on tonight, right from the start of the game!"

Sure enough, our line started the game, and as soon as the puck dropped, Posa, like a rabid warthog, made a beeline towards Jack Brownschidle, a very good, solid, and dependable veteran defenseman on the Blues. Posa attacked him like 10 drunken sailors on shore leave, pounding on the generally sedate Brownschidle.

When the festivities were over, Brownschidle, as he adjusted his face shield, calmly said to Posa as they skated toward the penalty box, "Hey kid, you're gonna have to beat up a lot tougher guys than me to stay in this league."

Victor was called up to the Blackhawks the previous year for two games while still playing junior for the Marlies. He did indeed go to Saginaw the next day and, unfortunately, never did make it back to the NHL. He became just another number in the hockey abyss. But I had at least gotten him to play all out in that exhibition game and I stuck with the big club.

Jimmy Ralph or "Ralphy" was one of the best goalies I faced in junior hockey. This will come as a surprise to many because of his shtick of self-effacing humor concerning his goaltending abilities on his color commentating stints on radio and television. Ralphy is hockey's version of Bob Uecker in baseball. The fact of the matter is that to even be invited to a NHL training camp means you are one helluva goalie. I got to know Jimmy at a few OHL All Star games in junior and we both became property of the Chicago Blackhawks. For two weeks every training camp, we went out for dinner together. I say that it was only two weeks because that was the maximum time he spent with the big club before being sent off to various ports of call in the minors.

Our first training camp together was a memorable one. The medical testing back then was done like you were on a conveyor belt. Your heart was tested at one station (EKG), your eyes at another, nose and throat at another, and teeth at yet another. It was, literally, 80 guys going from station to station. I don't think the Navy Seals go through that.

Everyone was in groups of two and Ralphy was my partner. Naturally, one of the stations was the rectal examination/ prostate check. Back then, it was just the lube 'em up technique and away you go. As Ralphy was bent over in the "position," he blurted out, "Hey Ludzy, I didn't worry about the finger up my ass until I felt two hands on my hips!"

Now, it is an old line I know but I had never heard anyone say it when they were *actually* getting it done. The doctor was not impressed in the least. Needless to say, I was laughing my ass off, no pun intended.

Every night for Ralphy's short stint with us, I would grab Larmer and the three of us would go out to a little area called the Italian village. Jimmy was unbelievable. He is well known now as an after dinner speaker and it doesn't matter if he is with one other person, or a group of 100, he is the same. Jokes, impressions, and interaction with the other patrons would continue throughout dinner. Everything but tap dancing. I always felt I should leave a tip for Ralphy at the end of the night.

Jimmy Ralph: During our first training camp together after a tough day of practices, Ludzy and I got an invitation from none other than the infamous Tony Esposito to go out for a 'few' beers. It was an odd invitation from a player of legendary status to two young rookies. But we jumped at the opportunity to swill a beer with Tony O. He made $300,000 per year and drove an Excalibur to and from practice. Ludzy and I were driving a Dodge Ram and a rusted out T-Bird from a different decade.

The fact he asked two relative youngsters out for a drink should have sent signals blaring. Any veteran halfway smart, after the day we had put in, would have just packed it in for the day. Tony was a bit of a cantankerous and snarly guy. But, hey, it was Tony Esposito.

Jimmy Ralph: We were in the midst of a professional beer drinker. The first sign of trouble was when he put his finger in the air and ordered nine beers, and that was just to get us started. The combination of being dehydrated from practice and having nothing to eat was a recipe for disaster. Our side of the table looked like a log rollers convention. Tony Esposito was always five or six beers ahead of us. Thank the Lord that the Hotel Bismarck was 60 to 70 feet across the street. We crossed over oncoming traffic, and who do we see huddled waiting for a cab to go to dinner in front of the hotel but Orval Tessier, Bob Pulford, Jack Davison, and Cliff Korall. You never saw two guys put their heads down like we did and pray no one asked us to talk.

During Ralphy's second year in training camp around the third or fourth day, he had an outstanding afternoon session in net. He made spectacular saves and was virtually unbeatable. He was still a very young goalie but was definitely outplaying the veteran goalies, including Skorodenski, Bannerman, Esposito, and Janecyk. His confidence was at an all time high. Ralphy called me in my hotel room at the Bismarck and wanted to go out for dinner right away. We met at the elevators and at the next floor, an old scout named Smitty, who was a good guy who always had a cigar in his mouth, stepped in.

Smitty looked at Jimmy and asked, "Say, Jimmy, can you see out of that mask of yours? It doesn't look like it!"

After putting on a Vezina-like display that afternoon, Ralphy was really puzzled why the scout would say that.

"Hell, seeing the puck is a prerequisite for a goalie, isn't it Ludzy?" Ralphy shot back.

And wouldn't you know it, during the scrimmage the next morning, Ralphy was throttled for eight goals. As each goal went in, he would say to his teammates, "Thanks a lot guys, thanks for the effort. I really appreciate it!"

Ralphy had the roommate from hell during one camp. He was a big fat farmer from out west with a premature balding head. He had more gas than Saudi Arabia. His farts were known to clear entire dressing rooms, never mind the tiny rooms at the old Bismarck Hotel. He burped, blew his nose in the sheets, and didn't flush the toilet. Ralphy had made all of his complaints known to Larms and me and, needless to say, we thought it was hilarious. Ralphy was fit to be tied. Ralphy was so sick with disgust, he wanted to ask for a new roomie. He was so desperate, he was prepared to room with us and sleep on the floor. The coupe de grace was the time when Ralphy went back to his room to grab a nap and found his roomie, his fat carcass laying buck naked on the bed, pleasuring himself. Ralphy was somewhat startled and asked him if he wanted to be alone. His roommate said it was no problem; he would just go use the bathroom.

Ralphy immediately came back to our room and screamed, "That's it! I have had my fill of that guy!"

When he went back to his room, he found a sample of his roommate's DNA wrapped in a towel. Fortunately for our friend Ralphy, he was able to secure a new roommate pronto.

All players, especially goalies, get ready differently for games. Tony Esposito did not talk the day of the game, to anyone. You never had to guess who was starting in net. He would not shave, and his head would bob and weave all day. Tony would be totally focused in a zombie like state, and he was big on visualization before it was popular.

Jimmy Ralph: Even in exhibition games, he would not talk. It was like he was in a trance. Every five minutes or so, he would twist his watch around on his arm and show me what time it was, so I knew how much time I had before warm up. No talking, he would just show me the watch. And he would tap the top of the watch as if he was nervous that I was not further along in my dress.

Early in 1982, we were in New York and playing the Rangers. Steve Larmer's mom and sister, Doreen and Donna, came to visit. Both women are the salt of the earth; they are just solid people. Steve and I made arrangements so they could come to the game. They had also come to a few games when we were in Moncton the year before. The morning after the game, Doreen called Larms and me and asked if we could join them for breakfast in the hotel restaurant. While we were eating, Orval and Bob Pulford sat a couple of tables over and appeared to be giving Larms and me the evil eye. It was so obvious that I remember feeling very uncomfortable, and was a little miffed that I could not totally enjoy my brief time with Steve's mom and sister. As we readied to leave, we both gave each of them a hug and a kiss goodbye. Shortly after, upon arriving at the LaGuardia Airport and getting ready to board the plane, Orval told Larms and me he wanted to see us before we got on. Tessier often wore a purple, beaver pelt fedora and pulled it down over his eyes when he was in a serious mood. We looked at him and his hat was pulled down. We must be in trouble, as only his nose was jetting out from beneath his hat. He gave us that hairy eyeball look. We meekly followed him. He took us right outside the terminal and stared us down before exclaiming.

"As we speak, at this moment, you two arseholes are both suspended from the Chicago Blackhawks Hockey Club."

His face was beet red, and he was almost shaking with rage. Orval's nose had the propensity to turn as red as W.C. Fields' proboscis when he got in this state. The early New York commuters at the airport were getting a full fledged reality show right before their eyes.

I think Orval was looking for a response, but both Larmer and I stood there stunned, trying to think back over the past 20 hours as to what we had possibly done to extract that statement from Tessier. He seemed surprised that we said nothing to defend ourselves so he continued.

"It's not bad enough that you bring those two broads on the road with you and hide them in your room, but then you have to insult everyone by prancing them down for breakfast in the morning right in front myself and the GM!"

We were stunned! Finally, Larmer could only utter disgustingly, "That was my mom and sister."

A stunned Orval was quick to respond. Under the circumstances, one would have expected that at least a mild apology would have been in order. But with a slight tilt of his head and an adjustment of his hat, he simply bellowed, "Get on the fucking plane."

As we got on the plane and took our seats, I could not resist turning to Larms and saying, "Larms, Tessier thought we were both with your mom and sister...which one do you think he thought I was with?"

"Shut up, Ludz!"

One of the most important things for a rookie is to be accepted by the other players. So on another trip into New York City, Tom Lysiak, Darryl Sutter, and Greg Fox took us to various establishments. The veterans also teach you that you have to pick your spots. That is to say, you have to know when you can go out, and conversely, you have to know when to shut it down and give your body a rest. We had two days off in New York, so the veterans figured it was safe to take out the young guys. We went from bar to bar to bar from 12 noon until 1:00 am. We all probably had a little too much to drink. Finally, on the way back to the hotel, we grabbed a sandwich at a corner deli. Later that night, I heard Larmer get up, groaning and moaning, and he stumbled to the bathroom and got sick.

He stumbled back into bed, lit up a cigarette and exclaimed, "Damn pastrami sandwich!"

One trait I learned from Tessier that I tried to incorporate into my coaching years later was that nothing that Orval did or said to you was personal. By that I mean, one day he could tear a strip off you for your play or actions and the next day it was over. I would think I was going to be persona non grata for days for something that I had done, and he would simply come up to you and start a normal conversation the next time he saw you. He had made his point, and it was time to move on. He would never hold a grudge.

Orval Tessier: When I was playing myself, I felt that was the way I wanted to be treated. I played for some great coaches. I played for Punch Imlach. And that guy could be tough on you. But, 15 minutes later, he would ask you to go for a sandwich. I also played hockey for Hap Emms. Now, here was a tough guy too. But his record in junior hockey speaks for itself. When a coach got on me, I had to take it, but I always appreciated the fact that when I met him the next day, it was a new day. I figured I'd better pattern myself a little bit after those great coaches.

He also could laugh at himself if you caught him in the right mood. After getting to know him a lot better, I used to joke with him concerning his baldness and his convenient use of the infamous comb over, or "bacon strip technique," to hide some of the bare patches.

He would get a haircut and I would ask him, "Hey Orval, you just get a haircut? How much was it?"

"Ten bucks," he would proudly crow.

"Oh really? Nine dollars to find it and one to cut it?"

He would chuckle, shake his head, and walk away in disgust.

In Chicago, as in Moncton, he had his own peculiar way of speaking.

Jimmy Ralph: Orval had a unique way of always putting the word 'hockey' into every sentence he could. He would say things like, 'Jim, put on that hockey mask, put on those hockey gloves. Pick up that hockey stick. Play yourself onto the hockey club. Your hockey life depends on it,' and 'that's a true hockey story.'

One of the things I have always tried to do is dress well. Sometimes, I had a few hiccups with respect to my apparel.

Orval Tessier (1982-83 Jack Adams Award, NHL Coach of the Year): We were in the playoffs against St. Louis, and Ludzik had this grey suit he kept wearing all the time. The suit looked okay, but he kept wearing these brown shoes with it that didn't match too well. He was getting it from everybody so, instead of going out to buy a pair of grey shoes, he painted them grey! Of course, when the paint dried and he walked in them, they cracked and looked ridiculous. Here's a guy in pro hockey wearing painted shoes!

I've got to admit that Orval Tessier was not a dull man. He enjoyed friction, loved to talk loudly, and was actually pretty funny, even if he did not mean to be. One time he was quoted in a Chicago daily that when things got boring around the dressing room or he felt some complacency had set in around the team, he was going to order up a Catholic versus Protestant scrimmage.

Murray Bannerman, who was Jewish, found this hilarious. "I guess I've got the day off when that happens."

It never did happen.

Another statement that went under the radar occurred during a press conference after a road game versus the Detroit Red Wings. Apparently someone on our club complained about the beds in the Pontchartrain Hotel. When confronted by a reporter and asked to comment on the ship shoddy excuse, Orval, without missing a beat, chimed in with, "Well, they should try just having one person in the bed." It was a statement to suggest he believed extracurricular activity was afoot.

We had an overnight fiasco one time in Philadelphia. Two guys rooming together from the club got into an early morning (3:00 am) fracas with patrons in an adjoining room. We had defeated the Flyers that night and were feeling pretty good about ourselves. The original cause of the rhubarb was never confirmed, but eventually a security guard was called to the player's room, knocked on the door, and was told to "fuck off" in no uncertain terms. The guard, realizing they were part of the Blackhawks contingent, immediately put out an SOS.

"Call the coach," he pleaded over his walkie talkie.

Within five minutes appeared the very familiar sight of one Orval Tessier. Now, let me tell you, even at the best of times, Orval was not an oil painting. But at 3:00 am, he looked very rough and disheveled – speeding along the hallway like a barreling bowling ball, bare feet, blue pants, and an untucked white undershirt. His comb-over was now flapping like a scarf in the wind. Tessier arrived on the scene like an aggressive Columbo and quickly took charge of the Philly standoff.

"Open the fucking door, now," he screamed. There was no response.

The completely befuddled security guard was now trying to calm the loud and blustery bench boss. Orval was having none of it.

"Open that door. I want to see who's in there," Orval told the guard.

Twenty or so teammates, clad only in underwear, were all peering out their doors and sneaking into the hallway to get a close up view of the proceedings. The episode had also attracted the attention of the other guests who were on the floor, who probably thought it was a terrorist attack. "Get the fuck back to your rooms," roared the rampaging Tessier. Suddenly, a bellow that would attract a bull moose could be heard emanating from the room.

"Aaaaaahhhhaaaaaaaaa, two married guys." And then, as if he was condemning them even more, "And two Catholics!"

I got introduced to Roger Neilson in my early NHL days. He was an associate coach with the Blackhawks. I'm not sure how enamored Orval was with Roger being in that position, but that's the way it was. Orval was a pure motivator, not an X's and O's guy. Everyone knew that was Neilson's specialty. Shortly after I had met Roger, we were having a film session with the whole team. Orval told all the defensemen that he wanted all shots from the point to be on the ice so they could be more easily deflected.

Roger, being the studious one, said, "Well, Orval, actually we did some extensive review in Vancouver, and the ideal height is six inches off the ice. If it is along the ice, it has more of a propensity to get deflected wide of the net. Six inches allows the puck to get to the net more often and get deflected more often at the net, which will also permit more rebounds."

They started to get into it right in front of everyone and then, a little later, we were going over tape from the night before, and wouldn't you know it, Al Secord scored on a deflection from a shot that was right along the ice.

Orval shot back to Neilson something like, "There you go. What do you think of that, Captain Video."

Neilson simply replied, "You got it, Mount Orval," which became Orval's nickname after he spewed lava all over the place about us not having hearts.

Roger had a dog named Mike. The dog was treated like a human being and accompanied him everywhere. I would describe the dog as a Husky-Lab mix, and it was pure white. It was like no other dog I had ever seen. It went from team to team with Neilson at his various NHL stops. The dog would have free reign in the stadiums and rinks where he coached, and I wouldn't be surprised if Mike had a say in who made the clubs. Let's just say the area where Chicago Stadium was located was not the best. In fact, it was a bit of a freak show with pimps, drug addicts, transvestites, warlords, and pit bull fights. When you parked your car, it was $5 plus another $5 if you wanted it to be there when you got back. We used to always tell Roger that if he didn't keep a better eye on Mike, he would come out one day and look across the street and see Mike roasting on the spit of a barbeque. I really believed Mike would one day end up on the menu at "Clydes BBQ, Bail Bonds and Pawn Shop," your convenient one-stop store.

Roger was one of the most unprecocious men I have ever met. Bob Pulford had lent him a Mercedes to drive, and when he returned it, there were scratches all over it where Mike had been jumping in and out of the car. Roger wouldn't even have noticed that. That kind of stuff didn't interest him in the least. I even heard at some of his stops, he used to ride a bike to the arena just to get a bit of exercise. Apparently, he did it a lot in Philadelphia, of all places.

When he was coaching the Philadelphia Flyers and I was coaching in Tampa Bay, we had a close game one night but they beat us late in the game. Roger came around to talk to me after the game. He was wearing one of those funny bright ties he always wore and mentioned that he had a bad flu bug. Looking back, I think it may have been the beginning of his cancer because he didn't look very well at all.

He was an assistant coach of the Ottawa Senators the last time I saw him in person. I was in Ottawa as coach of the Mississauga Ice Dogs. He was not going to be around much longer, and he knew it. It was a really tough visit for both of us. Everyone loved Roger. He was always in tune with the players. He was a fun guy, and the thing that I took from him was that you didn't have to be a prick to be a good coach; if you knew what you were talking about, and he did know what he was talking about, you could be effective. He did not drink, smoke, or swear, a rarity in our profession. He was a man of fertile imagination. For example, on a penalty shot he was known to pull his goalie in favor of a defenseman. Upon hearing the whistle to start the penalty shot, the defenseman would attack the stunned shooter. When Roger pulled his goalie in the last minute for an extra attacker, he would have his goalie leave his goalie stick across the crease as he peeled off to the bench. Both rules were amended because of Roger.

He was a religious, moral person, but he never pushed his beliefs or way of life on you. I took from Roger that you'd better be technically correct when you were talking to players because you can fool some of the people some of the time, but you can't fool hockey players if you don't know what you're talking about. I really miss Roger.

Over the years, of course, you get to know some of the referees and linesmen pretty well. The great majority of them are just great hockey fans and great people. John D'Amico was a classy, classy linesman who just flat out loved the game. He was as strong as a bull.

It was a simple moment but one that I will always remember. Quite early in my career, we were playing in the Gardens and D'Amico, as he lined up for the drop of the puck before the opening face off, happened to be standing beside where I was sitting on the bench and said in what seemed like reverent terms, "Hey Ludzy, Hockey Night in Canada… Chicago Blackhawks…Toronto Maple Leafs…Maple Leaf

Gardens…on a Saturday night…in the middle of winter…it doesn't get any better than this baby."

Remembering that comment still gives me goose bumps. I would have another encounter with John D'Amico near the end of my playing career in Rochester. Funny enough, we were both inducted into the Etobicoke Sports Hall of Fame in 2009.

I had an encounter with another referee early in my career, Ron Hogarth. It happened against the St. Louis Blues and involved Doug Gilmour. I think it was Doug's first year in the league. I was asked the year before to present an OHL trophy to the league's leading scorer, who was Gilmour of the Cornwall Royals. So here we were the next year, on a Sunday night in Chicago Stadium in the last minute of the game, and Gilmour and I were lined up for a face off. The puck was dropped and Gilmour and I got tangled up battling for the puck in Hogarth's feet as Hogie was unable to get out of the way. My stick accidentally came up and clipped Doug in the mouth. He lost a couple of his chicklets.

I turned to Hogarth, and yelled, "Hogie, get out of the frickin' way, you're too fat!"

Hogarth just looked at me and glared. As we were going off the ice after the game, he said, "Yeah, Ludzy, I'll be renting a tux for your induction into the Hockey Hall of Fame."

I quickly came back with, "Well, if you have to, for you, it will be a 52 extra stout!"

I felt bad about clipping Gilmour's teeth, so I went around after the game to Gate 3.5 in Chicago Stadium and said I was sorry. Classy, even early in his career, Gilmour said "No problem." He knew it was an accident. It was the only time I ever apologized for anything I did on the ice.

Orval Tessier's run as the Blackhawks head coach came to an end after one and a half years, in the spring of 1984. He was greatly criticized in the playoffs the year before when he insisted that what our team needed was "18 heart transplants" to beat the Edmonton Oilers.

"We'll probably contact the Mayo Clinic for about 18 heart transplants before Sunday. I don't know if we can get it done. There's usually a waiting list for those things."

With that hot exchange in a post-game playoff tirade Orval Tessier, frustrated, exhausted, and more than a little pissed from a 8-2 spanking that was seen coast to coast against the dynamic Oilers, signed his death certificate as a Blackhawks coach. That was bullshit and everyone knew it. Orval was just trying to be Orval Tessier.

The fact of the matter was he had used that same line a couple of times during the regular season but it didn't get much reaction from the press because we were not in Canada, so he wasn't chastised for it.

Hey, their fourth line winger Jaroslav Poszar, a Euro and an extremely talented player, grabbed our heavyweight champ Secord and gave him an old fashion beating right in Chicago. We were speechless on the bench.

Funny thing about those Oiler teams in the 1980s. They would have, in my opinion, throttled the 1955 Wings, the Leafs of the early 1960s, and Scotty Bowman's Canadiens of the 1970s. No disrespect to anyone, but those teams would have been attacked like a band of gypsies on a leg of lamb. Anyway, a little insight into an athlete's psyche. Everything is structured, especially on game day. Get up, breakfast, team meeting, morning skate, afternoon nap, etc. The one thing I remember about the Blackhawks was that the stereo, which would blast music from 4:00 pm on game days, would have to be turned off at 6:00 pm sharp, and would stay off for the remainder of the evening – a practice I believe was observed by 20 of the 21 NHL teams then in the league. The Oilers however, whose dressing room was directly beside ours in Edmonton, cranked their stereo up to unfathomable decibels and the walls of our room would quake, vibrate, and tremble under the stress of the Edmonton discothèque. As our club quietly tried to put on our game faces, the footloose and fancy free Oilers had all the frivolity of 20 guys in a strip club. They were cocky, confident, and could back it up. Just before you went on the ice to start the game, the Oilers could be heard as a club in unison letting anyone but the hearing impaired know what they thought of you. I'm not sure if it was planned by the cocksure coach and GM Glen Sather, but you never know. The Oilers would have one guy read the starting lineup, "Starting in goal for the Chicago Blackhawks, number 35, Tooonnnnnyyyy Esposiiiitttttoooo." On cue, the entire Oiler band of merry men, like an organized choir, would 'boooooo' loudly and add a few chirping comments. "Old bastard," one Oiler would shout, and a scattering of other gems would follow. "Five-hole," another would bellow, and for good measure an unidentified voice behind the wall would add, "sonovabitch can't see." This ritual would go on for the entire opening lineup. "Stinks," "can't fuckin' play," "gutless," "get on him," and that's being kind. Conversely, they would pump their own tires, "Starting at center, number 11 Mark Messier," followed by a quick expulsion of cheers and comments. "Big night," "run 'em over," "we're gonna kill 'em." Hey, it isn't bragging if you can do it.

I loved playing those games against good competition. I especially enjoyed playing against the Great One, and trying to antagonize him as much as I could. I never really knew if I had any effect on him at all.

Paul Coffey: Gretzky knew I was good buddies with Ludzy. He came in after one period in the playoffs and said, 'How can you be buddies with that asshole.' Gretzky said Ludzy was one of the most irritating players he played against. I found it kind of funny.

It was like pitting mules against thoroughbreds. You could have had Scotty Bowman, Fred Shero, and Al Arbour all on the bench but, when push came to shove, if you didn't have the horses, you were done. You didn't race a Volkswagen

Bug at the Indy 500 unless you knew one hell of a shortcut. Nobody was going to beat those teams. Nobody.

Orval Tessier: When I was let go, I just shut the door. I never made a statement. I didn't throw stones at anybody. I just walked away from it. It probably cost me another job somewhere else in the NHL. I don't doubt that whatsoever. I could have mentioned quite a few things, but that would've meant me singling out some individuals, and it wasn't going to serve my purpose any by criticizing anyone in the organization. Some members of the press turned against me because of some individuals. The team was very upset at me because I wouldn't take a scouting job, but I felt at that particular time, I deserved better. I never said a word to anyone in the press; I just kept great memories of Chicago and the majority of the people I was associated with.

Tessier's success came from the fact he portrayed himself as a mean tough guy who didn't take any crap from anybody. During his two-year tenure, he had taken the Blackhawks farther than they had been since Billy Reay was the coach in the early 1970s. However, after being relentlessly berated for the "heart transplant" quote, the next year, he appeared to mellow and was more of a nice guy with his players and the media, which in my opinion, caused him to lose his edge somewhat and therefore his effectiveness. It hurt me deeply to see the man I had learned to appreciate and respect lose his fiery and bombastic ways. I have always felt that Tessier deserved a longer term as Blackhawks head coach but, as I would find out years later, in the coaching ranks, what is apparently deserved is not always what transpires. Of course, I called him immediately after he got fired to express my gratitude for all he had done for me and especially for giving me a chance to play at the NHL level. Who knows what my career path would have been if it weren't for Orval. I think the only time I got mad at Larmer was after Orval got fired. Steve didn't see the need to call him right away. I thought he should have called immediately.

"After all Orval has done for you and the chance he gave you, you would think you would at least have the decency to call him right away," I lambasted him.

It's kind of sad that two of my favorite men in hockey, Orval Tessier and Don Cherry, got along like a cobra and a mongoose. They really despised one another. I think they had a few rough encounters when they played on the same junior team. It's really too bad. They are both great guys but something happened and they could never get along. I actually know what solidified that hatred. When Orval won the Jack Adams Coach of the Year Award in 1983, he reportedly said that the trophy would mean something except that Don Cherry's name was on it, too. So, after the "heart transplant" comment, Cherry didn't say anything at the time. He was just laying in wait. He knew Orval's comment would come back to haunt him like a four-week old tuna sandwich. And, wouldn't you know it, when the Hawks struggled out of the gate the next year, Cherry pounced on him like a wounded puma. I don't think they've ever talked since. Rule #66: When picking a fight, make sure he's not at the top of the food chain.

I never really understood why, after my junior encounters with him, I took a strong liking to Orval Tessier. Orval later told me that I was one of his three favorite players of all time that he had coached. John Wensink was number two. That meant a lot to me. On more than one occasion, he also told me I was the only hockey player he would have allowed his daughter to marry. I never knew quite how to take that compliment. Either it was a great condemnation of hockey players in general or shows how little Orval really did know. Somehow, the thought of the blustery Tessier as a father -in-law conjures up some hostile images. Perhaps I liked him because he bore a striking resemblance to my father, both in stature and personality. Near the end of our hockey relationship, I discovered an eerie coincidence – my father and Orval Tessier were born on exactly the same date: June 30, 1933.

After Orval was unceremoniously dumped, Robert Jesse Pulford stepped in to take the helm. He actually coached me twice in my tenure with the Blackhawks. A good man, he was a person who chose his words carefully, to say the least. When he coached or was under some type of stress, he would unknowingly purse his lips together and blow hot air out of his lips for about 10 seconds that sounded like the flaps on an awning in a wind storm. When I was growing up in Toronto, Bob Pulford was bigger than life. A rugged, all purpose player, who had a handful of Stanley Cups with the Leafs. When I got to Chicago, he was like a father figure to a lot of us. I always looked forward to him coming in the dressing room after a game, especially if we had won. He would go by each player's stall, rub their head, and give them a little nod. I lived for that post-game ritual. He was the only coach I ever had that would come in after a loss and stand in the doorway and say, "Sorry boys, I didn't coach very good tonight. I didn't have my A+ game."

A lot of the players would think "Oh, screw off, Pully," but it was Pulford's way to regroup the troops and make you feel a little sorry for him that you had lost for him. He had a way to make you feel ashamed if you did not win.

Pulford was an old school guy. He was not a systems guy at all. His pre-game oratories included statements like, "You gotta think about winning; you gotta think about scoring. You have to want it more than the other guys."

The pressure to win each night was always visible on Pulford. He could not camouflage his intensity with his flushed cheeks, the wringing of his hands, and the odor of the three cigarettes he had just ripped through in five minutes during the intermission before he came back into the room and implored us to "think about it." In other words, it was all about will. And he was right. When will meets skill, it's tough to beat.

Whenever you talked to Pully, he would usually be smoking. He could inhale a cigarette like no man I have ever seen. You would stand there, watch him inhale, and wonder where all the damn smoke went because it wouldn't come back out. You knew it went somewhere, but I could never see it escape! You could always tell when he had been through a difficult day because he would come downstairs from his office and you could see orange nicotine stains on the top of his white hair. When he was just the general manager and not on the ice at practice, the players learned, the hard way, to hide their cigarettes when they were on the ice. Pully had no qualms about raiding each guy's package for three or four darts each while they were on the ice.

Pully was a tough contract negotiator. I fancy myself a bit of a hockey historian, and I always found it funny that Pulford, who had many flare ups with Punch Imlach in his Leaf days, wasn't afraid to use Imlach-like tactics when he negotiated with players. You weren't going to push him around at the negotiating table. I had one of the most popular agents at the time, Gus Badali, but it didn't matter to Pulford. Pulford knew exactly what he was going to pay you and didn't stray from that number. And let's be honest here, the good Lord and the 12 Apostles were not going to get me one extra cent. For a player like Larmer, he would tell him he was playing with Secord and Savard, so he *should* score. He could get any right winger to take that spot. So Larmer probably didn't make what he deserved while he was in Chicago, at least not in the first few years.

Pulford was a pretty even keeled gentleman who had seen it all before. We were on a western swing and a bunch of players were playing pool in the afternoon at a local establishment. Rich Preston and I were partners and were holding the table pretty good. I was married the summer before, and Mary Ann had given me a beautiful watch as a wedding present. I remember switching my watch from my left hand to my right hand because the glare from the table deflected off my watch into my eyes while shooting pool. It was a move I would regret later in the evening. I left the pool place with Dale Tallon, the color commentator with the Blackhawks at the time. As we went to get our coats, we saw that one of our players, Dave Donnelly, was getting into it with the bouncers. He lost his claim check and they wouldn't give him his coat without it. Tallon stepped in and said he was with the Blackhawks group, and they ended up giving him his coat. The cab ride back to the hotel was $15, and Tallon threw in $10 and told us to make up the difference and add a tip, which I thought was more than fair. I don't know whether it was the "war juice" he had been drinking that night, but Donnelly started to lip off at Tallon and told him he should pay more of the fare. Donnelly, usually a quiet guy, now turned into a belligerent, big mouthed, bully. Tallon, one of the nicest guys in hockey, was excellent at verbal sparring matches. They really started jabbing at one another. It got heated to the point where I thought it might get physical so I threw my two cents in, and Donnelly and I started going at it. I tried to calm the situation down, but Donnelly and I ended up going to the back of the hotel and having a little dust up. I walked to the back of the hotel and looked skyward at the full moon thinking I should have just paid the cab fare. I got in several good shots but my watch, which I had put on my right hand an hour earlier, went flying into the bushes or water, and we couldn't find it.

Dale Tallon: Ha! I almost forgot that. Oh, that was funny. I think Ludzy was more pissed off about losing his watch. I first met Stevie when he was about 14 years old. I lived in a condo that was part of a complex called the Masters. Pretty exclusive. I would always see this kid all the time in the weight room. He seemed to know everybody there: the guards, the pool cleaners, the cleaning staff. He and I finally met and after a bit I say to him, 'Hey, what unit does your family live in?' He looked around and whispered, 'Actually, Mr. Tallon, I don't live here at all. I just use the weight room.'

The next time I saw him was five years later, and I was the Blackhawks color man. Ludzy came over to me and shook my hand. 'Remember me, Mr. Tallon?' You don't forget guys like Ludzy.

The next day Darryl Sutter rented one of those Geiger counter machines that you can find coins in the sand with. I think we found four or five watches in our search but none of them were mine. Darryl was convinced there was no way I was going to tell Mary Ann that I had gotten in a fight and lost my wedding watch. But I am not like that. I told her the true story the very next morning. Of course, she thought I was an idiot, but I told her everything.

Darryl and I were neighbors in Chicago, so the wives took turns picking us up from the airport. Mary Ann picked us up after this road trip and the whole way home Darryl kept asking, "Ludzy, what time have you got there Ludzy?"

Darryl Sutter was quoted in the Chicago Tribune speaking about me. "He's got spunk, he's a cocky kid. He doesn't show respect for other players or other teams. He's our Polish prince now."

As luck would have it, the next day after the fight with Donnelly, I had scheduled a lunch with Pulford to discuss the possibility of playing more center, which was my natural position, rather than left wing. The whole team knew about the fight. Donnelly had a black eye, and I knew Pully knew. However, for the full two hours during lunch, not a word was spoken about the fight. That was Pully's style.

Finally, as he was getting the bill at the end of the lunch, I couldn't stand it any more and calmly commented, "I guess you heard about the fight between Donnelly and me?"

Pulford just took one of his big inhales of his cigarette that could be heard 20 feet away and said in his own halting way, "Yeah...I...heard...did you talk to him?"

I responded that I had not. Pulford calmly responded, "Well, you'd better talk to him because he doesn't look very good."

And that was Pully's way of not making a big deal out of it. I was not proud to have gotten into a fight like that with my own teammate. But Pulford was well respected by all the players and was a good, honest man.

A proud moment for me occurred when I was coaching with the Florida Panthers and Pulford came to see me before the game just to say hello. Rick Dudley, the Florida general manager stood with us and Pulford, not a gifted conversationalist, jumped in when Dudley, who had also coached me in Buffalo, made a joke about my lack of goals in the NHL.

Pully, as if going back in time, reached out and ruffled my hair caringly and said, "He knew what he did, and did it every night."

Rick Dudley: It was really nice to see, and of course, I had to say, 'Yeah, he knew what he was doing, but nobody else did.'

I felt like I was 23 again.

The Gutsy Cowboy...Hailing from Viking, Alberta, one of seven brothers. He was the personification of true grit. Darryl Sutter emptied the fuel tank each and every game and performed with, and inspite of, injuries that would have sidelined mere mortals. Pictured here with Darryl. That's Steve Larmer kissing my Mary Ann.

I have always been a huge wrestling fan. When I was growing up, I closely followed the likes of Haystack Calhoun, Sweet Daddy Siki, Bobo Brazil, The Sheik, and Lord Athol Layton. I just loved the carnival like atmosphere.

We took it one step further in my neighborhood in my mid teens. We built a makeshift boxing ring in my basement, put up ropes, brought in extra chairs from everywhere, and even sold tickets. We called it the MWBA – the Markland Woods Boxing Association Championships. It was real boxing, not wrestling. A bunch of us had built the ring in the morning and then pretended nothing was going on when my dad came home for lunch. He couldn't figure out why we kept telling him he'd better get going or he'd be late for work. The timing was just right. Just as he headed down our street, around the corner came three guys with their hands taped and a crowd following them. We had a great afternoon with everyone having two or three fights each. The characters included Mulhado, Ken Seims, and Ray Dostanic. There were some pretty good "summerhays" thrown that afternoon and more than a couple of knockdowns. I won the tournament with a knockout over a fellow called Brian Beaky Rowe. Beaky went on to become a merchant marine. We tore the ring down and got rid of all the extra chairs before my mom and dad returned home. There was not much evidence except for the 15 half inch holes in the basement paneling.

In the late 1970s, one of the famous wrestlers was Tony "Cannonball" Parisi, a native of Niagara Falls. The Cannonball moniker came from his patented finishing move to his wrestling matches. He'd climb up to the top rope, and with complete precision, he would explode off the rope, with the speed of a falling elevator, and land on his semiconscious foe's sternum. That was his immensely feared cannonball move. It was his signature move. Tony was a short, stout man, and if he was an inch shorter, he would have been a perfect circle. I once witnessed him eat an egg salad sandwich that was four weeks old. It was green, moldy, and appeared to have things growing on it. It was absolutely the grossest thing I have ever seen anybody eat. He didn't care.

"Ludz, you only live once," Tony would constantly implore.

Like I said, he was from the Niagara Falls area and owned a hotel and bar on the famous Clifton Hill downtown. When I was in junior, he did a great job of teaching me how to work out properly to get bigger and stronger because I was a pretty skinny youngster when I first came to Niagara Falls. By the early and mid 1980s, he was promoting and organizing wrestling matches. I would have dinner with Tony, and after he had consumed four bottles of wine at dinner, he would sing classic Italian opera. He had a beautiful classical voice. He would then start delivering head butts and applying sleeper holds for fun to all those around him.

Tony was a fun guy and a great storyteller. He had hundreds of stories. The funniest story he ever shared with me concerned a trip a bunch of wrestlers took to Japan. The principle in the story was a 625-pound fat man from Arkansas, Haystacks Calhoun, who always wore bib overalls that needed an acre of denim to tailor. On a flight from Toronto to Japan, the other wrestlers laced Calhoun's chocolate pudding with two bars of Ex-lax. After gobbling up his dinner and drugged dessert, the aftereffects of the pudding took three hours to manifest.

"Something ain't right down there neighbor," moaned the human blimp as beads of sweat rolled down his hillbilly beard.

The other wrestlers were choking back laughter and went into a state of delirium as Haystacks, doing the sideways shuffle down the aisle, knocked over young and old, big and small, to reach the toilet and relief. The 625-pound giant realized all too quickly that there was no way, no how, his cramping carcass would fit into the airplane toilet. What transpired in the next 60 seconds speaks volumes for the stewardesses and the ability to improvise in desperate situations. The two lucky stewardesses grabbed two big dark blue blankets, and held them up like a shower curtain while Calhoun desperately tried to free himself from the confinement of his overalls. Tony and the other wrestlers, no doubt having consumed copious amounts of alcohol, almost lost control as the big boy finally wiggled out of his straight jacket like clothing and, holding a garbage bag behind himself, relieved himself for 20 minutes. Cannonball Parisi told me that the tears of laughter quickly dissipated and were replaced almost instantaneously with gagging and nausea as the putrid smell of crap from a 625-pound man began to waif throughout the plane. I always thought that would be a great TV commercial for the Kitchen Catcher.

One Friday night, I came home and my wife said, "You know what you are doing tomorrow, don't you?"

I proudly replied, "I most certainly do…it is Stephen's (my first son) christening."

"Yes it is," Mary Ann replied, "but it is also the day that you promised Tony Parisi you would referee one of his wrestling matches. It's all over the Niagara Falls Review."

I had actually forgotten I had agreed to it a couple of months before. I don't go back on my word for anyone, so I went down to his restaurant in town, called "Big Anthony's," and asked him if we could work around my christening schedule, so I could go to the baptism, come and do a match, and then go back to the big reception we were having. Tony agreed, of course, and said he would give me the midgets. He would work around my schedule, and whenever I could get there, he would put on the midgets. As I left his restaurant, I detected a smirk on his face.

So right after the christening, I headed straight over to the wrestling matches at Oaks Park and went into the dressing room. Tony was waiting for me and introduced me to the wrestlers. Tony warned me they liked to play games with the referees. By following wrestling for so many years, I was aware that the referee can become the sideshow in the match. Tony said the midgets would try to kick and bite me in the ass, and would definitely try to pull my pants down.

So I figured I'd go over and have a chit chat with the wrestlers to show them who was in charge. One was a somewhat older, gruffy guy with big overalls named "Hillbilly Bob." The other guy was a little old guy who had massive scabs on the top of his melon. I couldn't yet figure out why. I decided to go to Hillbilly Bob who seemed to be in charge of things. I laid it on the line, and in my best Clint Eastwood impersonation, told him, "Look, pal. I have to live in this town in the summer time. So if you start to embarrass me in front of this crowd, I'm going to pick you up and fling you over the top ropes!"

This little bastard looks down, no, I guess it was up, at me and says, "Oh yeah, well you better make sure that I (and he slaps his hands together) don't throw you over the top ropes!"

I looked at him and I was about to say something but something made me stop. I thought to myself, "He just might do that and then I would be in real trouble." So I let it go.

Just before we were being introduced, I walked by the snack bar, which happened to be manned by my former landlady and asked her for a roll of tape, which I wound around my waist as tight as possible so these little madmen would not be able to pull my pants down.

So off I went into the ring with no preparation whatsoever. Being a fan, I knew that the winners were predetermined, but I had no idea who was supposed to win the match I was officiating. They instructed me to simply count "one, two, three" when required. I quickly realized the match was professionally choreographed. Being that close to the action, I saw that both wrestlers talked continuously throughout the match. The older wrestler, the one with the scabs on his head, called the entire match. I had obviously never been that close before but it was amazing to hear them call every move during the bout. The coup de grace of the match was when Hillbilly Bob picked up the old guy, with the scabs don't forget, lifted him right off the ground by his feet, let his head touch the ground, and then spun him like a spinning top on the canvas. The guy literally spun around for 30 seconds on his head. His scabs opened up, and blood started seeping out. I quickly counted one, two, three, jumped out of the ring, ran to the exit, and got in the waiting car driven by my best friend, Kirky, and my sister, Karen. We made a mad dash back to my son's baptism reception. That was my first and last foray into the ring as an official, but it was a lot of fun.

Unfortunately, Tony died of a heart attack in 2000 at the age of 58 at the coffee shop he went to every morning in Niagara Falls. He was one helluva man.

There were a lot of character guys in Chicago when I got there. Tom Lysiak, a fellow Pollack, was a man that everyone always wanted to hang out with. He smoked a cigarette like James Dean. He liked to drink Cutty Sark scotch. He was a Joe Namath kind of guy. Everyone wanted to go where Tommy was going. Everyone wanted Tommy's approval, and I mean that in a good way. He called me "Lec," after Poland's solidarity leader of the time: Lech Walesa, because of my Polish heritage and because I wore a charcoal overcoat that Tommy thought looked like it was bought in downtown Warsaw.

Tom had a way of making people do things they would probably not normally do. One playoff series against Detroit, we had just eliminated the Red Wings in Detroit. Bomber, Lysiak's nickname, decided to take me to a good restaurant to celebrate. I knew Tom realized he was coming to the end of his career. After a great dinner, we went out for a couple of celebratory drinks and got back to the famous Pontchartrain Hotel at about three in the morning. Walking into the lobby, I was surprised at seeing the famous 7'4" wrestler Andre the Giant passed out on a couch in the hotel lobby. The bellman had just thrown a big bed sheet over him as there was no way to move him.

When I saw Andre the Giant, a living legend to me, lying asleep on the hotel couch I had one of the strangest feelings of my life. I *almost* got the overwhelming urge to go up to him and pull one of his big, huge, black nostril hairs right out of his nose and then run away as fast as I could. Strange, eh?

In Chicago, Roger Neilson was very keen on the conditioning aspect of the game. Not unlike Bert Templeton, he was ahead of his time when it came to off-ice conditioning. We were given the option of running 5.5 miles on up hill, down hill roads, or you could ride bikes – but you had to go 25 miles. Most of the guys were pretty good at doing something. Lysiak, who I doubt ever trained a day in his life when not forced to, was not the greatest proponent of this part of the sport. I think his training schedule consisted of cutting back to one pack of cigarettes a day. Tommy took his pack of cigarettes with him on his bike ride and leisurely sauntered along like it was a Sunday afternoon family outing. One year in training camp, Lysiak pulled up to the Bismarck Hotel, threw his keys to the doorman, and spied our trainer, Lou Varga, whistling for a cab.

"Hey, sweet Lou," he yelled at him. "You wanna pick me up some skates tomorrow morning at Gunzo's?"

When I was a young boy, I would see the name 'GUNZO'S' printed on all the Northland sticks that the Hawks would use. Mikita, Hull, Magnuson. Everyone seemed to use the same sticks that were actually pretty shitty. All those great black and white pictures and you always saw that name in bold lettering on the shaft: GUNZO'S. I always thought that was an odd name to have printed on all the whippy wood. In reality, it was simply the name of the sporting goods store that all our sticks went to before they came to us at the old Stadium.

Ordinarily Varga's sour demeanor and prickly personality caused the players some trepidation when asking for anything, but Varga came running over to Lysiak to ask him exactly what he needed.

"Just pick me up a pair of Super Tacks," he told the trainer, "and get'em about a size 11 or 12, maybe a little bigger. I don't want anything biting my ankles."

Keep in mind, most players are extremely finicky about their skate model and size. Tommy was not concerned in the least. However, when the first day of camp came, he would dominate. He was just that talented.

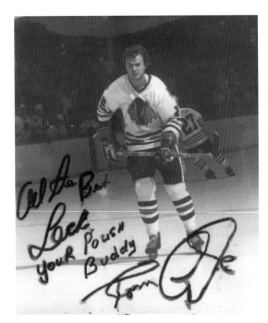

The Easy One...from High Prairie, Alberta came a simple superstar named Tom Lysiak, known to friends as "Bomb." This picture hangs over my bar in Niagara Falls. Tommy would love that. My Polish pal swashbuckled through life. Nobody drank more scotch, smoked more cigarettes, and had more fun, and anyone who tried to keep up to him was making a big mistake. He was usually the best player on the pond, hangover or not.

Lysiak could also be a pretty tough cowboy. He used to say if anyone gave him a hard time, he would just give them a good old fashioned Albertan "High Prairie Haymaker." Tommy had a slow drawn out way of speaking, often sounding like he was singing a song when he spoke. He was not afraid to comment on the toughness or ability of a fighter. Once when we were going on a west coast swing, Jerome Dupont announced to the club he was going to pick a fight with the toughest guy on each of the teams we were going to face. A daunting task indeed. First stop was in Winnipeg, where Jerome promptly picked a fight with tough guy Jim Kite, who just as promptly laid a beating on him. Next stop was Calgary. Jerome looked around and searched out Nick Fotiu, who swiftly threw him around like a rag doll. Finally, in Vancouver, Jerome decided he had enough and abruptly dropped the gloves with Canuck tough guy Stan Smyl. Stan beat the living tar out of Jerome.

Between periods, Lysiak took a couple of long puffs of his cigarette, stood up, and slowly spoke, "Jerome...I greatly admire your courage...but I question your judgment. You gotta learn to fight son, or your face is going to turn into a pile of goo!"

Jerome didn't fight for quite a while after that, and I didn't blame him.

I went to help Lysiak move his stuff out of his place when he was going home after his last year in Chicago. He knew he wasn't coming back, and I knew it also. He told me something that always stuck with me.

"Lec," he said, "hockey is a funny game. I love ya, but I'm probably never going to see you again. It's not because I don't want to, it's just because that's the way hockey players are. They're very tight for a short period of time, and then they never see each other again. Always remember that. Never forget that."

And I've never seen him since. I did speak to him again, though. Lysiak had an outstanding career but is probably best remembered for intentionally tripping linesman Ron

Foyt on Halloween night, 1983. Lysiak was upset at being continually waved out of the face-off circle. He kept imploring Foyt to drop the puck and quit being the show. Finally, after about the fifth time of being thrown out, he switched face-off spots with Darryl Sutter. As soon as the puck dropped, he went straight for the face-off dot and flipped Foyt ass over tea kettle. He received a 20-game suspension, and to this day, has shown no remorse whatsoever. Knowing this, I played a prank on him when I was coaching the Vipers. I got his phone number in Rutledge, Georgia and disguised my voice.

He answered the phone and I began, "Mr. Lysiak, this is Mr. Foyt. I don't know if you remember me or not."

"Yeah, I remember you," he said curtly.

I couldn't believe my ruse was working. I continued, "I just wanted to tell you where my life has gone since then. As you know, I was fired at the end of the season because of that episode. My life spiraled downhill. I couldn't hold a steady job after that. I became a drug addict. I became an alcoholic. I was in and out of detox centers. My wife left me. And my kids have disowned me. All because of that night."

Lysiak responded, "Yeah, well you should've dropped the fucking puck then! What else do you want?"

"Bomber, it's Ludzy," I laughed. I had gotten him hook, line, and sinker.

"Oh Ludzy, you son of a bitch."

Tommy Lysiak lived every day to its fullest. He never got cheated. Lysiak married a beautiful girl named Malynda, and resides in Georgia.

Another name, one more familiar with hockey fans of the 1980s, is Behn Wilson. He was simply one tough hombre. Behn was the type of guy that if he came up to you in a bar and asked you to move over, you would look at him and tell him to take a hike. But by the time you rattled 10 shots off his head and his hair hadn't even moved yet, it was too late. You were thinking twice about your actions.

Behn was a great guy who liked to pretend he was a "learned" man. Actually, he was quite intelligent and therefore garnered the nickname "The Thespian" from his teammates. In actuality, he probably had a PHD like the rest of us: Pool Hall Diploma. Most of us didn't think too much of it at the time, but Behn was one of the few who would question Alan Eagleson when he would come and visit our team and explain how great our retirement situation was in our Players Association. Eagleson would cut Behn up left, right, and center when he questioned what Eagleson was saying. Unfortunately, most of us wanted to just play hockey and leave the business to others. Obviously, we all should have taken a keener interest. Behn evidently could tell everything was not copasetic.

The Scary One...the visage of number 23, Big Behn Wilson, in a blood thirsty mood provided many sleepless nights for countless athletes in the NHL during the 1980s. Nothing could have been as frightening as Behn navigating into scrums in search of fresh prey or an old score to settle. Once aroused, as he was in a Chicago training camp in 1986, the results were predictable and sickening.

Hockey fans remember him as a tough, hard nose defenseman for Philadelphia and Chicago, who thoroughly enjoyed punching people so hard that their faces turned into a bloody, pulpy, mess. However, the thing that Behn *loved* most was to score goals. On September 24, 1983 in Minnesota, a fellow named Randy Velischek, a Montreal native who played 10 years in the NHL and measured in at 6'1" and 200 pounds, tripped Behn when he was on a rare breakaway. Behn went tumbling into the boards. He wasn't so upset at getting sent sprawling into the boards as he was at losing a great scoring chance.

Wilson slowly got up and looked around and in his slow, laboring, way of speaking, looked at each player and questioned, "Who…did…that…? Who…did…that…?"

The more sour he got, the more he stammered. To fess up and also to save his other teammates from annihilation, Velischek meekly admitted it was him. He really had no choice. The rest of the North Stars were all pointing at him anyway. Wilson then attacked him with a fury few have ever seen. Velischek, a solid NHLer, was looking for a hole in the ice in which to hide. If he had been carrying a drill press and shovel, he would have buried himself. He wanted nothing to do with Behn. When Behn got upset, he was like a man possessed. His eyes would flip back like a shark about to devour a sea lion. Behn continued to pummel Velischek, who just tried to hang on for dear life. The North Stars implored the linesmen to break it up. Behn kept pouncing on him like a prison guard on a convict. Behn was given the unanimous decision. Wilson was a strong, strong man who did not look physically strong but was strong as an ox and could take a punch, a key prerequisite required to be a resident tough guy. He took his craft seriously. Behn had a book on all the gunslingers in the league and studied up on any "unknowns." It was not unusual for Wilson to go over to the opposition before a game to investigate the unfamiliar names.

"Who is this fucking Lavelle kid? What's his deal?" Behn would ask like a Secret Service interrogator.

Someone would tell him, "Hey, Behn, the kid scored 75 goals in the Quebec league last year, has 12 penalty minutes; I don't think he's going to ask you to go!"

Behn had a great tilt with Wendel Clark of the Leafs. Wendel got the jump on him and got in what seemed like seven or eight solid blows. Wendel's punches sounded like an axe hitting a piece of wood. Behn got in a few shots later in the fight to even it up a bit. We went into the dressing room after the period expecting to see Behn either getting stitched up or at least being treated for some lacerations on his face. But there were no cuts. He was looking in the mirror calmly applying a little Vaseline to his face. His skin was like Buffalo hide.

He was called upon to stand up for his position during one training camp. During that camp in the fall of 1986, a group of us were huddled around a small coffee table in the Bismarck Hotel, quickly gobbling down a below average breakfast, more out of habit than necessity. A few of the players were reading the sports section of the Chicago Tribune. Big bold headlines trumpeted the story about a rookie, drafted 35th overall, named Mark Kurzawski, who was supposedly really tough and was endeavoring to take Behn Wilson's job away from him. The youthful, potential assassin even had his picture taken with a Mike Tyson like scowl, just in case Behn had trouble identifying him. Kurzawski was a defenseman, and Behn was slotted to play left wing in the morning scrimmage. That would have put the mercury on Behn's thermostat on the rise. At the breakfast table, Behn ordered his usual piece of blueberry pie with a coffee and did a double take upon seeing the headlines concerning Kurzawski. Behn looked a little disshelved with his messy red hair, two days of facial growth, and he also had a sore back from the long run the day before. He was transfixed on the article. His eyes appeared to explode out of their sockets a couple of times.

Finally, a slight grin came to his face. He put the paper down and limped out of the coffee shop with his pie and coffee still in hand. Everyone at that table, and I mean everyone, knew it was going to be an ugly morning at the old Chicago Stadium. Wilson looked like a heat seeking missile in launch mode ready to attack. I vividly recall that this Kurzawski lad looked confident, calm, and a bit cocky. He may have been a tough kid from the streets of Chicago, a real strong guy who had plowed through a maze of pugilists, but he had no idea he had now entered another echelon of insanity and viciousness. In other words, don't grab for the check if you can't pay the bill. And Behn was cashing his receipt.

The inter-squad game, red versus white, was scheduled to start at 8:15 am. At approximately 8:16, Benjamin Alexander Wilson made a direct beeline for the youngster. Behn took a two-handed baseball like swing at Kurzawski's arms and pulled his hockey stick out of his grasp. He then tossed it into the stands in the general direction of the Chicago Blackhawk scouts. It was something out of World Wrestling Entertainment.

As he skated around the rink in triumph he yelled, "There's your tough guy, fellas!"

Behn Wilson proved the law of the jungle. Only the strong survive. He was at the top of the food chain and not ready to be supplanted just yet. Mark Kurzawski never played a game in the NHL.

Behn was the best I've ever seen in scrums. In what he knew was going to be his last year, he would enter a scrum, grab two players with his big paws, and bellow out, "This …is…my…llllast…yyyear…bbbuttt…I…plan…to…tttake… sssomebody…with…mmme!"

Not many stayed around to ask Mr. Wilson's retirement plans.

"Big Daddy" Bob McGill, who you would think was a big muscled, full bodied lad because of his nickname, had an average sized frame for a hockey player. He was one of my favorite guys to have a beer with after the game. He could recount stories with the best of them.

One afternoon in Quebec during a game against the Nordiques, Big Daddy and Rick Vaive, aka "Squid," went at it. McGill might have been the only player in the NHL at the time using a Cooper stick. The guys used to get on him pretty hard about that. During the warm up, we were doing the usual dump it in, breakout, three on two come back in drill. Big Daddy was having a tough time completing his passes to Vaive on the breakout. When we came into the dressing room after the warm up, Squid started to bust his chops.

Examining Big Daddy's stick like a diamond cutter on 16 karats, Squid yelled, "Hey, Big Daddy, why don't you start thinking about changing the curve on that Cooper stick of yours, so you can start making a couple passes on my stick!"

Big Daddy, never one to back down from a verbal or physical assault snorted, "You just worry about Squid, and I'll worry about Big Daddy!"

Vaive tried to explain his comment, "No, I'm just saying, well, maybe, if you got the right curve on your stick, you could make a pass."

Big Daddy was starting to get a little pissed, "These sticks have done Big Daddy just fine over the years!"

Squid shot back, "Well, if you think that's fine, then that's another story!"

We all thought we should step in to stop the argument because we were about to go on the ice. Both Big Daddy and Squid were great teammates and fun to be around.

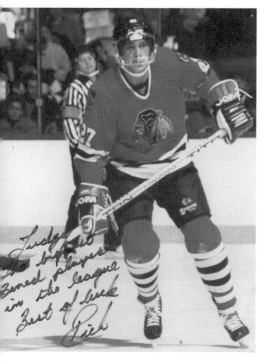

Rick Vaive: I used to call Ludzy the Big Boned Man. Ludzy was a classic example of a guy who you would play against and hate, but when you played with him, he was a real fun guy. When I was with Toronto, he was always stickin' ya and stirring up shit. We later became good teammates.

The Pure Scorer...the one and only Rick Vaive a.k.a. "Squid," whose sticks were the weight of a telephone pole. He paid the price and attacked the net like a fat man on a bowl of fettucini.

Chicago is a great sports town with the Cubbies, White Sox, and, of course, "Da Bears." Jim McMahon was the punky quarterback who owned Chicago in the 1980s. I got to be an acquaintance of his during my time there. In the several times I met him, I got the distinct feeling he would have loved to be a hockey player. He used to play Sunday afternoon with the Bears and then bring his son to the Blackhawks games on Sunday night. He would often come into our dressing room after the game. He was a free spirit who spoke his mind and did not worry about any repercussions.

On the weekend of January 4, 1986, the Blackhawks were in New York, but I had to stay behind because of a broken foot. A couple of friends of mine, Willie and Vic Burt, came down to watch the National Football Conference playoff game against the New York Giants. Avid football fans will remember there was a controversy brewing between McMahon and Pete Rozelle, the NFL commissioner at the time. McMahon wanted the right to wear advertising on his headband and Rozelle wouldn't allow it. So in the playoff game, McMahon simply wrote "ROZELLE" in big letters across his headband in protest.

The night before the game, I went out with my two buddies to catch the atmosphere in downtown Chicago before the big game. We went to a couple of large establishments and then I said I knew a smaller place, called Z's, that might be a little quieter. So we went over there and were having a drink when my friend Willie said, "Hey, see that guy over in the corner there by himself. He looks an awful lot like Jim McMahon."

I looked over and because I knew Jim pretty well by that point, I said that was definitely him. The two guys with me expressed some serious doubt that Jim McMahon, before the biggest game of his career, would be out at 11:30 pm drinking beer in a downtown public bar. I didn't want to interfere but I walked over, and sure enough, it was him. He was standing alone, with his hat pulled down, and sipping on a beer. I introduced my two friends, who were awestruck at meeting McMahon at such a place and time. He obviously just wanted to relax and have a few drinks by himself before the big game. The rest of the team was sequestered in a downtown hotel. McMahon couldn't have been more pleasant and cordial to us. He was surprised my two friends had come all the way from Toronto to watch the game. We didn't want to bother him too much so after 15 minutes, we left him alone and went to another bar.

Willie: Ludz and I were standing there, and I looked over and saw this guy leaning against the bar having a beer all by himself. It was around 11:00 pm. Ludz said that it was Jim McMahon, but I told him he must be mistaken. He's going to play the biggest game of his life tomorrow. But sure enough, it was him, and we had a nice chat. I couldn't resist asking the waitress how many beers he had partaken in, and she said six or seven. We went to another bar and I couldn't resist going back into Z's around one, and he was still there!

Next time I saw McMahon, he said when he got up the next morning, he went and had an Egg McMuffin for a pre-game meal.

The next day, at 1:00 pm, the Chicago Bears, led by Jim McMahon, went out and beat the New York Giants 23-0. McMahon, with his "Rozelle" headband on, threw for two touchdowns and led the Bears to a dominant victory. The Bears went on to win the Super Bowl that year by beating the New England Patriots 46-10.

I was able to get to know the Sutter family quite well. The Sutter story is obviously well known in the hockey world, and I must say that everything that everyone has heard about them, about their toughness, resilience, and fortitude is true. The one Sutter I probably knew the best was Darryl. He captained Chicago most of the years I was there. We were neighbors in Lombard, Illinois. Every day we were at home, we drove the 45 minutes to the rink and back together. Usually Larmer and Rick Paterson came with us. He was a great captain, leader, and person. Many people don't know he couldn't get any interest from professional teams early on, so he went and played a year in Japan. Near the end of his career, his knees were shot, but he refused to give up. Several times, he had a syringe put into his knee on game days to have it drained of the enormous amount of fluid that had accumulated. Even with the excessive treatment, he would play that night in enormous pain. Obviously, a lot of players play through pain, but Darryl would have to be rated at the top of any list.

As I have been associated with quite a few of the Sutters during my playing and coaching career, I am sometimes asked which one of the Sutters I liked the best. I really think they are a great family. All the brothers are true competitors and great guys, but the one I probably loved the most was their father, Louis. He would come over to my house at Christmas time, and you didn't need to sit with him for more than five minutes to realize why the Sutters turned out the way they did. He was a tough, rough guy who pulled no punches. As many know, the dynasty almost never started. Most people are familiar with the story about the first Sutter who left Viking to try out for a junior team. Brian was the second eldest. Gary, the oldest, always stayed home and took care of the homestead with Louis. Brian went to try out for Red Deer and got cut a couple days into camp. He called his dad and told him to come pick him up; it was over; he had been cut. Louis told him he was not going to come and pick him up. His dad told him to go back in and tell the coach that he needed another chance. Louis told Brian to tell the coach he could help the team. The coach obviously saw something in Brian's eyes and gave him another shot. And lo and behold, the Sutter saga began, and the rest is history.

One night in Orlando, Duane "Dog" Sutter came down to see me before a game between my Detroit Vipers and the

Orlando Solar Bears. The Sutters had their father Louie there sitting in the stands, so we went over to him and had a nice chit chat for a few minutes. I happened to say to Mr. Sutter, "Hey Louie, there's an Irish guy who's always lipping off to me during the game, and he's a real sonofabitch. He sits right behind our bench." The antagonist I spoke of was very real, but I was just joking about taking care of him. As quick as you could say 'Viking, Alberta,' Mr. Sutter rolled up his sleeves and said, "I'll keep him quiet, Ludzy." Dog and I just looked at each other and laughed. I really thought the world of all the boys.

Brian cut a path for his brothers to the NHL jungle. I think Brent was perhaps the most naturally gifted, but they all had one similar characteristic in their DNA – they worked hard.

Duane Sutter lived with us for about two months when he first came to Chicago, before his family had a chance to move from Long Island. Some would call him a prankster. Some would call him a SOB, in a kind and loving way. After he moved into his own place, he still used to come over to visit us at night sometimes, just to shoot the breeze. When he left to go home, he would secretly flip the thermostat up to about 90 degrees Fahrenheit. I would wake up at about 4:00 am, barely able to breathe. One time, I could hardly open my eyes the heat was so excruciating. He had turned it up full throttle. I'm not sure why he found that so funny, but he did it on several occasions.

Al Secord, a great, beautiful guy, is now a pilot somewhere in Texas. He was one of the most highly conditioned athletes I had seen up until then. He looked after his body like no one's business. He was a scoring machine in the NHL until he came down with an abdominal injury, which he couldn't get fixed up satisfactorily, and it effectively ended his career.

Al was a tough guy who loved boxing. That is partially why we formed a strong friendship. By today's standards, or I should say any day's standards, our "gym" at the Chicago Stadium was pretty sparse. A Wall Street stockbroker's office would probably have had more equipment in it. We had two bikes, a fistful of dumbbell weights with which to do curls, a Windwell bike, and a speed bag. In one of Orval Tessier's speeches, where he was lambasting us for this and that, he told us he thought our recent rash of injuries was at least partially caused by the use of the weight room. He loudly exclaimed, "The weight room is out of bounds for all players. It is now padlocked!"

He roared on, "You guys are more concerned about looking good at the beach than playing hockey!"

That type of attitude was tough for a guy like Al, who prided himself in being in tip top shape at all times. He body was as hard as a rock; in fact, his nickname was "Rock." He was cut like a north end bus seat.

In my rookie year, Secord saw me fooling around with the speed bag and approached me. "Ludzy, you wanna go a couple rounds with me?"

I remember Tom Lysiak warning me, "Don't be stupid, Ludzy. He's gonna kill ya, and if you do happen to catch him with one, he'll then proceed to kill ya AND bury you."

I did a lot of boxing growing up, so I wasn't really too concerned. We worked out an arrangement where we would box three rounds. It was a real good scrap. I thought I held my own pretty good. I would honestly say it was probably an even fight. At the time, Al was one of the heavyweights in the NHL. I was not.

The Chicago Tribune was doing an article on me at the time, and I stated that Secord was the clear cut winner in our fun exhibition bout. Al walked in the next day with the article in hand and said, "I like that."

I think I gained his respect that day. Secord was very serious about being a student of the game. He learned how to skate technically correct and learned how to shoot like he had written a "how to" manual. Without that type of dedication, he knew he would have been lucky to score 25 goals in NHL. So I was not surprised one night when we were leaving the rink in Minnesota and a fan yelled out, "Hey Secord, you're the worst 50-goal scorer in the NHL."

He simply responded with no emotion whatsoever, "You know it."

The Man-made One...For four to five years, Al Secord dominated the NHL in a most convincing fashion. A man who could scare netminders with his wrist shot, drive to the net like a freight train, and pummel the opposition's top thugs into a helpless heep. The "Rock," as we called him, when fevered up, could not be halted.

We were good friends, especially after our little boxing match. We always had a lot of fun together. He was from Espanola, Ontario, and I used to go up to his golf tournament in the summer. He would come down to my hockey school in Niagara Falls. He was one of the greatest examples of dedication I had ever seen.

Another big tough guy on the Blackhawks during the 1987-88 season was Glen Cochrane. At 6'2" and 210 pounds, he was a big bodied guy with a Sergeant Slaughter-like jaw, who had a 10-year career in the NHL. He was as tough as Tuesday. He was a great teammate and made many friends. One evening in Toronto, about six of us went to a famous downtown steakhouse. Cochrane and I walked to the restaurant. On the way, I bought two muffins to eat after dinner. The server was a loud fellow who presented the meal as if he was introducing the Duke and Duchess of York. As the tuxedo wearing waiter was presenting two meals at the table, Cochrane stabbed a steak off one of the plates still on the big metal food warmer, and replaced it with one of my muffins. As luck would have it, the plate was just about to be presented to Steve Larmer.

The waiter proudly barked, "Breaded steak," and gracefully put the plate, which now had a muffin on it soaking in steak juice, in front of Larmer.

Larmer politely smiled at the waiter and immediately began digging in. Grampa Larms surveyed the muffin with complete contempt. He touched it, poked it, and pushed it around his plate a bit before registering his verdict.

"This is a fucking muffin, not a steak," he crowed.

The whole table just roared with laughter. Larmer was not amused.

Glen Cochrane spent only one year with the Blackhawks, but he just didn't care about anything. He was funny and very unpredictable. One night in Chicago, we were getting blown out something like 6-1. He scored a goal with about three minutes left in the game, and he went nuts. He put his stick between his legs and rode the length of the ice in celebration before 18,000 stunned fans. I think he even kept the puck. When we got back to the bench, I caught my breath and leaned into the big man and said, "Cocker, it's fuckin' 6-2 and..."

"Hold on to that thought, Ludzy pal," interrupted the man with the lantern jaw. He wanted to hear his name called over the PA system. There was a disappointing weak response from the Chicago fans, as most were putting on their coats and exiting the stadium.

"Hey, I don't care. It's my first goal in about four years," he replied, after I finished my comment about his celebratory war dance after a prolonged scoring drought. I had to laugh. He was a hell of a guy, one of the best to go out for dinner with; in a tough business, he was always laughing and having a great time. I was the victim of a prank in a bar that involved Cochrane when he was playing for Philadelphia earlier in his career. One night in Philly, I had a fight with Ray Allison, and while in the penalty box, I had a verbal exchange with the Sasquatch-like Cochrane. The tale of the tape showed that it was a slight jump in weight classes for me and out of my league, but as Cochrane skated by I warned, "You're next, Cochrane." It was a bit of a stretch. I had enough trouble trying to dispose of Allison. Teammate

Curt Fraser, who was a good friend of Cochrane's, was sharing the penalty box with me at the time for his battle with Bob Hoffmeyer. He did a double take, "Ludzy, we'll need a shovel to scrape you off the ice if you fight that guy. Stay away from him."

That same night, we all went out for a bite to eat, and in walked Glen Cochrane. He stood at the doorway until he caught my attention; he was a massive monstrosity. He started his voyage towards me with blood in his eye. The guy was pissed about my "You're next" comment. He slowly walked the long way around the bar, and I didn't take my eyes off the guy. Teammate Jack O'Callahan, standing beside me, whispered, "This don't look good Ludzy." No shit. Cochrane saddled up beside me and let out a lion like roar, and started laughing as he extended his hand, "I'm next, am I?" he asked. Just then, the mastermind of the act, Curt Fraser, entered the bar cackling like the Joker. If you're going to give it, you have to take it.

Cochrane was the central figure in one of the most disgusting and disrespectful chapters in player degradation I have ever witnessed. Glen Cochrane was a meat and potatoes guy. He worked the pits on the ice and fought any and all comers. Our pension, which is somewhat of a joke to begin with, calls for you to be fully vested when you reach 400 games played. That was the magic mark. "Cocker" was at 399 games when he was demoted to the minors by Mike Keenan. One more NHL game and he would supposedly get $250,000 at age 55. The massive Cochrane was reduced to tears, understanding full well if he did not report to the minors, he would be suspended and thus lose the opportunity to be recalled and get the precious game in. It was like the proverbial carrot in front of the donkey, and it happened during Keenan's reign of personal assaults. Fortunately, Pulford did the right thing and traded Cochrane to the Edmonton Oilers, where he got in 12 more games to end his NHL career.

Curt "Fras" Fraser was a unique type of tough guy. His hands were huge with fingers the size of Polish kielbasa. His body fat was maybe five percent. He was also a skilled hockey player, but where some tough guys would fight to beat the other combatant within an inch of his life, Fraser was not like that.

I had been assigned the previous year in the playoffs to watch Bobby Smith when we played the North Stars. I did a fairly good job neutralizing him, and we went on to win the series. You gotta do what you gotta do during playoff time, and let's just say at the end of the playoffs, Bobby Smith, who was a great player, was not a card carrying member of the Steve Ludzik fan club. The following September, we played the North Stars in a pre-season match up. I am convinced to this day Smith got Fraser and me mixed up. He harassed Fraser throughout the contest and near the end of the game Smith inexplicably gave him a huge shove, which Fraser could not ignore. There are things I do not know nor can I explain, such as what is in a hot dog or why Keith Richards is still alive at 65. Add to that list why Smith chose to drop the mitts with Curt Fraser. But Smith and Fraser did indeed drop their gloves and went at it. Smith was 6'4" and had a condor like reach on him, so, at least at the start of the tilt, he was holding his own. Fraser then grabbed Smith with his right hand and threw a left, which traveled, at most, 12 inches to Smith's nose. Fraser's first left disintegrated his nose, and the next three or four bombs may have leveled some small cities in France. I don't think I have ever seen a face destroyed like that. When the carnage was done, Bobby Smith was left in a heap, and the blood covered a two foot square. After the game, I joked with Fraser, "Hey Fras, you should have used a gun, it would have been cleaner."

Dino Ciccarelli skated by and said, "Let's just call the game."

There was only a minute to go anyway. He was right. It was one of those fights that made you almost feel sorry for the other guy – almost. Shortly after that, the North Stars traded Smith to the Canadiens. I often thought that one of the reasons was because the North Stars didn't think a player could take a beating like that and be the same player afterwards.

We went out after the game in Minnesota, and Fraser, who was a diabetic, turned to me and said, "Ludzy, why did the guy do that to me? I think he thought I was you!"

He went on, "These hands won't heal for a long time." Being a diabetic, the healing process takes longer.

Bobby Smith learned Lesson #112: When taking a receipt, make sure you get the right guy. I had wished Smith had gotten the right guy, so Fraser did not have to go through that pain. Smith picked the wrong door and it was almost fatal.

One of the biggest acts of bravery I saw in my career was seeing Fraser, during one playoff run, getting injections to freeze his ribs when they were broken. He went into the medical room, and you could hear him screaming as the needles went into his ribs. He would have to do this every period. Fans do not realize all the pain that players play through in a season. Curt Fraser was as game as they come. Unfortunately, he was traded that summer to the hated Minnesota North Stars.

I always had a lot of fun with Fraser. Maybe it was because you knew you were going to have ample backup if there was trouble. One night on Long Island, we were just walking back to the hotel. The Nassau County Coliseum was literally just across the street. We were walking across the crosswalk in the hotel area, which we thought was a safe area as far as traffic was concerned, but when we looked up, there was this black Cadillac zooming at us like a bat out of hell. It hit the brakes at the last second.

I just turned toward the car and yelled, "What the fuck are you doing?"

The guy starts to get out of the car. You know you're a big man when you get out of a car and the whole chassis bounces up and down about six times, rendering the shocks useless. He must have been 450 pounds and one mean looking son of a bitch.

He glared at me and said, "What d'you say, motherfucker?"

I called it like it was, "Hey Fras, what did you say to that guy?"

"Let's go, Ludzy," Fraser simply said. Always was a good backup guy to have around.

Cutting to the net around Hall of Famer Bernie Federko.
Goalie Mike Liut is about to close the door.

Everyone looks at hockey players today and says that they should not complain about anything. In many ways, they are right. But there are also negatives that come with the territory. My dad, Ted, had been sick for a year or so and died somewhat abruptly in October 1984 at the age of 51. Ted Ludzik was my greatest booster, my number one fan, and like most fathers, my harshest critic. He was the first son to Polish immigrants, Stefan and Mary, who came to Canada in 1928. By the time Dad was 18, he was a bush pilot in the Arctic Circle.

My father may have been the most complex man I've ever encountered, and even today, at age 48, I have a very difficult time describing him. He had a lot of hard miles on him. He finally just ran out of road.

Immediately following the 1984 semi-finals against the Oilers, where I personally witnessed Gretzky's skills reaching their zenith, I feverishly drove from Chicago to Toronto as my mom had said Dad was not doing very well. My mom and sister Karen are both nurses. They warned me to brace myself for what I was going to see, but no amount of warning could have helped. Dad's body had been ravaged beyond repair. Years of alcohol abuse and hard living took him from a massive 260 pounds to a skeleton of 125 pounds. His once huge forearms were now the size of a garden hose. I sat beside him on the old couch in the family den, and with great difficulty, he struggled to push himself up into a sitting position. He seemed surprised I had rushed home so quickly, as he did not see the urgency. "The Bear," which was the name given to him by my close friends, reached over and grabbed his cigarettes and fought with his hands to light the butt. He then commented on the recent series against Edmonton.

"Could someone not have belted that little bastard!" he growled, obviously referring to number 99. That was my dad.

I was married that summer on July 28, 1984 to Mary Ann Czaplicki in Niagara Falls, Ontario. That morning Dad pulled out all of his chest tubes and IV's and just walked out of the intensive care unit at Mississauga General Hospital and drove down to Niagara Falls for the wedding. My mom, being a nurse, warned him that he was just crazy. To his embarrassment, many people at the wedding could not recognize him. He could pass for a man of 80.

Steve Wilson: I had been away and not seen The Bear for several months. I literally felt faint when I saw him. I could not believe it was him. I remember asking someone if that was Ludz's uncle.

I can sum up my father best by saying, "To those who did not know him, no explanation will do. To those who did know him, no excuse is needed."

My father passed away on Halloween night, his favorite time of the year. I had lost my biggest fan. We were on a western road trip, and I flew home for the funeral. The day I buried my father, I got a call from our general manager Bob Pulford.

He asked, "Any way you can play tomorrow night in Vancouver?"

Obviously, I would have liked to have spent at least a couple of days with my family, but I felt it was my duty to go. The Bear would be the last man to want his son to miss action. In retrospect, I should have insisted on staying at least one more day.

I met the team in Vancouver, and on my first shift, I got into a fight with Grant Martin. Martin was a guy I used to get into it with in junior. He had a habit of slashing you if you beat him on a face off. That night, I lined up at the face off and said, "Any shit from you tonight and you're gonna eat Sherwood."

I was in a foul mood and was mentally drained from the previous two days. I was playing, but it was like I wasn't even on the ice. I was mad at the world, mad at the

Vancouver Canucks, and mad at Pulford. I was even mad at my father.

Martin slashed me on the face off, so that was it. I was so upset I don't remember the altercation very well, except that I was kneeing him in the head, which I normally wouldn't do to anyone. There was no reason why the Blackhawks should have made me play that game. I should have been with my mom and sister, and my wife.

Mary Ann Ludzik: I was back in Chicago by then, watching the game, and I just cried.

Steve and Mary Ann

When Alex Ovechkin went home to see his ailing grandfather, there were some who were critical of him going back home during the season. Thinking back to my situation with my father, I vigorously defended him on The Score television show with Steve Kouleas. Ovechkin was right to do whatever he felt he had to do, and the Washington Capitals are to be commended for allowing him to do so.

A couple of years later, I had just come back from breaking my foot and got my only hat trick of my NHL career in Washington. I sat in the dressing room after the game thinking my dad will be so excited to wake up the next morning and read in the Toronto Star about my three goals. It wasn't until a few moments later, that I realized that wasn't going to happen. The next night, I broke my foot again, blocking a shot from Mike Milbury.

Injuries are obviously a part of hockey. As a young boy, I never had a really serious injury. I was taught that you didn't stay down. If you could get to the bench, you better get there. My thought process was that I couldn't be hurt badly. The reason I felt that way was because I was always able to persevere through any injuries I had and was able to just keep playing. In the OHL, I took everyone's best shot, which included being cut, punched, body blasted, slashed, speared, and cross checked. I was resilient enough to take it all. But like a car with a touch of rust on it, I started to show some kinks in the armor. I broke my collarbone while playing in Chicago. We were playing against Montreal, and I had just beaten Craig Ludwig on an icing call. He just hammered me against the boards. The glass in Chicago had a lot of give to it, but not enough in this case. Instantly, I couldn't breathe. As I slowly made my way to the bench, all of the Hab players chirped at me.

"Take that, you fucking asshole," someone yelled.

When I got to the bench, I asked our trainer, Skippy Thayer, to cut my shoulder pad. It felt like it was up near my ear and felt awkward. He responded that it was not my shoulder pad near my ear, it was my collarbone. Our team doctor, Dr. Louis Colb, said he thought both my shoulders touched when I hit the boards. My collarbone snapped right in half. Dr. Colb came to the hospital to set it. The doctor assumed I had been given morphine, so he went ahead and set it. Unfortunately, I had not been given the painkiller. I think that was the closest I've ever come to fainting. I was in the hospital for a couple of days.

<u>John Kirk (best friend)</u>: It was tough for all of us who knew Ludzy to watch him just kill penalties and play a checker role. Then when he started to play a more active role, he started to get some real bad injuries. He paid the price to follow his dream. Ludz tried to go through you instead of around you and eventually the toll on his body was devastating. A couple of points here. Ludzy was a chameleon as a player; he could adapt, he could do anything you wanted, or play anyway you wanted. He learned that from his dad and had not forgot it. Secondly, his 'fuck you, I'll do anything to win, clean or dirty' was, and is still on display today. Remember, I had to walk to school with the guy, and you had to be ready for action all the time. Hey, I'm the guy's best friend for 46 years, and this is all I get to fucking say…bullshit.

I had several great, enjoyable years playing with the Chicago Blackhawks. The team, the fans, the players, and the Stadium were all unbelievable. Sometimes, I had asked for more ice time. On more than one occasion, I asked to play my normal position of center. But, all in all, it was a pretty good existence and living. Like all good things in life, however, everything must come to an end at some point.

That happened to me before the 1988 season, when Mike Keenan became the coach of the Blackhawks. I knew he was either going to love me or hate me, but I didn't have a good feeling. I really thought it was not a good sign when he said to me one day, "You're not good enough to be a Blackhawk!"

A little harsh, but that was the way Mike was. Hey, there may have been better Blackhawks over the years, but none were prouder. The writing was definitely on the wall when I only played in two of 11 exhibition games. I think I scored in one of those games in St. Louis. I thought I had been around long enough to deserve to have an opportunity to at least fight for my job. But I think Keenan was set on getting rid of some of the old guard, such as me, Bob Murray, and a few others. He ended up getting rid of everyone except Keith Brown and Larmer.

Years later, I was coaching San Antonio in the AHL, the farm team of the Florida Panthers, and Keenan was with the Panthers. He was now my boss, and I got a real good look at and got to experience firsthand, his hockey psyche. I realized if Mike got it in his head he didn't like you, or didn't want you, you were done. For example, with San Antonio, he just didn't like Steven Weiss. I don't know why; he was one of our better players. When I asked him why, he would just respond he didn't like him, and would give no other reason. Same thing with Nathan Horton. He didn't like Horton, but couldn't tell anyone why. And, unlike Tessier, who would let it go after a few minutes, once you got in Keenan's doghouse, you were done like dinner.

Even a player of Steve Larmer's ilk incurred his wrath. Before the third period one night in Winnipeg, when we were losing 5-1 to the Jets, an incoherent Keenan stormed into the room, and in a blitzkrieg, booted a young Jacques Martin off the bench for the third period, and demanded he relay a message to Jack Davison, our assistant general manager sitting in the crowd.

In front of the whole team Keenan pronounced, "I want Larmer traded tonight for any fucking goalie in this league."

As we prepared for the third period, Larms turned to me and said, "Ludz, I hope it's not here to Winnipeg."

"Hey Grampa, you always loved the fish and chips here," I countered.

We ended up winning 6-5, and I'm sure Mike figured it was because of his defeathering of us in the dressing room. At that point, he really didn't like Larms. I always thought that

Mike Keenan was good for the lazy Larmer. Keenan pushed him off the ice to condition himself and got a lot of the fat off Larmer's hide.

Many people in the hockey world ask me to compare Bert Templeton to Iron Mike Keenan. There is no comparison. Bert was a naturally tough guy who cared little for any frivolity. As I got to know Mike Keenan better, I soon realized he was actually a very nice guy who had difficulty continually holding up the guise of being a tough taskmaster. He wanted so badly to fashion himself like Scotty Bowman, but could not quite pull it off.

One thing I will say is when Keenan took over a team, the trainers were a little sharper, the room was a touch cleaner, the bus drivers and even the pilots were right on time, and everyone picked up the pace. That's a lost art that Keenan has the ability to bring out.

The whole situation with Keenan coming to Chicago illustrated how disruptive hockey can be to the lives of the families involved. In the fall of 1988, my wife was pregnant with our second son, Ryan. He wasn't growing in the last few months of the pregnancy so there was a little stress. After he was born, he was very sick and needed emergency surgery to save his life. Right around that time, I got sent down to Saginaw. My wife, meanwhile, was back home in Chicago, putting the house up for sale, packing boxes, taking care of our two-year-old son, Stephen, and keeping regular doctor appointments for Ryan. She finally ended up taking care of everything and then moved lock, stock, and barrel down to Saginaw. We no sooner got settled and I got called to come back up to Chicago. Keenan had no empathy for family situations whatsoever.

He might as well have said, "Here's 25 cents. Call somebody who fucking cares."

Doug Wilson said about his time with Iron Mike, "No team won more and enjoyed it less." Wilson was eventually moved to San Jose and is now the GM of the Sharks. He is a class man. Never saw Dougie have a bad day, at least he never showed it.

The Entertainer....the most electrifying player I ever saw was Denis Savard, a high energy, explosive, dancing master who weaved his magic show nightly at 7:35 pm with a standing room only audience in the smoky confines of Chicago Stadium. His road show was equally as good. He could start on a dime and leave you five cents change. Few were better.

When I coached, I always made a point to know exactly what was going on in my players' lives. If you don't care about them, why in hell should they care about you and be 100 percent committed to the team. That's all I'll say about that.

I came back to Chicago for about 20 games. It's the perfect place to discuss the greatest player I have ever played with. I met Denis Savard at my first Blackhawks training camp, but over the years, I got to know him very well. Denis was like a meteor on and off the ice. He never stopped. He was a born hustler through and through. He was a street smart guy. Denis could shoot a wicked game of pool and run the table we had in our dressing room any time he wanted. The only guys that could occasionally beat him were Tom Lysiak and Jack O'Callahan. Even then, I think it might have been a set up.

Denis could also play cards, always won the biggest pots, and then announced to all how much he had won. Yes, mon ami, Savy wins again. He always had a wad of money on him. More importantly, he taught me that there were some players that are on a different plane than you.

When I went to my first camp, I was determined I would chop down this little third overall pick from Quebec and show him who was boss. I first laid eyes on him in the lobby of the Bismarck Hotel before our first skate and thought he was just a little tsetse fly. He used Canadian sticks, and the knobs of his sticks were taped like a goalie, with a big huge knob on the end, which was very unusual for a forward. But after watching him skate for the first time in person, man o' man, I'd never seen anything like it before. He was electrifying. I quickly became an admirer of his, even though I didn't want to. I wanted to show everyone I was a better player. Just like my first junior camp with the Flyers, there were four teams in camp, so sometimes you didn't have the early game. I was so enamored with him that even if I wasn't playing until the second game of the morning, I would still get up early and get on the bus and go to the rink, just so I could watch him play. At the time, I was too embarrassed to tell anybody that. Much like my admiration for Gretzky, I loved watching this 18 year old perform his trickery on ice. The two were opposite. Number 99 was sleek and angular, and like a great chess master, was always three moves ahead of you. Savard was like a human stick of adrenaline, ready to perform spinaramas and daring enough to do them.

I learned the difference between good and great; all men are in fact not created equally.

I just marveled that someone my age could dominate the scrimmage the way he did. I think he was hell bent for leather to show everyone he should have been the first pick in the draft and not Doug Wickenheiser. He could not speak English very well when he got to Chicago. So Rick Preston, being the team player that he was, set about to teach "Savy" one word a day. Preston made him use it in a sentence. On a bus ride early in the season in Quebec, Preston told Denis that "obese" meant smart. So when Tessier got on the bus Savard yelled the length of the bus,

"Orval, you are a very *obese* man!"

Orval stared him down and then they started to speak in French, so the ruse was up.

Savy was just a special, genuine person. He loved to gamble. He would come up to you on the plane and open his hand and show you a pile of change and say, "Ludzy, if you guess within 25 cents, I'll give you all the change I have in my hand."

You would take a guess because you knew Savy loved to do it. After you guessed, he would crow, "Aaaahhhhh, so close."

Laughing and giggling, he would count the change in the palm of his hand to show you how close you were to winning it. He was like a weight guesser at a carnival. He would even bet on whose bag would come out of the baggage claim first at the airport.

Savy was a great player, and I always felt a little sorry for him when we played the Oilers because he wanted so much to be as good as Gretzky. He would always say, "I'm not Gretzky; I'm not Gretzky."

Everyone would always tell him it did not matter. He was a great player in his own right.

Savard, like most French Canadians, was passionate and hot blooded. His temperament would allow him to achieve seemingly unreachable heights of greatness on the ice, and at the same time, get him into periodic trouble. Enter Mike Keenan to the Chicago organization.

When Keenan came to Chicago, he had not yet earned the moniker "Iron Mike." He would get that while in Chicago. It was pilfered from "Iron Mike Ditka" of Chicago Bears fame.

It was an uncomfortable match right from the start: Keenan and Savard, like the Hatfields and McCoys. Savy was a great friend to all and a great teammate to every player. He made sure everyone was a part of the scene. Savard also had a special knack of recognizing the achievements of others. And he was genuine about it. "Hey Ludz, great job on the penalty kill late in the third, baby," he would say. He was, quite simply, a high energy guy, and the greatest player that I ever played with. Any of the 20 Chicago Blackhawks who witnessed the battle between Keenan and Savard in the old Chicago Stadium during a "practice" session will never forget it.

It was during a "red/black" practice. What is a "red/black" practice you might ask? Simply put, it was 10 players in red jerseys, 10 players in black jerseys, no pucks, no drills, and the knowledge that this would be punishment for a poor performance the previous night. In reality, it was simply the coach getting his pound of flesh. As we stepped on the ice and began skating around the glistening ice, no one had to guess what was going to be in store. Anxiety reigned supreme.

As Keenan strolled onto the ice with no stick in hand, a whistle tightly clenched between his teeth, and a full cup of coffee in hand, we watched tentatively as he made his way to the player's bench. With black jerseys at one end and red at the other, the volatile Keenan began playing a sweet rhapsody on his whistle. Down and back, down and back, down and back, were his orders. This went on for 45 minutes non stop with bodies strewn all over the ice. Rick Vaive, a physically strong athlete, crumpled to the well worn ice in a discombobulated state of dehydration. Squid cramped up, and the sight was something to behold.

Rick Vaive: It was pure hell. I cramped up and was flat on my back with my legs in a sitting position. I had been in a few bag skates in my day, but this was a disgrace. I didn't have to be in shape anyway. Keenan just used me for the power play. He never even called my name, just used his foot to nudge me. I am glad Ludzy finds this story funny.

The ever caring Keenan, looking down at the 43-goal scorer in complete contempt, ordered the trainer to "get that piece of shit off the ice." The trainers, looking like rodeo clowns, scampered out to the stranded Vaive and dragged him like a 200-pound tuna off the ice.

At around the same time Denis Savard, who could skate for a calendar month and not get tired, had seen enough. As the "reds" were whistled to go down and back for what seemed like the 100th time, Savy decided he would not stop at the end boards. He just did a quick pivot like a Leprechaun and headed back down the ice in the other direction. As the "blacks" were about to engage in their next down and back, the shrill of Keenan's whistle halted us.

"RED, GO AGAIN," he bellowed out as the whistle exited his now permanently pursed lips for the first time in 45 minutes.

Savard knew full well why the "reds" had to go again, but being stubborn, repeated his rebellious action. This time, he performed his patented "Savardian spinarama" move, which he had made famous in Chicago. It was now a showdown between the fiendishly fiery Keenan and the tempestuous Savard. It was like two rams butting heads, neither giving an inch. Keenan was holding to his guns, as he should, and Savy would not flinch. Savard, the born poker player and street smart kid, was playing a game of Texas Hold'em with the dealer being Keenan. Unfortunately for Savy, the house usually wins.

"Big Daddy" Bob McGill: Keenan made the big boys pay, too, not just the third and fourth liners like most coaches.

It was a confrontation with the bombastic Keenan and the equally temperamental superstar. Keenan, throwing his now thoroughly frozen coffee to the ground, demanded that red go again. Savard jumped out to the lead again, determined to repeat his performance of not stopping at the other end. This time, however, he was hotly pursued by Doug Wilson. As Denis was about to rebuff Keenan's orders of stopping at the boards for the third time, Savard was given a solid jolt by Wilson, who forcefully brought Savard to a halt at the boards. Savard, an avid horseman, was about to spit the bit. Tearing off his red, sweat soaked jersey and throwing it to the ice, Savy seemed to be in an exorcistic state. Shoulder pads, elbow pads, stick and gloves littered the ice, which looked like a garage sale for used equipment. Keenan had pushed his racehorse to the brink of both dehydration and mental breakdown. As Savard yelled almost incoherently, a few words could be deciphered.

"Get me the fuck out of here," he screamed quickly, as he banged on the exit door like an inmate in the asylum trying to escape.

It mattered little that the young man from Point Gatineau, Quebec had been the "guy" for the Blackhawks since his rookie year. A lot of people forget the fact that before Denis Savard donned the Blackhawks jersey, 10,000 was the attendance norm at the Stadium. The minute Savoir Faire danced on the ice with the famous number 18 on his back, the crowds quickly swelled to 20,000. He was now in Mike Keenan's sights, and it would not take long to extradite the very popular Savard from Chicago. The seeds of that exodus were planted the day of the bag skate. Like I said, simply the best player I ever played with, bar none.

During my brief time in Saginaw, I had another encounter with the lovable John D'Amico. Many times when a player has been in the NHL and sent down to the minors for one reason or another, young up and coming players try to prove themselves by challenging players that have already been in the NHL. Such an incident happened to me one night in Saginaw, when I played against a fellow named Guy Jacobs. He kept goading me all night.

"Come on, old man, let's go. You don't have it anymore."

"Hey, I just want to play hockey. Go fight with somebody else," I repeatedly told him all night.

Naturally, we ended up in a little skirmish and both of us got sent to the penalty box. He just wouldn't give it up, and when he yelled that he was going to poke my eye out during our next encounter, I had finally had enough. That was personal. I climbed over the Plexiglas in my penalty box, through the timekeeper's area, and over the Plexiglas again into his penalty box and laid a beating on him. I had popped my cork, and as soon as the ugly mess had been stopped, I instantly realized I was in deep shit.

As luck would have it, John D'Amico, who was then in charge of discipline in the International Hockey League, was in the stands watching the game. He came down after and wanted to know what had transpired between Jacobs and me. After telling him the Coles Notes version and explaining that I had just lost my mind, John calmly said, "You know Ludzy, to see something like that is probably a 10 to 15 games suspension, minimum."

I just stood there in silence as he looked ruefully skyward.

Then he finished, "Thank *God*, I didn't see it," and he walked away into the night. Always liked that John D'Amico.

Leaving the Windy City

On November 29, 1989, I was traded to the Buffalo Sabres for Jacques Cloutier and a couple of draft picks. Although I played 11 games with Buffalo, I was soon sent to Rochester, where I was named captain. There I became involved in one of the biggest melees of all time. If it had happened in the NHL, it would be a well known story. It was my first game back from a hand injury. Don Lever, Rochester's coach, said it was the scariest thing he had ever seen. We had been warned that Binghamton liked to pull shenanigans like this. It was an unwritten rule, and is now a formal rule in most hockey circles, that you did not go on the opposition's side of center during warm up. It was like a badge of honor to defend your turf.

Rudy Poeschek, who hailed from Terrace, BC, played his junior hockey with the Kamloops Blazers and measured in at 6'2," 220 pounds. He was nicknamed "Leather Face" for a reason. He was a legitimate heavyweight in any league. Playing against the Binghamton Rangers was like being in a tank full of sharks. They had a few other tough guys, including a young Tie Domi. Joe Paterson and a young gunslinger named Pete Fiorentino rounded out a roster that left many a player using a putty knife to scrape the crap off their underwear after a game. Poeschek was known to skate by center ice during warm up and take the legs out from under unsuspecting opponents. This night, Poeschek was patrolling the red line when he started kicking out the backs of our guys' skates. One, two, three, four guys got upended. I could see him out of my right eye and waited for him to slip me the nine of hearts. As I turned to give him a spear in the midsection, he bent down and I shish kabobed him on the forehead with the blade of my stick. The blood started to flow quickly. I meant to get him in the gullet, but it was his fault to begin with. I refused to go quietly into the night. Normally, it would take five or six fellows to stop Rudy. The sight of this guy with a head the size of a medicine ball bleeding profusely was like watching Frankenstein's monster come to life.

In those days, there were no officials on the ice for warm up. They were having a leisurely cappuccino in the stands when heaven turned to hell in a flash. The officials came scampering on the ice in their civilian clothes and street shoes. One of the linesmen, who was an off-duty cop, got hit with one of Poeschek's bombs, which was intended for me, and had a seizure on the ice. Finally, after about 10 minutes of absolute mayhem, although it seemed much longer than that, the officials and policemen finally convinced Rudy to go back in the dressing room for the extensive needle and thread work that was required on his melon. Back in my dressing room, I was taking off the small amount of gear that still remained on my body after my encounter and suddenly heard the Binghamton fans starting to roar again, so I assumed the battle was still in full swing. I returned to the ice. Meanwhile, Poeschek was in his dressing room getting the first of 30 stitches put into his forehead. He reacted when his trouble making trainer ran breathlessly back into the room and told the volatile player that his nemesis Ludzik was back on the ice. In a rage, the massive Poeschek pounced off the examining table and made a mad dash for the ice surface and his pound of flesh, namely mine! Oh baby, he still had the needle and thread dangling from his wound as he charged the length of the ice like a bull on a matador. But as luck would have it, he could not see very well. The blood was as thick as pea soup and had gotten into his eyes. It was like pin the tail on the donkey.

Dave Baseggio (teammate): I could not believe the mayhem. Ludzy chopped Poeschek right between the eyes. I was a good friend of Ludzy's, and used to watch him when he starred in junior. In fact, his future wife lived right next door to us. Ludzy was a dirty hockey player; hope he's not pissed at me for saying that but he was not a nice person on the ice. Rudy's head opened up at least six inches. Blood was gushing from his forehead. Ludz was tossed out of the game, which had not even started, and when he went into the shower, he took a shovel with him in case that nut Poeschek came into the dressing room looking for revenge. Ludz was escorted out of the building with our bus driver, Billy the Kid, who was a former biker and always carried a gun.

Billy the bus driver was a tough old buzzard and genuinely great guy. He went out to our bus and brought his 45-caliber revolver into the dressing room. He noticed me looking at it and said, "Don't worry Ludzy, it's not loaded."

I told him, "Not loaded! Billy, I was actually worried you may not have enough bullets to get me outta this goddamn asylum tonight."

In a strange twist of fate, I ran into Rudy again when I was coaching in Tampa Bay. He was trying to make a comeback in the NHL. We talked for about 15 minutes about that debacle in Binghamton. We both had a chuckle over it, but after seeing the size of this man and staring at the telltale scar across his forehead that I had been responsible for, I questioned my judgment.

"What were you thinking?" I asked myself.

Shutting It Down

Way back at the start of my career, I watched Tony Esposito at the end of his. He was clearly past his prime, and it bothered me greatly to see him booed mercilessly. I told Mary Ann that if I ever got to that point in my career, please give me a nudge, just a little tap on the shoulder, and tell me that it is time to go. I had suffered several bad physical injuries and had some liver difficulty, where I had a stent put into the liver duct.

I actually had a good, solid season in Rochester and was about to be exposed in the waiver draft. We were in the playoffs and it was in the second round against Binghamton when I started to feel really sick. The team actually thought I might have food poisoning. One morning, I could not get up. I could hardly move, and my urine was black. It felt like an elephant was sitting on my chest. I still went to the rink for practice but my wife phoned our trainer, Kent Wisebeck, and told him he'd better take a look at me. She told him I could not stand erect, and had not slept a second that night. My wife is a paramedic by profession, so she is very efficient at doing diagnosis.

Kent took me in the back room, did a quick examination, and said I'd better get to the hospital. They ran a battery of tests. One of the problems I have always had was that it took three or four times the usual amount of anesthetic to knock me out. That made the testing all the more difficult. The long and short of it – I was diagnosed with sclerosing colangitis, which is a scarring of the ducts in the liver, as I best understood it. The tests involved a mild form of surgery

(ERCP: endoscope retrograde cholangiopancreatography) to probe my liver. It was apparently the same disease that killed Walter Payton. The head doctor actually said I would need a liver transplant as soon as possible. I had just played 25 minutes of hockey the night before, for crying out loud! I was in complete shock at this diagnosis and Mary Ann was crying at my bedside.

I was going in and out of consciousness, and she proclaimed, "Tell me this is just a bad nightmare."

Throughout my career, I was fairly fortunate with the physical injuries associated with the game, but near the end, I was really falling apart. Doctors were shooting cortisone in my wrist every two weeks just so I could hold my stick. I had a broken wrist to go along with a shoulder separation. And the grand daddy of them all: a broken sternum. That was all in one year!

<u>Mary Ann Ludzik</u>: The broken sternum was it for me. By the end, I could not stand it. He could barely get out of bed in the morning, and he would still play 25 minutes a night. Actually, the prednisone he took when he was 16 years old to help him with his Crohn's actually came back to haunt him later. The liver damage, the broken bones – it's a bad drug that we understand more about today. We knew little of the side effects years ago.

I was quickly transported from Rochester, New York to Toronto's Wellesley Hospital. My guardian angel, Dr. Marcon, who had seen me through my tough battle with Crohn's as a teenager and throughout my life, was once again there for me. As it turned out, I did have scarring of the ducts and a plastic stent was placed inside. The entire ordeal left me weak beyond belief, and I did not know if I had another comeback left in me. I spent the summer recuperating and was not sure if I would be able to play again.

The next September, however, I had the opportunity to play in Austria for a team called the Zell am zee Ice Bears. I was a little hesitant about going over because I heard that if you were an import and not playing well, they would throw you under the bus. But my teammates turned out to be one of the best groups I had ever played with. The coaching was brutal, but my family really enjoyed the experience for a year.

My wife would marvel at the 3,000-metre mountains in our backyard, the picturesque scenery, and the beautiful way of life that existed in Austria. When Mary Ann and the boys first got to Austria, the first thing she wanted to do was to go grocery shopping. Eggs, bread, meat, and butter were not a problem. She ran into difficulty however when she could not locate the toilet paper in the store. She tried in vain to ask the German speaking manager, "Where is the toilet paper?" He seemed to be stumped; it was like playing charades with a blind man. A little exasperated, my beautiful and cultured wife pulled out all the stops and acted out a pantomime, worthy of Marcel Marceau, to visually demonstrate her request, "Where is the toilet paper?" The shopkeeper instantly recognized the 'I need toilet paper' signal and quickly directed her to the bathroom supplies section. As we exited the store, I told my wife, "It could have been worse, you may have needed tampons."

The end is near in Europe. I'm 32 years old and my body, and wife, are telling me enough is enough. With the elasticity of Evel Knievel, I roll out of this cartwheel unscathed.

I had played hockey since I was three or four years old. I was now 32 and had never had a coach I disliked until this experience. Suffering from small man syndrome, this little runt could not coach a chimpanzee up a tree with a handful of bananas. Having him at the wheel of a hockey club was like hiring a taxi cab driver to drive in the Indy 500.

But I decided to stay the complete season and played pretty well, I thought. But that was it. I was done.

I was not sure what I was going to do next. I had run my hockey school in Niagara Falls for several years and had a small silk screen business going. I had been in partnership with my old Niagara Falls Flyer trainer "Mobes" for 10 years with the business. As I mentioned, he was the son of my billets when I played junior in the Falls. I knew him as a fun, extroverted guy; a sort of John Belushi type, who always lived life to the fullest. Unfortunately, it didn't work out like I would have liked. Even though the school was still doing well, I decided to shut it down.

It wasn't until around Labor Day of 1992 that Rick Dudley, then with the Los Angeles Kings organization, called me and asked if I would be interested in coaching the Muskegon Fury of the Colonial Hockey League. I got to know Dudley a bit when I was traded to Buffalo. He now had a little bit of clout. All the Colonial Hockey League teams needed NHL teams to feed them with players. So Dudley phoned the owner of the Fury, a young, baby faced guy named Tony Lisman, and told him the coach he wanted him to take was me. Bruce Boudreau coached the team the year before and we had a bit of a rivalry, as he operated a competing hockey school in St. Catharines, a 10-minute drive from my hockey school in Niagara Falls. Gabby Boudreau is a good guy and a good coach. I heard he had told Lisman he should be careful of me because I was a take charge kind of guy who would want everything his way, that I would be difficult to get along with. As it turned out, I don't think Lisman and I had a major argument in the two years I was there.

But I was not just given the job "carte blanche." By this stage in my career, I now knew what that phrase meant! I went down for my interview with Lisman, and in preparation, I asked several people that knew me to put in a good word for me. Darryl Sutter, Orval Tessier, Bob Pulford, and a few others all sent faxes through to Lisman saying they knew I would do a good job for him. I learned afterwards that Dudley had basically told Lisman if he wanted players to feed down from the Kings, he'd better hire me as coach. There were three people in the interview process. I tried to come across as confident and sure of myself. I had no coaching experience. I found out later that Lisman was a little leery of me because, after interviewing me, he thought that I was a little too cocky. But businessman Billy Cooper, who was Tony's brother-in-law and was asked to sit in on the interview, thought differently.

Billy Cooper: After Ludzik left the interview, Tony looked at me and said, 'Yeah, kinda cocky, isn't he?' I remember like yesterday what my response was: 'Cocky? This guy is a great guy. He's confident in himself; I wouldn't call him cocky, and Tony, we better hire that guy because I guarantee you that guy's going to be in the NHL in less than five years.' I actually underestimated all the things he would accomplish.

So with strong encouragement from Billy Cooper, Tony took a chance on me.

The team did not have that confident air about it the year before. I wanted to change that. The management group became very close over time and had a great relationship. I figured the Colonial League would be the perfect league for me to start in. For my personality, I knew it would be way better than taking an assistant coaching job with a team somewhere. I knew I would have to do everything from planning the hotels, meals on the road, bus trips, and the small items of a team that often get overlooked. A great deal, I figured, for $35,000 a year. That is why I sometimes have little respect for some NHL coaches that do not pay their dues to get there. You can't get to heaven without going through a little hell.

I wanted to get to Muskegon on my first day around noon. That meant I had to leave my Niagara Falls home around four o'clock in the morning. I distinctly remember feeling like Christopher Columbus. He was pretty sure the world was round, but there was a little trepidation in setting out that the world just might be flat. I know that's a weird analogy but that was how I felt when I set out on that dark and dreary morning in September. I knew I wanted to coach and was very confident I would develop into an excellent professional coach, but there was a part of me that was a little anxious about the task in front of me.

The trip from Niagara Falls to Muskegon proved eventful. As I went through Brantford, Ontario, home of Wayne Gretzky, I was clipped by a transport truck and my car spun into the ditch. I was okay but my car was all banged up. Fortunately the car, loaned to me by a dealer friend of mine, was in good enough shape to carry on. I made my way to Windsor. Just as I crossed over the Ambassador Bridge, one of my tires exploded and went as flat as a pancake. I remember thinking, if this is a foreshadowing of things to come, I'd better just turn around now and head back to the Falls. My car limped up to US Customs in Detroit. I felt like Jethro Bodine driving the Beverly Hillbillies' truck.

The guard took one look at my car and flat tire, and she calmly said, "Pull over, sir."

"I can't pull over," I pleaded. "My tire just went flat."

"Pull that car over now, sir," she said louder.

So I pulled over and was told they would not let me in the US with a car in that condition. Embarrassingly, I turned around, and my car bumped and grinded back over the Ambassador Bridge to the Canadian side. Luckily, I was able to coast into a hotel – the Holiday Inn right near the bottom of the bridge. So I got out and wasn't sure how I was going to get a proper tire on, but I began to jack up the car. This was when one of life's coincidental moments happened to me. I noticed a gentleman walking towards me. He was dressed in a short sleeve shirt, tie, and no jacket. I instantly recognized the carved, chiseled face. There were not many others like it. His face could hold three days of rain with all his scars. It was none other than Terrible Ted Lindsay, one of the greatest left wingers of all time. He was there for a funeral.

Lindsay said, "Hey, can I help you out with that tire?"

Of course, he had no idea who I was and got a good chuckle out of it after he found out. He actually helped me put a spare on and then drove me to a tire shop to have the damaged wheel fixed and, as quick as you could say 'Terrible Ted,' I was on my way to Muskegon. Little did I realize that in my five years coaching in Detroit later on, Lindsay and I would go out to lunch frequently. He was the most black and white guy I have ever met. I really enjoyed his company because he did not feel the need to appease anyone. He just said what he thought.

One time I mentioned, "Hey Ted, St. Mike's is coming out with a junior A team."

"There's no fucking need for that. They shouldn't do that!"

Another day, he just exclaimed, "I'd like to get one shot on Hasek. I'd just snap it over his fucking shoulder. He goes down way too much."

You could see why those great old players were so great. They didn't back down from anything, or anyone, and always had the attitude that they were better than the next guy. Ted Lindsay never lost his combativeness. There are stories that he was banned from some Old Timers games because he just couldn't turn off the competitive juices. Hell, I remember him being aggressive in a charity wheelchair game we were involved in, which resulted in a kid being banged out of his wheelchair.

That first year in Muskegon was a great experience for me. I learned so much, and because it was in the Colonial League, any mistakes I made were not magnified. I could just chalk it up to experience. I was indoctrinated into the ways of professional hockey quickly. I got to know Norm Krumpschmid the year before when I had played in Austria and invited him to play for my new team. In training camp, he suddenly contracted meningitis and was sent to the hospital for a week.

I was summoned down to the owner's office one day. Lisman insisted, "Ludzy, get this Krumpschmid out of town. Get him out of the hospital. Put him on a bus, taxi, I don't care."

I asked, "What? Why?"

"I got no insurance on these guys, Ludzy. He technically hasn't signed yet, and I got a $15,000 bill coming from the hospital. I don't have the money to pay that."

Welcome to coaching in the pros, I thought to myself. There was no way I was going to let this guy go. First of all, I had all but given a verbal commitment to him that he would be on my team and, second of all, I didn't want Norm and his family to have to be burdened with a $15,000 debt. I told Tony I would go home and think about it and get back to him. Even though I disagreed with Tony on this, Lisman was a good guy who I knew did not want to leave Krumpschmid out on a limb. He just didn't want to pay himself.

Mary Ann and I thought of the idea to get some signed sweaters and raffle them off between periods at the Fury games. I called Gretzky, Larmer, Paul Coffey, Ray Bourque, Cam Neely, and some others. Most of them sent a couple of signed sweaters. That is the type of fraternity hockey players have. Even though Krumpschmid wasn't a known name to these guys, they were more than willing to help out. So Mary Ann would go between periods and sell tickets to raise money for his hospital stay. It worked really well.

Mary Ann Ludzik: It was amazing. Every game we raised $1,000 to $1,500. It doesn't take long at that rate to raise $15,000. The players who donated sweaters didn't care which level of hockey Norm played. They just wanted to help out.

Norm Krumpschmid: I got really sick with meningitis. I lost about 15 pounds in a few days. Coming from the Canadian system, and after playing in Europe where the

team covers everything, I just assumed I was covered. My wife helped Mary Ann and Ludzy, who were great, with raising money for me by selling the jerseys.

So we raised the money, and one day Lisman calls me into his office and says, "I just got a call from the hospital and they are labeling it as a charity case. They don't want any money. So this will be great. I will be able to spend the money any way I want."

I said, "Hold on a second. We raised the money. We're gonna put it back into the players. We're gonna fix up the dressing room. We're gonna buy some weight equipment, some bikes, and put it all back into the team."

Tony did agree that this was the right thing to do. Hopefully the players that donated the sweaters thought we spent their donations wisely. Krumpschmid recovered, came back, and had a good year for us.

The first game I ever coached was in Flint, Michigan. I met Bobby Hull a few times throughout my NHL career with the Chicago Blackhawks. I have one thing to say about him. Every hockey player who ever took a paycheck in the pro, semi-pro, or European leagues owes a debt of gratitude to that man. He was the one player who had the balls to go to the World Hockey Association, which allowed many others to follow. That greatly enhanced the earning power of all professional hockey players. He opened the vault for all the players and only he had the combination. When I was growing up, he was the most charismatic player in hockey, a man who brought a Hollywood feel to the game. I don't think I ever saw a picture of Bobby Hull where he did not look like the best player on the ice, with his blond hair flowing – a toupee or not.

Everyone heard a lot about Bobby's personal life, but I never saw any of that. To me, he was a funny, personable guy. I actually developed a pretty good impersonation of him, if I do say so myself. That prompted Bobby to talk to my buddy Larmer at a banquet one night.

He grabbed him by his tie and said, "Tell your buddy Ludzy to stop impersonating me all the time."

In the Old Timer games in Chicago, he used to ask to use a couple of my sticks. Of course, I said that was okay. He used to take them and fix them up a bit to his liking and in his deep growling voice slowly declare, "Nowww, you gotta be a superstar to use these bad boys!"

At my first game in Flint, Bobby was there promoting a beer company. He had what looked like a four-hour lineup to sign autographs. He was very cordial to everyone. When I went to say hello, he was nice enough to offer to come down to talk to my players before the game. Bobby Hull wanted to talk to my players before my first professional coaching debut! Of course, I took him up on the offer. Unfortunately for me, there was about two hours between the autograph session and the time he would give words of wisdom to my players, and in that time, Hull had time to tip a few beers – partake in the nectar of the gods, so to speak. Hey, he was there to promote a beer company. As he came into the room, he got his feet tangled up in the hockey bags and almost fell over. That was probably the highlight of the dressing room visit. Let's put it this way, that night his oratory was not worthy of the Smithsonian Institute. And we ended up getting blown out that night.

Another encounter I had with a legend – he was a legend in my mind anyways, and a trailblazer – was with Carl Brewer.

Brewer was involved in that famous Leafs, Red Wings trade, where among other players, the Red Wings acquired the rights to Carl Brewer. As a kid playing ball hockey, we would always do pretend big league trades to even the teams out. In our neighborhood, everyone always wanted to trade the rights to Joe Bulger, a kid who more often than not did not show up to play. One night, in 1998, my wife and I went out to dinner at the Casa d'Oro in Niagara Falls, the town I have lived in most of the time since the age of 17. In walked Carl Brewer with his girlfriend, Sue Foster. He sat right beside us. It was one of those intimate Italian restaurants, where the tables were about 12 inches apart. Now, I am not one to walk up to celebrities I don't really know. I know what it's like to be out in public and want some privacy. But growing up around hockey and always joking about the famous trade that included the rights to Carl Brewer, I could not resist introducing myself.

"Hello Mr. Brewer," I said. "My name is Steve Ludzik, and we have a bit in common. I coached in Detroit; you played in Detroit; and we have both been to Austria for hockey."

I guess he was in a hockey mood. He pushed his table right beside ours without even asking. A few years later, he actually put this encounter in his book "The Power of Two," and mentioned that two bottles of Beaujolais wine were involved. Well, I must say that was not a true statement. I believe there were at least four bottles involved. We just had a tremendous time. At one point, I mentioned how much he was a trailblazer in helping the players against the likes of Alan Eagleson. Brewer said he was still upset by the fact that not one player had issued a sincere thank you to him. That really bothered him. He put his name and reputation on the line in battling Eagleson and getting the monies that the players deserved. I turned to the waiter and called him over.

"I've got the bill. That's my thank you to you."

He got pretty choked up and said he had not gotten any money for me. Obviously, he had put his neck out, which positively impacted all players going forward, including myself. I felt that was the least I could do. When I found out he put this encounter in his book, I thought it was kind of special.

Carl Brewer was a rebel and didn't care what anybody thought of him. He set his own tune and didn't care if the beat was off. More importantly, and the reason why I always liked him, even before I met him, was the fact that he just *loved* being Carl Brewer.

As soon as I got to Muskegon, everyone started warning me about my first trip to Thunder Bay. It was one of the most intimidating places to play in the world, people would tell me. Some of my players were petrified to go there. My motto was to believe half of what you see, less of what you hear. But in this case, there was no exaggeration. It was like having the old Broad Street Bullies out on bail. You felt as if you were swimming in a pond of water moccasins. Keep in mind that to play in the Colonial League in the first place, one could not be faint of heart.

They had a fellow on their team whose name was Vern Ray. He worked on the railroad lines, was from the northern town of Nipigon, was 6'2" and tipped the scales at a behemoth 270 pounds. I was sure there were pictures of this guy in the post office. They had a good player named Jerry St. Cyr and another named Bruce Ramsay, who was just an assassin on skates, plus another dandy: Chad Rollins. And filling out this band of assassins was Mel Angelstad, another big boy who always had massive penalty totals.

Being the new boy on the block, I really couldn't comprehend all the talk that went on about this team. The first month of the season, Thunder Bay came to Muskegon to play. I wasn't quite sure what to expect. Looking back on that first game against them, I remember that the carnage was unnbbelllieevvaaaabblleeee! What a debauchery. During post game, I was pretty much in a state of shock answering to a crowd of reporters...okay, one guy!

After the game, I went to Tony Lisman and asked him, "Who wins this league?"

He responded ruefully with a smile, "Oh, Thunder Bay is at or near the top every year."

I told Lisman that we were not running a petting zoo here. I realized if we were going to win, I had to change the culture and dynamics of the team, and fast. Rule #1 that came to mind in that situation was, "If you're going to play with the big dogs, you'd better make sure you have a couple of pit bulls in the kennel."

I made some quick movements. If Thunder Bay was the team we were going to have to beat, I didn't want my best players scared to death. If it took fire to beat fire, I decided we had to load up. I quickly decided on a course of action. So...I made the trade for...a most intimidating player... *Andy Bezeau.*

The Indestructible One...Andy Bezeau was an indomitable force who sadly never got the opportunity to play in the NHL. You would only have to see him play one period, one shift, or one second, and you would quickly realize that this was a force of nature. At five-foot-nine, he feared no man, but even the Beezer was a touch concerned one night in Fort Wayne and their assassin lineup.

He was one of my favorite players of all time. It is extremely unfortunate, in my opinion, that the casual hockey fan does not know the name of Andy Bezeau. Rick Dudley, who I am very close to, in spite of him firing my ass in Tampa Bay, has seen numerous ports of call in his playing, coaching, and managing days. He would agree that Andy Bezeau was one of the toughest players he has ever seen. He was all of 5'9," if stretched on a rack and weighed in at 183 pounds. But in a bar fight, he would make a marine sergeant pause to think whether he should jump in or not. He was a poor kid from New Brunswick. I was somewhat familiar with Bezeau. He had played for the Niagara Falls Thunder.

In 1989, he actually hitchhiked with his buddy from his home in New Brunswick to Niagara Falls to play for the Thunder. Bill Laforge was the coach there. I think he picked Niagara Falls because he knew there would be motels where he could stay, although he probably just slept on a park bench. The only problem was he had not informed the Flyers or Laforge that he was coming. Bezeau showed up at the first day of training camp and Laforge said he admired his moxy and heart, but he just didn't have a spot for him. He had a snowball's chance in hell of making the team.

Bezeau's response was simple and direct, "Just line up all your big boys tomorrow morning one, two, three and I'll take them all on."

So Laforge decided to at least put him on the ice, as he had come so far. And, sure enough, he demolished the three tough guys at camp without so much as a scratch on his face. Laforge told Bezeau that even though he liked his style and guts, he just didn't have a roster spot for him. So again Bezeau was told he was not required.

The next day Bezeau returned and told an irritated, but quizzical Laforge, "Look, I'm staying here. I'm not going anywhere." It was like a scene out of "An Officer and a Gentleman."

Bezeau was lucky that Laforge was a coach that admired that sort of gumption. Laforge was a bit of an outcast himself, whose high jinks and love of mayhem often brought him up on disciplinary reviews in front of David Branch, the OHL Commissioner. Bezeau went on to become one of the scariest guys in major junior A hockey. He had a reputation as being a one-punch knock out artist. In that first year with Niagara Falls, he played 60 games, scored 20 goals, assisted on 19 others, and had 206 minutes in penalties. He also recorded 15 points and 73 penalty minutes in 16 playoff games. Not bad for a walk on.

I saw a lot of so-called tough guys in my time, but he was the real deal. He had a face on him that would make Sonny Liston pause in a bar fight, and had the ferocity of a pit bull. I wanted him so badly, I traded three players for him: Mark Turner, my highest scorer; Lorne Knauft, an all star defenseman; one other player; and future considerations. The only way the owner allowed me to make the deal was that I got $15,000 in return as well. I think the cash was delivered in a paper bag.

Tony asked me again about the deal before we pulled the trigger, "Are you absolutely sure about this?"

I simply said, "Look, this guy will be the most popular guy here from your side of the fence. You will sell way more tickets, and from my side of the fence, he will change the culture of our team."

We made the deal. And we never looked back.

After making the deal, Marcel Dionne, who was the general manager in South Carolina of the ECHL at the time, called me and said, "Ludzy, you just signed your death warrant.I told Bezeau when he left here to go and throw his skates in the garbage can and go be a taxi cab driver, because he's uncontrollable."

His former coach, who was my old pal Rick Vaive, called me and said, "Good luck Ludzy. He's brutal."

So now I was getting worried. When I met him for the first time after the trade, I was somewhat startled, but not surprised. Bezeau's hair was long and greasy. He wore a jean jacket, jeans, and old work boots. In short, he looked extremely disshelved. I hoped I had not made a huge mistake.

I looked at him and told him the way it was, "Andy, I don't know what has happened to you along the way, but it appears to me you have lost respect for the game and yourself. You may have played for some undisciplined coaches along the way, which may have precipitated this, but you're gonna get your pride back. And you have to get your respect for the game back. First, cut your hair and shave; and I want you to wear a suit and tie to the rink. I want you to look half decent because right now, you look like a fucking bum right off the bloody street."

I was more than a little concerned when he looked at me and calmly spoke.

Andy Bezeau: I told Ludzy I hoped he didn't sell the farm to get me.

My main concern was I knew his hockey skills had deteriorated over the past few years. He was used primarily for fighting. He was like a pit bull thrown into combat every night. He seemed disgusted with the game itself and the people in it. He was sickened by what he had to do to make a living.

I also told him he didn't have to fight for me. He should work on drawing penalties sometimes. Andy Bezeau did not need a road map to find his prey. I think he respected the fact I was not ordering him to fight at every turn. Almost every coach he ever had pushed him into his fights. I think he was relieved I did not do that to him. Other teams turned him into a human attack monster that would react like Pavlov's dog. That respect became mutual quite quickly.

Andy Bezeau: Whatever Ludzy asked, I never had a problem doing it for him. I had problems with what other coaches told me to do, but I had huge respect for Ludzy.

If you really, truly want to coach and be an effective one, the X's and O's are but a small part of the equation. You gotta find out what makes a guy tick, where he was born, how he was raised. It turned our team around. No one pushed us around anymore, and it allowed all the other players to grow an inch or two. One man with courage makes a majority.

Norm Krumpschmid: When Bezeau came in, that really changed everything. Nobody really talked to him at first because he was just a scary guy. He played for Brantford and met us in London, Ontario for his first game. He was already in the locker room when we got there and was quietly getting ready. Ludzy started him, and first shift, he took a run at the defenseman Paul Holden (a 6'3," 210-pound brute) and put him through the end boards and then proceeded to tear the living tar out of him. We were all on the bench laughing at Bezeau. 'Look at that madman,' we hollered. But we were sure glad he was now on our team.

After having him with Muskegon, he ended up following me to the Detroit Vipers and then came to training camp with me with the Tampa Bay Lightning, where he broke his elbow on Steve Webb's head.

You only had to play with him, or against him, for one game to realize he was a player that was more than a tough guy – a unique player that I have not seen duplicated before or since. To make such an utterance is saying something.

In his professional career that spanned from 1991-2001, Andy Bezeau racked up 3,947 minutes in penalties in regular season and playoffs, his high being 618 in 1995-96 with the Fort Wayne Comets. Fans loved him, teammates loved him, opposing coaches loathed him, and opposing players feared him.

Andy Bezeau: I think the guy I fought the most was Bruce Ramsay. I think we fought 35 times. At first, we really hated one another, but after a while, it was just a competition to see who would win. It got to the point where we would have beers together.

This is not a "Bezeau" for the Hockey Hall of Fame book, but one night when he was with the Vipers in the IHL, he knocked out Captain Robin Bowa, a legitimate tough guy from the Fort Wayne Comets. We went back to Fort Wayne two weeks later, and sure enough, the Comets bulked up with four paid assassins from the East Coast League. You know the guys: 6'3," 230 pounds, "from parts unknown." They were simply going to try and put Bezeau's ten toes up.

Fort Wayne did little to disguise their quest for revenge. All four were activated on game day. A telephone call to the IHL office fell on deaf ears. The only way to stop the proceedings would have been if the four were refused at immigration or had arrest warrants issued against them. No such luck. Prior to the game, even Bezeau, who would normally be anxious before a game, was oddly quiet. I did not let Andy participate in the 20-minute warm up. It would have been suicidal. Before the team took the ice I, as usual, went over our game plan and key points. As the buzzer went to signal us to go to the ice for the start of the game, I told everyone to sit down.

I stood before Andy Bezeau in front of the whole team and said, "You have nothing to prove tonight. You do not have the green light to fight. If you really are as tough as we think you are, go draw us four or five penalties tonight. Tell those guys you'd really love to fight, but Ludzik has the red light on you, and we'll win 6-1 easy. But I'm asking you to suck it up for us."

I put Bezeau on to start the game. As soon as the puck dropped, three cement heads from Fort Wayne dashed towards Bezeau.

Bezeau stood his ground and said, "Sorry boys, not tonight. I'm under house arrest."

The three goons and 7,000 fans were incredulous. It was like Patton yelling "Retreat, retreat." This went on for 60 minutes.

After drawing yet another penalty for us, Bezeau yelled down the bench at me, "Ludz, give me the green light just once. I'm going fucking crazy!"

I walked down the bench and leaned into him and ordered, "Beez, stay in the game, red light."

I think the final score was something like 8-2 for us. Let the record show Bezeau gave us six power play opportunities.

On the plane ride home to Detroit, Bezeau, with a post game beer in hand, walked to the front of the plane and simply said, "Thanks." And then he turned and walked to the back of the plane. Even the toughest guys sometimes need a spot to lie down.

Bezeau lived hard off the ice as well, but I respected him a lot because what you saw was what you got.

Rick Dudley: Bezeau is the toughest human being I have ever known. This is not a regular human being. This guy...he is void of any fear; he is void of any pain. If he doesn't feel pain, he doesn't feel anything. The time he hit the boards head first was mind boggling. I thought he was dead. One night, he went to run a guy, the guy ducked. He went over top of him and went straight, head first into the boards, and he just crumpled on the ice. I left the box upstairs and was heading downstairs because I thought he was dead. He was lying motionless quite a while. As I walked by inside the glass, all of a sudden his legs started to twitch. It was unbelievable.

Andy Bezeau: I think it was a guy by the name of Darcy Simon, but I'm not sure. All I remember is I went in head first and my left foot hit me in the back of my head.

A year later, he cornered the player that had ducked and disintegrated his nose with one punch.

Thanks to the Internet now, one can search "Andy Bezeau" and sit back and enjoy. No tough hockey player could put Bezeau down, but a 45-foot fall off a roof onto a driveway in 2000 gave him a grade two concussion and injured his pelvis and back. That ended any chance of a professional comeback. Bezeau, married with two girls and a boy, currently lives in Rothesay, a suburb of Saint John, New Brunswick and is currently running successful hockey schools in the area. I talk to him often. He is one unforgettable man.

To go along with Bezeau, I picked up some other players who went to the same school of hockey. I acquired Jodi Murphy, under suspension for life from the Sault Ste. Marie Greyhounds. In two seasons with Muskegon, Jodi scored five goals and amassed 328 penalty minutes. I picked up Justin Morrison, a pepper pot from the Kingston Canadians. In 1991, in Kingston, he had 44 goals, 57 assists, and 222 penalty minutes. For me in 1994-95, Justin had 86 points and 224 penalty minutes. Beauty! I also got Gary Coupal, a 6'2," 205 pound tough guy, suspended for life by the OHL from the Sudbury Wolves. Coupal had been a defenseman and turned into a fighting forward in order to make the Sudbury Wolves. Halfway through his final year, he was involved in a high sticking incident and received a match penalty. The league came down hard and suspended him for the balance of the season and the playoffs. We picked him up. I also had Kevin Barrett who contributed 307 penalty minutes.

The whole culture of our club did change. We were now going to be the hammer, not the nail. Many a night, while walking down the aisle of the bus before a game, I felt like a lion tamer before we went in the cage to entertain. Our guys were crazy. We were now the hunters, not the hunted. Those tough guys let our best players play without fear. We walked in the front door and left through the front door.

There has been an evolution of sorts with regard to enforcement in the game of hockey. In earlier years, with the likes of Milt Schmidt, Ted Lindsay, Rocket Richard, and Gordie Howe, if a player had a beef or an altercation with someone, they took care of it themselves. I recall the story of rookie Ron Ellis being greeted with a friendly hello from Gordie Howe at a faceoff.

Howe said something to the effect, "Hey, Ronnie, you're having a pretty good year."

Ron was shocked the mighty one even knew his name, "Why, thank you very much, Mr. Howe."

As the puck was dropped, Howe gave Ellis a butt end to the chops for no reason, knocking out a few teeth, which required some immense repair. That was Howe's welcome mat. I met Ellis years later, and he confirmed the gory details of his encounter with Howe.

Later on, in the 1970s and 1980s, with Guy Lafleur, Marcel Dionne, Mario Lemieux, and Wayne Gretzky, there evolved a need for the best players to have enforcers. Teams didn't want their "franchise" players having to worry about, or exert energy, on handling their own dirty work. In the minors, there was a combination of the two styles, which made for some hugely entertaining games.

I have never been one to shy away from altercations with referees when coaching. It is my Achilles heel. This started early in my coaching career with Muskegon.

<u>Norm Krumpschmid</u>: We were in Flint, Michigan and Ludzy was pissed off at the ref, and the game was over. We're standing down by the dressing rooms, which were below the stands, and a fellow came over and handed him the game tape. He took it from the guy and said, 'What the hell am I going to do with this,' and he smashed it on the ground right in front of everybody. It's one of those old VHS tapes, and he picked it up and took the tape and walked over and tied it to the ref's door. He wrapped it tight and then took the rest of the tape and unwound it as he walked at least 75 yards to get to the exit door. The tape was continually unwinding. He walked out the door, out to the parking lot, and tied

it to the door handle of the ref's car and then got on our bus!

That did happen. The referee that night was sleepwalking for 60 minutes; he was just royal red ruby rotten. I got a call the next day from Bob Myers, the commissioner, who thought it was pretty inventive.

That first year in Muskegon, we were often short on both talent and manpower, thus necessitating some extracurricular skullduggery. One night it was so bad, I had to put my trainer, Mark Roof, in net. The only goalie available to me that night came down with the flu and could not get off the bus. Rock Belli was his name. I didn't care how sick he was, I couldn't believe that for the good of the team, he at least didn't try to suck it up and try.

I went on the bus and said, "You've got to be fucking kidding me. We're going to battle with a trainer in net, and you're just sittin' in here with a cold and flu."

It went against all my gut instincts about sucking it up. Right then and there, I knew we would never win a championship with this guy in net. Anyhow, Roof had played goal in practice for us and was willing to give it a shot. Unfortunately, the Roof man let in eight goals in 58 minutes, so his career goals against in the Colonial League was 8.23, but he gave it his best shot. Our players tried to protect him like a mother hen over an egg. A great team effort, except for the slightly fevered goalie rolled up in his sleeping bag on the bus.

Actually, Roof was kind of proud of himself for being willing to step between the pipes and talked to the reporters after the game with a cigarette in hand. I had to step in and tell him to get his ass back in the room and treat all the injuries in there. He did. I hope he kept the receipts for his goalie equipment.

The first year we lost in the first round of the playoffs to Brantford. We were definitely outmatched but not outworked. Our goaltending let us down. My gut instinct, after witnessing Belli bail on the team when he was "sick," was to go all out to get another goalie. But I thought we could hide him a bit and overcome any inadequacies with hard work. That experience taught me to always trust my gut instincts, especially with respect to goaltenders. If you don't have a goalie, you are paddling upstream in a wicker canoe; you have no chance.

I also had to come up with some unique ways to gain some extra rest time for our players during the games. One time, I got an empty tin of tobacco chew and filled it with coffee grinds, fresh from Tim Hortons, and gave it to my trainer to put in his pocket. At the appropriate time, I would give him the signal, and he would fire it onto the ice and it would explode. By the time the ice crew came on the ice and cleaned up the mess, we had achieved the required five minute break. I think I utilized that stunt effectively five or six times. I even tried it when I was with the Vipers once, but I made the mistake of giving the tin to the assistant trainer as he was going back to the dressing room for something and told him to throw it on the ice. He did a great job but made the mistake of being as proud as a peacock of the job he had done and stood there admiring his handiwork. He was summarily grabbed by security, all the while yelling, "The coach told me to do it!" That was the last time I did it in Detroit.

I used coffee grinds because, even though they are usually very fine, they come off the ice very easily and will not cause any player to hurt themselves. I have heard of pennies and other coins being thrown on the ice by coaches, but I knew that was very dangerous.

Probably the piece de resistance for gaining the extra edge was the stunt I pulled with stick gauges. I always figured there must be a way to utilize them to my advantage. I was sitting in my office one day and thought if I could file down a stick gauge and then give one regulation one and one filed down one to a friendly penalty timekeeper, I might gain a fraction of a inch, so to speak, in a game that would be enough to win. So one day in Muskegon, I took a stick gauge and filed it down on a skate machine. What that would do was to cause a perfectly legal stick to be measured as having too big of a curve, and therefore, the opposing team would incur a two minute penalty. If I picked up a towel and flung it over my shoulder momentarily, that meant the penalty timekeeper would pull out the illegal stick gauge because I was going to call for a measurement. If the other team called for one on us, the normal regulation one would be used. We used that trick five or six times in Muskegon. That one stunt graduated nicely to the Vipers in Detroit. One night, Daniel Shank from the Las Vegas Thunder, after being called for an illegal stick, looked at the gimmicked gauge sideways, upside down, back to front, but it was filed with the precision of a cue ball, so there was no way the shenanigans could be uncovered. I'm pretty sure Rick Dudley knew I was pulling that prank occasionally, but he just looked at the situation with the proverbial one eye open.

<u>Rick Dudley</u>: Ludzy is the most inventive guy I know. This was part of his ingenuity.

Starting in Muskegon, I have always tried to treat all my players with the utmost respect and dignity. It always bothered me that just because you put a track suit on, wrap a whistle around your neck, and prop a baseball cap on your head, that you are considered a coach and you automatically command respect and it is owed to you. That is complete crap. My opening statement to players at training camp was always, "Relax, we will cover all areas of the game and do it constantly, and if there is an area of the game that you don't understand, it is my fault, not your fault. If you do not have your routes on the forecheck or know your coverage down low, that's my fault. There are no gray areas." I egotistically wanted each and every player that played for me to say that I was the best coach he ever had and that's what motivated me.

After my first year in Muskegon, I was offered a job by the Chicago Blackhawks and Jack Davison to coach in the East Coast League, but I had given my word to Tony Lisman that I would give him two years and do everything in my power to get him a Colonial championship. I thought we had built a good enough team by the second year to really challenge for a Cup.

By the end of my second year in Muskegon, we were tough enough to match up with Thunder Bay. They still had a few more tough guys than us but it was pretty even.

Andy Bezeau: Going into Thunder Bay during the season, they had about six tough guys, and we had only three or four, so each of us would just fight twice each. If you did well against one guy, you knew the next guy was coming!

The final series between us was just good hockey. Of course, it was rough, but the hockey was fast and furious. During that final series, I noted on the schedule that if we won Game Six in Muskegon, we would have a long, long bus trip for Game Seven back in Thunder Bay.

So I went to Tony Lisman and said, "We've come all this way. I don't want to put these guys on that long bus ride for Game Seven."

Lisman said, "Okay, we'll fly."

After we won Game Six, I said to Lisman, "All right, when are we flying out?"

He responded that he had said we would "try" to fly, but there really wasn't any money in the budget for a flight. That left a bitter taste in my mouth, but we had no choice. Off we went on the long bus trip. We ended up getting beat in Game Seven. The boys gave it a gallant effort, but it was not to be.

During the last minute of play, when the game was no longer in doubt, the Thunder Bay fans started to unroll a banner at the top of the stands, written in four-foot high letters, that went from blue line to blue line and said:

"LUDZIK...START THE BUS!"

Being the visiting coach in Thunder Bay was a memorable experience. They had a fan that used to harass me behind the glass at the bench. I later learned he was a doorman at a local bar. He used to try to entice me to attack him. On my last trip into Thunder Bay before that final series, the owners of Thunder Bay, the Cavas, actually called me in my hotel room and invited me out to dinner. Everyone kind of knew I would be moving on the next year. They took me to dinner and brought along the doorman that harassed me behind the bench. They said they enjoyed our team coming to town. We were a good draw for them. It turned out to be a very enjoyable dinner. They were a classy group of guys who knew how to win.

After that second year in Muskegon, Rick Dudley, who had been watching me, asked me to come to the Vipers of the IHL and be his assistant coach. The plan was for me to be his assistant coach the first year and then take over the reigns the second year. Dudley was getting tired of coaching and being general manager at the same time. At one point during that year, he got so frustrated that he ripped an industrial water fountain right out of the wall at the Palace of Auburn Hills, which was no small feat. I thought being the assistant coach sounded like a great plan, at least as far as I was concerned. The team, however, did not perform as well as we would have liked.

With about 36 games left in the season, Dudley and I went upstairs and had a drink after losing yet another game. He exclaimed, "I don't want to coach this team anymore. I'm done."

I tried to talk him into continuing. I said that maybe we could turn the corner and so forth, but he had obviously thought it through and said, "No, I'm done."

He wanted me to take over immediately and he would concentrate on his management duties, which were becoming his passion more and more as time went on. What I think finally put him over the edge was when one of his scouts highly recommended a player from Ottawa, and Dudley brought him in. After watching him for one shift, Dudley knew the player had no hope. It was then Dudley realized he would have to take a more direct, active role in recruiting.

Duds said to me, "Ludzy, I would have only had to have seen this kid for two shifts to know he could not play at this level."

No one was better at quickly evaluating hockey talent than Rick Dudley. I think we won over 30 of the next 36 games and had a great finish to the season. Unfortunately, those wins were not official wins for my coaching stats. I really couldn't have cared less. It was a lot of fun.

In the first round of the playoffs, we were down 2-0 to the Indianapolis Ice in a best of five series. I kicked one of our best players, Daniel Shank, off the team. He was just a bad apple. He was more interested in "chicken hawking" and padding his stats than seeing us advance in the playoffs. We promptly won three straight to win the series. I think Duds had coached for so long and was such an intense individual that he couldn't understand when players weren't as competitive and intense as he was. He once drove a big truck from Detroit to Niagara Falls to help me move furniture from my home. He loaded up the truck, and drove back with me to Detroit, and then went back to the Palace of Auburn Hills and ran five miles on the treadmill. That's not normal. He should have been tired. I think I was a good counter to Dudley that year. I was able to read, with that group at least, when to put the pedal to the metal, and when they needed me to back off a bit. I'm not bragging here but if you look at our time in Detroit, we had a lot of successful seasons, and we had a lot of fun.

One of the greatest youngsters I ever coached was a 17-year-old Russian named Sergei Samsonov. He gave up a lot to leave Russia and his family. His father was a taxi cab driver and Sergei could not speak a word of English when he came over. Sergei wanted to play in the IHL because he wanted to show and prove to everyone in hockey that he was the best 17 year old on the planet. He did not think he would be able to do that in junior hockey. We were able to get him, even though he was property of the Ottawa 67's. He thought if he could play against men at 17 and play well, he would be better served in the long run. His theory proved to be correct.

When he first came to Detroit, he roomed in a hotel with a comrade that was also trying out for the Vipers. His friend spoke English and helped him with the language. In the first week Samsonov got to Detroit, he was struck with food poisoning and taken to the hospital. I got a call at four o'clock in the morning from his friend that he was in the emergency ward in Pontiac, Michigan. Now, that is not the prime real estate area in Detroit, especially at that time of the night, but I quickly got dressed and headed down to the hospital to see if I could be of any assistance. When I got there, I saw a scared young man. Sergei was just lying on a gurney in the middle of the hall. He was vomiting continuously, had bad, as opposed to good, diarrhea, and had a look of fear in his eyes. He didn't know what was going to happen next. I noticed he kept pulling on the band on his wrist, the identification bands the nurses put on you when you come into a hospital in North America. He seemed almost frantic to get this band off his arm. He appeared almost more upset at the band than the effects the food poisoning was having on his body.

After trying to make Sergei feel more comfortable with some small talk for about 10 minutes, while he was waiting to be seen again, I asked his interpreter, "Hey, do you know why Sergei is so focused on the simple band on his wrist?"

His friend responded, "Yes Ludzy, I do. In the Soviet Union, when you are ready to die, they put a band on your wrist to identify you!"

I explained simply, "Well, tell Sergei that in North America you do not have to worry until they put a tag on your toe, and then it's way too late to worry!"

Sergei Samsonov: Geez, I didn't remember that. But, yeah, we had to call 911 and I was really afraid. It turned out to be really nothing, but at the time I thought it was really serious; they rushed me to hospital. Ludzy was there for me. We can laugh about it now, but it wasn't funny at the time.

The other thing I remember about Sergei was he was probably the most respectful teenager I have ever coached.

Around the arena, I don't care if the players call me Ludzy, Ludz, Steve, Coach, whatever. Sammy, my nickname for him, always called me "Coach" without fail. I believe in the Soviet Union, it is disrespectful to call your coach anything but "Coach," especially for the younger players.

Once, halfway through the season, I walked by Sammy who was just pouring himself a cup of coffee and I said, "Hello, Sammy."

Sammy just quickly looked behind him and saw me and said, "Hello Ludzy!"

He quickly realized he had called me by my nickname and was so embarrassed, he quickly scampered off through the dressing room door. That kid was just a pleasure to coach and to be around. With the language gap and his skill level, I had to be careful not to burden him with too many systems, while at the same time making sure he followed the basic systems the team had put in place.

Sergei Samsonov: Looking back, it was probably the best thing that happened to me. I just came straight from Russia and didn't speak much English. He just let me play. I was very fortunate to come to a coach who didn't give me a lot of X's and O's. He was a very disciplined coach and very system orientated but I definitely had a long leash. It was tough getting used to the professional game as a 17 year old, but I could make mistakes and I wouldn't get benched.

You just don't hold back a thoroughbred. To demand Sammy to dump the puck in every shift, well, it would be like asking Secretariat to pull a milk wagon. You would break his spirit.

The year he first came over to play for the Vipers, he was eligible for the draft. As it turned out, he was an integral reason why we were driving for the Turner Cup. In the first two rounds, Samsonov played well, but in the third round, we played the Pittsburgh Penguins farm team, the Cleveland Lumberjacks, coached by Rick Patterson. It was a big, mauling team that had acquired some NHL pick ups for the series. Sammy, with his strong but small stocky frame, was getting clutched and grabbed all over the ice and having a tough time getting going against such a team.

I went to Sammy and said, "How do you think you're playing, Sammy?"

In the best English he could muster he said, "I play no good, Coach; I play no good."

I knew he would continue to have a difficult time against the Lumberjacks and would probably continue to be ineffective. If such a performance continued, it would hamper his draft status, never mind our playoff status. On top of that, if he got a little rest, he would be fresher for the final round.

So I said, "Listen, Sammy, here's what we're going to do. We're going to make up a story that you hurt your back. You are struggling right now. If we come out and simply say you're going to be a healthy scratch, it will hurt your draft status. What I'm going to say is that you hurt your back and you're injured. I want you to sit upstairs and watch. Don't worry, we'll beat these guys. Then I want you ready for the final round of the playoffs."

Well, as the story goes, Samsonov, while he wanted to play, he never complained and our team dug in and won the next two games versus Cleveland to win the series. A fresh

Samsonov was in the first game of the final series against Long Beach, and we won 4-1...my Sammy got all four goals. You can look it up.

Sergei Samsonov: I was so tired by the end of the season because, you know, I wasn't used to playing all the way up 'til June. The seasons in Russia were done by the end of March. By the time the third and fourth rounds came along, I was absolutely exhausted. That little rest helped, and I remember in the first game of the finals scoring four goals; I can't say it was spectacular play by me; it was just right place at right time.

We went on to win the Turner Cup, and it was a most satisfying experience.

Sergei Samsonov: Being my first year and winning the championship, it was lots of fun. We also had a bunch of great veteran guys who helped me get through the year.

One night in the IHL in Atlanta, Brad Watson was refereeing. He was actually a good referee and a good guy, but this one evening, I didn't think he was calling a particularly good game. His performance was absolutely dreadful in my humble opinion. I yelled at him to come over to the bench. Some officials will come, some will not.

"Hey, Brad, come here for a minute, will you?" I beckoned.

He came over, and I leaned over and spewed venom in his face and made sure I was literally about two inches from his face. I yelled about this call and that call and not being too coherent about it, I must admit. Watson finally stopped me.

"Ludzy, I didn't come over here to hear you spout off about nothing. What do you want?"

I leaned in a little closer until I was almost touching his nose and yelled, "Well, Mr. Watson, I just want to let you know that for the past three days I have had the worst flu in North America, and I hope I just gave it to you."

Most referees have a good sense of humor and he said, "If you think the first period was bad, wait until you see the second and third!"

My actions were trumped by my passionate general manager, Rick Dudley, whose indignation was registered when he demolished a table in front of Watson's dressing room that night.

Bob McCammon, who coached in the NHL, AHL, and several other ports of call, was in charge of discipline for the IHL when I coached the Detroit Vipers. I was still a young coach and pretty abusive of officials in general. Bob McCammon asked Rick Dudley if he could speak with me. I knew Bob liked me because I believed there had been some interest in me from the Flyers when he was the coach there. He sat me down for about an hour before the game and went on about how much he respected me but that I had to lighten up on the officials during the games. He also requested that I be careful of my comments about officials after the games to the media. He also talked about the fact that I sometimes delayed my line changes to the outer limits of the rules to get my players a little extra rest. McCammon just kept going on and on ad nausea. To all those points to which he spoke, I was most likely guilty, guilty, and guilty.

After he was done, he went to Dudley and was a little exasperated as he said, "Duds, I spoke to Ludzy for about an hour about all of my concerns, and I'm not sure, but I don't think he listened to a word I said!"

Dudley, who knew me very well by that time, replied to the effect, "Take the 'I'm not sure' part out of your comment, and you're probably bang on."

Duds was right!

Another time, Rick Dudley and I bumped into McCammon at a restaurant after a game. I was really getting fed up with the officiating in the IHL at the time. I know most coaches complain a lot about the officials but I felt that in the IHL, there were an inordinate number of incompetent ones. McCammon took my comments personally and started to strongly suggest that "you coaches" love to complain about officials and blame everything on officials but do not offer one solution to the problem whatsoever.

I stopped him in his tracks and said, "You want a suggestion. I'll give you a suggestion. Go get Wes McCauley."

Wes, son of the late referee John McCauley, played for me in Muskegon and was now refereeing in junior B leagues in Ontario and a little bit in the OHL.

"You say you want players, but you really don't...go get a guy like that!"

To McCammon's credit, he looked Wes up, and McCauley became an excellent referee for the league and is now in the NHL.

Wes McCauley: Ludzy put in a good word for me. When I got to the IHL, I didn't referee one of Ludzy's games for quite a while. We were in Indianapolis when I reffed Ludzy's Vipers for the first time. They had a pretty experienced team -- either guys that had played some games in the NHL or veterans of the IHL. So I made a controversial call against the Vipers, and normally the players would have been all over me. But there wasn't a peep. I guess Ludzy snapped and said 'That's enough outta you guys. You guys won't say a word to him.' About seven or eight guys skated up to me and said, 'Jesus, I don't know who you are, but are you his kid or something?' Ludzy was a great coach who walked the line well. A guy who pushed you hard but let you have some fun. A guy that could snap, but you knew he would back you up. That's a fine line.

Even Jimmy the Greek in his wisest hour could not have predicted when I was six years old playing street hockey on Burnt Log Crescent in Etobicoke, pretending to be Gordie Howe, that I would have been the last coach Mr. Hockey ever had. You might have made a few sheckles if you made that bet. But so it came to pass. You can look it up.

I drew a portrait of Gordie Howe in Grade Four and thought it was quite good, but much to my chagrin, my teacher felt otherwise and simply wrote, "nose not long enough," and gave me a mark of 55 percent on the drawing. Every time I was with Mr. Hockey, he probably wondered why I stared at his beak for an inordinate amount of time.

Steve Wilson: Actually Ludz is a great artist; he can draw cartoons, paint with oils, and is as good as any of those caricature artists that draw at the carnivals. Never took a lesson in his life.

The late Colleen Howe, who everyone knows was the real manager of the Howe empire, thought it would be a great idea if Gordie could play professional hockey in six decades. A lot has been said about Colleen, but in my opinion, she was great for Gordie. All Howe wanted to do was play hockey. He never took a super keen interest in the business side. I met Gordie casually several times while coaching in Muskegon, and with the Detroit Vipers. After the basics for Howe's one game stint were agreed to, a meeting was arranged between upper management and the Howes to finalize the one-night contract. I told Dudley I really didn't think I needed to be there, but he insisted. So I went up to the boardroom. The people sitting around the table included Bill Davidson, the owner; Tom Wilson, the president; Ron Campbell, the vice president; and me. I sat right beside Gordie. Just as the meeting was about to start, Colleen got up out of her chair, pulled a tape recorder out of her briefcase, put it right in the middle of the table so everyone could see, and turned the switch on. The contract talk then began – nothing special, and Gordie and I ended up talking to each other while the meeting was going on.

He told me a story about Terry Sawchuk, and I laughed. Colleen looked over at her husband, "Gordie, can you just pay attention here for a moment please."

He did for a few minutes and then turned to speak with me again. What a great story for my grandkids. Gordie, like me, lost all focus during the meeting, so I excused myself and took Mr. Hockey downstairs to the dressing room. After showing him around, he asked if he could have a sauna. I got him a towel and went into my office. I actually forgot about him for a while and then raced back to make sure he was still okay in there. He was, after all, 69 years old at the time. He invited me up for a sandwich in the arena restaurant: the Palace Grill.

Gordie spoke very softly and made you feel like he was really enjoying your company. I got the distinct impression that he probably made everyone he was with feel that way. He mentioned he wasn't too comfortable with the hoard of reporters who would be there the next day, so could I meet him for breakfast across the street at "Muskies" in the morning before the press conference? I was very much awestruck by the personal time I was getting with Gordie Howe. I bragged to my wife that night how Gordie and I were buddies and recounted his stories to her.

The next morning, we met for breakfast as scheduled and walked across to the press conference. I must admit I wasn't too keen on the idea of him playing for us; I just thought it was a little too gimmicky for a legend like Howe. But when we walked into that press conference and over 100 people were there, I realized how big this was for a lot of people. On the podium, from left to right were Rick Dudley, me, Gordie Howe, Colleen Howe, and Marty Howe. Gordie got up to say a few words.

"Before I start, I would just like to thank a fine young man who has shown me around here the past few days and has been very kind to me. He has been very professional and made me feel at home here…the man on my left…Smitty!"

Was he was referring to me? Dudley, like an accomplished ventriloquist, without even moving his head or lips said, "WHO THE HELL IS SMITTY?"

Gordie called me Smitty a couple of more times in his remarks. When asked how much ice time he thought he would get, he replied, "It just depends on what Coach Smitty wants to do."

Finally, his son Marty handed his dad a note saying it was "Steve Ludzik." Gordie thought he was in trouble because he had let slip an inadvertent expletive. Now you can slice and dice the name Steve Ludzik any way you want: Ludzy, Ludz, Luder, Stevie, but there is no way you can come up with "Smitty."

With all the press and the excitement, Gordie had just gotten Smitty into his mind and so that was who I was for that press conference. It became a long standing joke between us. Just to get back at him a bit, every time I saw him in the building after that, I would call him Rocket, referring to Rocket Richard, who I knew he despised and who had lipped off in the newspaper regarding Gordie's appearance in this particular game. The neat thing was every time he signed something for me after that, he would smile and write, "To Smitty," so I have a nice collection "To Smitty" memorabilia in my basement. Strange but true.

I have a collection of Gordie Howe paraphernalia autographed to "Smitty."

To be a tough guy, or enforcer, in any hockey league is an extremely difficult job. It is like being a gunslinger in an old western town. I can think of a lot of things better to do than fight the other team's hit man. I don't think many want to do it, or should have to do it, but it is still a necessity on every team. Everyone sees the highlights of the big fights with lefts and rights flinging all over the place, but it is a tough position to be in. The majority of the time, if those players were not fighters or enforcers, they would not be on the team. They would not be able to make their respective teams on their skill set alone. That's just a fact. Interestingly enough, I have found over the years that most tough guys have similar traits. Most all of them are great guys who are not selfish in the least.

I don't consider a player who plays a minute and a half a game and is like a Doberman Pinscher on attack mode, worthy of being labeled a tough guy. I consider actual fighting as being on the last rung of the toughness scale. I judge toughness by a player's ability to take a hit, to give a hit, to play injured, and to make a tough decision at the hash marks to make sure the puck gets out when he is dead tired in the last minute of a game.

The problem for fighters is that to remain a good fighter, you have to fight all the time or you will lose your edge.

Dudley and I were driving to the airport after a game in Detroit to catch the team plane. For some reason, thinking it would be faster, Dudley took a route to the airport that included a stretch down 14 Mile Road, which is a very undesirable part of town. Of course, we were dressed in suits and ties, which didn't help either. After about six U-turns, I realized we were lost. That, and the fact Duds was grinding his teeth showing his frustration, was a sure sign that all was not good. All of a sudden we realized we were in the bad part of town. We were stopped at a light, and there were cars very close to us. So close to us they could have changed our oil. We noticed a truck behind us. Something just felt amiss. I looked in the right side mirror and saw this guy on foot coming up beside my door. He had a shaved scalp. I quickly realized he wasn't coming to wish me a Merry Christmas. As he got to my door, I quickly made a preemptive strike and quickly opened my door with my right hand and popped the guy in the head with my left. All of a sudden I felt a slight pop on my head. But I was more concerned about the guy I was now trading blows with. As I battled with my assailant, Duds, not one to shy away from any type of battle, removed the keys from the ignition of his brand new Nissan Sports Coupe, which he had just picked up the day before. As he dashed around the car, he saw an ominous sight. The truck in front of us had emptied, and the van in back of us had emptied. The red T-Bird that my assailant had jumped out of had us perfectly boxed in. We were being carjacked in Detroit. Our worst nightmare was now unfolding. Two guys versus 10. Not good odds. Unless the Iron Sheik and Dick the Bruiser suddenly appeared from our back seat, we were about to receive one hell of a shit kicking.

Duds yells, "Let's get going!" We jumped back in the car but, as it was a new car, he wasn't quite used to it yet. He had trouble getting the key back in the ignition. He finally did, and somehow he quickly maneuvered the car over a median and around the cars that were blocking us in, and headed down the road with the carjackers in hot pursuit. The undercarriage of his new sports car was in disarray. Dudley apologized for what happened. I said it wasn't his fault. We just got lost.

"Yeah," Dudley yelled, "but they broke a 40-ouncer over your head."

I then felt my head and looked at my hand with a pool of blood in it. Dudley now started egging on the hoodlums through sign language, as he knew the team was waiting on our private plane. With guys on the team, such as Bezeau and Banks, Duds figured they would have liked nothing better than to come out of the plane and rip some limbs off.

Rick Dudley: I started to get out of the car and then realized something was not right. There was a truck behind the car that was beside us with four more guys in it. I did not want Ludzy to get out of the car, but he opened the door anyway and hit this guy, and then another guy smashed a whiskey bottle over his head. That guy was not alone, I figured. We somehow got out of the situation, and then I wanted them to follow us, as we were going to the hangar where an entire hockey team was...that would have been kind of fun!

But the would-be carjackers must have figured something wasn't right when their potential victim was now waving them on. They eventually gave up the pursuit. We finally got to the plane, and I cleaned myself up, but the guys couldn't believe the hole in my head and how badly my hands were cut up.

Peter Cavaglia (player waiting on plane): We were waiting for the two of them. We saw Ludzy and his undershirt was covered in blood and there was glass all over his head and face. The stewardesses literally spent an hour picking glass out of Ludzy's head during the flight.

Mary Ann Ludzik: I heard about it from a parent on one of the boy's hockey teams a couple of days later. Apparently my husband had a death wish or something.

Mary Ann wouldn't speak with me for two weeks. She blamed me for the incident saying we should not have been in that part of town. Yeah, like I was driving!

We won the Turner Cup in 1997, and the next year, we were headed for two in a row. In the finals in Game Five in Chicago, we were losing 5-1 after two periods. Duds said he felt sick and left the building to go back to his hotel. He had seen enough. We seldom looked that lethargic. To be truthful my boss was sick, and our performance was sickening.

Dudley and my wife have always got along tremendously. Mary Ann was back in Detroit, and he phoned her from the cab on the way back to the hotel, telling her he wasn't feeling well and was tired of how bad we were playing. Even my two sons had seen enough and stopped watching the game and went to bed.

As my wife and Rick spoke, she said, "Hey, they just scored in the first minute of the third, 5-2."

They hung up and she called back a minute later. "5-3," she said.

Dudley yelled, "What?! Call me back if we get another goal."

Just as he was getting out of the cab, she called him back again and stated, "5-4, Duds."

By the time Dudley got up to his room, Mary Ann called back again and exclaimed,
"5-5 Duds!"

Dudley was beside himself, "YOU GOTTA BE KIDDING ME! That's it. I'm going back to the rink."

So he rushed back downstairs and hailed a cab back to the rink. Before he got back to the rink, he got the final call, "6-5 Vipers!"

Duds was very superstitious, like a lot of athletes, so he wouldn't enter the building until the final buzzer. The Vipers won in an amazing comeback and the general manager was pretty much in transit the whole time. Dudley was just so competitive and wanted to win all the time so badly. He just couldn't stand idly by and watch us play like horseshit. A lot like me. Not a great loser. There are guys who like to win. Give me a guy who hates to lose.

Andy Bezeau: Both Dudley and Ludzy were great to be around when they were in good moods, but when they were both mad, you just avoided them at all costs.

Duds had a pregame ritual with me that he would perform at about 6:00 pm every game. He would tap both my shoulders and utter, "Ludzy, I'm with you win or tie."

I have never liked losing. My digestive tract was unable to take it, pure and simple. One night while coaching Tampa, we played our hearts out against the New Jersey Devils and lost 6-5. We scored five goals against the big defensive juggernaut Devils and LOST 6-5! I went back in the coach's room. Dudley came in to join me, and there was this big fan that sat on the floor. I was fuming and gave it the biggest kick I could. The front of it, the protective guard, came flying off, but the fan kept going. Dudley laughed at me but I just kept kicking that fan until there was almost nothing left.

Rick Dudley: He kicked the fan and it bounced against the wall. I think Ludzy must have kicked it at least 11 times until only the nub of the fan was spinning around making a kerklunk noise every rotation; there were plastic pieces all over the place. It was the fan that would not die. I think I finally walked over and just pulled the plug. He was passionate. I had tears in my eyes. If you have not coached, you should reserve judgment.

Ira Kaufman (Tampa Bay Tribune reporter): There were a couple of nights at the Ice Palace when we heard some loud crashes coming from the coach's office before we got in there. We found out later it was Ludzik punching the walls, knocking things down. He took it very hard. He was extremely competitive. He expected everyone to compete.

Dudley should not be one to talk about outbursts. The faint of heart should not be in close proximity when something sets him off. We were playing the Cincinnati Cyclones in Detroit, a good team but one we usually tamed pretty easily. On this particular evening, we lost. We had a great crowd.

It was "Batman Night" at The Palace. The original star of the 1960s TV show, Adam West, was the special guest for the evening. Theme nights were the norm in The Palace. We had the likes of Ellie May Clampett from the Beverly Hillbillies, the Hanson Brothers from Slap Shot, and even Screech from Saved By the Bell made an appearance. I had gotten into a verbal set to with the assistant coach of the Cyclones, Al Hill, over the fact that he had grabbed my player's (Phil Crowe) stick as he skated by their bench. Al and I went at it for quite some time. Dudley, who was watching the game deteriorate from his perch in the press box, hightailed it down to the Zamboni area as we were exiting the arena after the game. Everyone was yelling at each other and the referees. It was a hotly contested game. It was bedlam all over the place.

Then I felt a hand gently massaging my shoulders. The voice said, "Ludzy, we don't need this crap. Let's go."

I had to do a double take. The face looked like my pal Dudley, but the soothing, calming voice made me think it must be an imposter. Rick got me calmed down a bit, and we headed for the confinement of our dressing room. This may be a good spot to explain that Duds and referees got along like a cobra and a mongoose. In other words, they were natural born enemies. The reason for our loss, in Dudley's mind, was the conspiracy against us by referees.

"They did everything except block shots," Dudley would say later.

On our way back to the dressing room, the officials unfortunately caught the eye of Richard C. Dudley, who quickly swooped down on them like a chicken hawk on a deaf field mouse. The three officials went into a state of panic and hurriedly unlocked their dressing room door and scampered inside, locking the door behind them. They just barely avoided the rampaging Dudley. After venting his anger verbally through the metal door, Duds gave it a couple of good kicks and then turned around and spied an industrial water fountain. I'm sure he had visions of wrenching the 200-pound cast iron structure out of the wall, like he had done the previous year. I was howling with laughter, mainly because of the calmness Dudley had exuded only moments before. With resignation, we both began to walk toward the dressing room. I noticed our head of promotions, Lynette Shady, walking towards us with an inebriated Caped Crusader under tow, now in civilian clothes. Batman would not have passed a bat breathalyzer at that moment. Duds had that look in his eyes that said "stay away from me," but as he walked towards Adam West with his head down, he took a cursory glance upwards and moved to his right to go around him. The bombed Batman was either stupid or crazy. He moved to block Dudley's path. Dudley shifted to his left, and Batman again mirrored his move, thinking he was being funny. I looked at Lynette with despair.

Duds, with his teeth clenched and his lips barely open, growled, "GET THE FUCK OUTTA THE WAY."

If Adam West had his utility belt, he would have reached for the bat rope and disappeared quickly, but as he now tried desperately to get out of Dudley's way, he dove sideways and headlong into a trolley, which had cases and cases of toilet paper loaded on it.

As we proceeded to the dressing room, I could not help but tell my friend, "You know, that was Batman you just accosted in the hallway."

"I don't care if it was fucking Superman," was Dud's curt reply.

With my job as a commentator on The Score, I like to do research on the Internet. I also get a lot of emails from fans informing me of their opinions on a wide variety of subjects. I get a kick out of the fact that there is often little difference between rumor, myth, and legend. I was always taught to believe half of what you see and less of what you hear. That is certainly the case in the hockey world, especially in the communication world we all live in now.

When we were playing the Chicago Wolves in the seventh game of the Turner Cup finals, there was no question the tensions were high. There was a huge rivalry between our two evenly matched teams. We were at the Rose Mount Horizon Arena, Chicago's home turf. The rumor was that I had stolen the Turner Cup from the arena lobby and took it down to the dressing room for the players to see. First of all, I would never do that. And second of all, it would be bad luck to do that, as most hockey enthusiasts know. And third, it never happened.

As anyone knows who was there, or read about it afterwards, there was a huge brawl at the end of warm up just as the players were leaving the ice. Two of my players were on the ice with four or five Wolves. It was all over a player shooting a puck into the opposition net at the end of the warm up. We were outmanned. I was just doing my shoes up in the back when I heard a roar from the 8,000 to 9,000 fans already in the arena. As the crescendo of excitement got even louder, I ran out to see what was going on. My first thought was that Dudley was getting into it with the fans. He had been a little on edge that day to begin with. Two police officers blocked my path to the ice, and two of my players were still getting the hell beat out of them by the four or five Wolves still out there. I asked rather loudly if the cops could move so I could let a couple of my players out there to save the two on the ice. The officer continued to block my way.

I had no option but to push the officer out of the way and said, "Boys, get out there and help those guys."

The officer and I got into quite an argument. Dudley came down to try to interject. He was so agitated that by the end of the first period, he was escorted out of the building and had to watch the rest of the game across the street in a bar. I always thought that the off duty officers were in cahoots with the team to make it difficult for us. The police station was directly across the street from the arena. History will show we lost that final game 3-0. It was 0-0 going into the third, but our players were really banged up. I was extremely proud of the effort throughout the playoffs. They fought like warriors. Dudley actually strutted his way back into the arena following the game and came down into the coach's room.

"Ludzy, I'm even more proud of this team than the one that won the Cup last year."

We were racked and savaged with injuries throughout the whole year and especially in the playoffs. We just didn't have the manpower to pull it off. To win, you gotta be good, and you gotta be lucky.

I always thought that playoffs were like the troops marching into combat in the Civil War. You know, row after row, and pity the poor sonofabitch that was the drummer. All he had was a pair of drumsticks to fight with. The point is you will lose guys along the way. It's a two-month marathon. You gotta stay healthy.

Dudley dragged me to the broom closet and said, "This is one of the greatest coaching exhibitions I have ever seen."

He went on to say he would not have been surprised if we had been eliminated one or two rounds ago. For Rick Dudley, who throws compliments around like manhole covers, that meant a lot to me.

Duds walked out of the dressing room area and into the Zamboni area, which was mobbed with Chicago Wolves fans that were in a state of ecstasy. He was cool and calm to begin with but then proceeded to get into an argument with the police officer that had tossed him out. I walked over to get a closer view, and we were both promptly escorted to our bus from the arena by the said officer and five or six of Chicago's finest. Dudley fought it tooth and nail all the way to the bus. He was getting literally pushed on the bus. As I have always said about my pal Duds, if King Kong and Richard go down an alley, the monkey's not coming out.

He still had one leg and foot off the bus, and one cop said, "That's it, old man, get your son and get the fuck out of Chicago!"

Folks, that is verbatim from a Windy City cop. Duds turned to me and said, "That's it! I'm going back!"

He came down off the steps and walked over to the officer, a young guy, who was standing by the bus door with a shit eating grin on his face.

"I don't have a dollar in my pocket, but I'm goin' tell you what I'm going to do."

And he reached into his back pocket and pulled out a credit card and continued, "Here's my credit card. I want you in the back room for five minutes alone. Just you and me."

And that's when the cops went to their walkie talkies. I quickly realized that the police station was directly across the street from the Rose Mount Horizon, where the bus was parked. Shortly thereafter, a swarm of six cop cars came careening across the street with sirens a blazing. You would have thought they had Al Capone boxed in. We were then "gently" escorted out of town.

At the time, if you read fan reports of the incident, it was said I two-handed a police officer in the face and instructed my players to pull off the shenanigans in the warm up. Neither, of course, was true. That was not my style...normally.

A couple of years later, when coaching in San Antonio, I ran into the same cops again. After getting to know them a bit, they admitted, "You know, that scene a couple of years ago was a bit of a set up."

I told them, "I always thought it was."

Detroit Vipers Rick Dudley, Buck Steele (scout), and Steve Ludzik with the Turner Cup

Hats off to John Anderson, who was coach of the Chicago Wolves at the time. He ran a well oiled machine that was deserving of the championship.

A couple of years later, I was an assistant coach with the Florida Panthers, and Clint Malarchuk was helping out with the goalies. Instead of buying a house and bringing my family down for the year, I was put up at the Ramada Inn Suites for my tenure. They did the same for my good friend, Clint Malarchuk. We both had bad backs, so we liked to go down to the hotel hot tub in the evening before we went to bed to shoot the breeze about what had gone on throughout the day.

One night, there were four guys already in the hot tub with a small keg of beer. Clint and I really didn't want to get involved in a conversation with anyone else, so we went into the weight room for a few minutes to wait until they left. Well, they didn't leave soon enough, and we really wanted a hot tub because our backs were killing us that day. We decided to bite the bullet and join them. No sooner did we get into the hot tub, the little pip squeak in the middle of the group, obviously intoxicated, looked at me and said, "Hey, I know you!"

That happens a lot in the hockey world, as you can imagine. Clint was just content on chewing his tobacco and sipping a beer.

"Where are you from?" I asked.

When he stated he was from Chicago, I said he must recognize me because I played 10 years with the Chicago Blackhawks.

The little guy squinted his eyes at me and ruefully said, "No, no, you're Steve Ludwig."

"Yeah, you're right, Steve Ludzik."

As soon as I said that, Clint jumped up with tobacco chew drooling all over his face and added, "You are! Holy shit! How ya doing? I always wanted to meet you."

Slurring his words, the squirt continued, "Yeah, I don't like you. You're the guy that stole the Turner Cup and brought it into the dressing room for your players so they could touch it before they went out to play."

"You know, buddy," I barked at him, "that's a great story, and I never denied it because I thought it was pretty funny. It never bothered me because it wasn't true. I'd love to tell you it happened but it never did. The Cup was guarded by four security guards in the lobby. What do you think I did? Go up to them and say 'Hey, look at the monkey on the ceiling' and just take it from under their noses!"

As with most fans you run into, once you talk to them for a while, they usually turn out to be pretty good guys, even if they root for a different team than you are involved with.

When you play and coach in junior and pro hockey, you make a lot of friends along the way. And if you are true to your word and have some gumption, you are bound to make a few enemies, too.

A man that has become extremely well known and famous in pro wrestling is Vince McMahon Jr. I give him credit. He is a modern day P.T. Barnum with muscles, who knows how to put on a big show. However, he and I had a little tussle when I was coaching the Detroit Vipers. It was the late 1990s, and we were in the middle of playoffs. The World Wrestling Federation (WWF), now the WWE (World Wrestling Entertainment), was in Detroit. The wrestling group had an unbelievable setup that included massage rooms with professional therapists and buffets of food that could feed a cruise ship. There was quite the entourage. The wrestlers, for the most part, are quite the physical specimens. All of them are used to working out every day. Long gone are the days of the cigar smoking, beer swilling, pot bellied maulers. When they were in Detroit, they sent a stage hand down to ask me if the wrestlers could use the team's gym at the Palace of Auburn Hills. Having known a couple of wrestlers, I said that would be no problem. My players were only coming in for massages that day anyway. Bret Hart was there and, being a good ol' Canadian boy, he was anxious to talk some hockey with the boys. We had about six or seven players in for treatment. They were getting ready to leave when McMahon's own private security guard came in and told our trainer that he and the players would have to go all the way around the building to get out. They could not travel the short route to the parking lot – the same way we left every day of the year, because it would "interfere with operations." I overheard the conversation, and the guard spoke in a very authoritative tone.

My nerves were raw. It was playoff time. I was putting in 16-hour days, looking at film, worrying about who was injured, deciding on match ups, and I looked at the guard and simply said, "Excuse me?"

The guard snapped, "You heard me. You guys are to go around the long way. Those are Mr. McMahon's orders."

That was it, "I don't know if you realize this, but you are renting the building off of us tonight. Our owner owns this building. So don't be telling us which way to go...because we are going THAT way. Our cars are there, and it is the quickest way out. For them to walk around, it would take them 15 to 20 minutes!" A slight exaggeration but I was making a point.

I was starting to get a little heated up, and all of a sudden, I noticed Vince McMahon coming nearer to us.

McMahon snarled, "What seems to be the problem here?"

I quickly snapped back, "What do you think we're doing, trying to figure out who's gonna win and lose tonight? You think we really care!"

He looked at me with that cocky side sneer of his and said, "Who are you?"

"Never mind who I am, who do you think you are telling my guys they have to walk around? I just let your guys work out in my workout area, and this is the kind of payback you want to give us, letting our guys walk an extra 15 minutes."

He kind of did a peacock swagger, and I started walking out the short way and said, "I'm telling ya. We're walking out this way. My boys are walking out the front way. That's the bottom line."

As we walked out, Ric Flair let out a big, "WHHOOOOOOO."

I spoke with Ric Flair a couple of years later, and he loved the fact I stood up to the mighty Vince McMahon. I made sure we walked out the way Vince McMahon didn't want us to. He kept that smirky grin on his face, almost like a Cheshire cat, that wrestling fans have come to hate. Actually, in some small way, I think he relished this little set to.

Fast forward a couple of years later. Wouldn't you know it, I was coaching in Tampa Bay and the wrestlers were in town. Sure enough, they sent a "roady" down to my office to ask me if they could use our workout center.

"You know, I think we can do that," I calmly said, "but do me a favor. I would just like to have Mr. McMahon come over personally and ask. I would like to say hi to him."

So a couple of minutes, later McMahon walked through the door. As soon as he saw me, he stopped in the doorway and slapped himself hard on the forehead.

"Oh nooo, not you!"

We both started laughing. We actually had a great conversation about wrestling. I now think he's a pretty good guy, just running a business. Like a lot of people, he is neither black nor white, but somewhere in the middle.

Heading to the Sunshine State

I first found out I was probably going to be heading to Tampa Bay while lying on a rubbing table in the dressing room at the Palace of Auburn Hills during the IHL playoffs. I was speaking to Jack Sights, Mr. Davidson's right hand man, and knew by the way he was talking to me that I was going to be offered the job. Out of respect for Rick Dudley, I waited until he was officially the general manager before I agreed to sign on.

One of my first mornings in Tampa Bay, I was driving with my wife, looking at the real estate in the area, and we were listening to a local radio broadcaster: Todd Alan Clem, aka Bubba the Love Sponge. We couldn't believe our ears. It was like Florida's answer to Howard Stern. Mary Ann asked me to turn the radio off. She found him both disgusting and perverse.

She bellowed out, "How can anyone listen to that crap? That's about the worst I've ever heard on the radio."

Meanwhile, I was laughing my head off. I responded that it was probably just his shtick and he was probably a really nice guy.

Mary Ann shook her head and turned down the radio and said, "This guy's a disgusting pig."

Ironically, shortly thereafter, someone from upper management at the Lightning happened to mention to me that if I ever got a chance, I should call up Bubba the Love

Sponge and introduce myself. I did and Bubba and I met for lunch and became quite good friends. He was a short guy who looked like he was 300 pounds. He was the King of Media in Tampa. Bubba had never previously talked about the Lightning franchise on air, and in fact, did not like them. He got to be a friend and used to call me at home to put me on his show. Mary Ann soon realized what a really nice guy he was.

<u>Mary Ann Ludzik "now"</u>: I hope I'm not wrecking his reputation, but he's a real Momma's boy – loved his mother. He is just a big ol' teddy bear, very polite, well mannered; just a nice, nice man. And he loved hockey.

He eventually got thrown off of public radio for supposedly slaughtering a pig on live radio, which was later proven to be false, and went to Sirius radio after teaming up with none other than Howard Stern. I heard he has another morning show in Tampa and is once again on the top of the heap in Tampa radio. Quite the character.

A new coach always has to look at the situation he inherited and start to fix those problems as best he can. You just keep correcting the previous problems until you get fired. Such was the case when Rick Dudley hired me to coach Tampa Bay. I did not like the state of the Lightning when I got there. I thought the practice routine was ship shoddy at best. To begin with, I had to start a serious pre-practice regimen to get it up to the level that I wanted.

After I took over, I honestly felt the work effort began to improve. We worked hard, for the most part, during games. A major problem I inherited was that the Lightning did not have a number one goalie. It was really hard to be successful without a bona fide top tender. We had actually decided we were going to go with Daren Puppa and Dan Cloutier. Puppa played a few games for us and was just awful. Remembering Orval Tessier's old line, I remarked to Dudley on a bad goal Puppa had let in, "Duds, I could have stopped that with my dick!"

Dudley phoned Puppa's agent and said, "We're not paying a million dollars for goaltending like that."

Puppa promptly got hurt in a career ending back injury.

And the thing with Dan Cloutier was he was inconsistent. One game or period, he might look like Terry Sawchuk, and then he would let in a horrendous goal the next period. Cloutier was a fiery guy who had a great left hand. The only problem was it was more memorable for punching faces than catching pucks. I'd never known a goalie that had a hockey card with TKOs listed, but every time I asked someone about him, it was always the same.

"Oh boy, is he tough." This was not of his doing, but it came from the media.

He struggled early in the year. Even when we outplayed teams and probably should have won, Cloutier would let in a softy. Of course, it was not always his fault, but the goalie is the last line of defense, every time. Although I could not show it, I sincerely felt sorry for Cloutier. He was a goalie in a bad situation. He was supposed to be the life raft and we threw him an anchor. He was very quiet and I have always believed that still waters run deep; you never knew what he was thinking.

One day he just didn't show up for practice. John Cullen, my assistant coach, called him but we could not get a hold of him. We were not playing well, and I really didn't want any more negative publicity for the team. So I told our trainer to put Cloutier's equipment on and just skate around during practice and stay away from where the reporters were sitting. It worked. No one noticed, which might say something about the sports writers, or about Danny's practice habits. Around five o'clock in the afternoon, Cullen finally got a hold of Cloutier. He said he was having a bit of a meltdown. Fair enough. He also mentioned that we had 13 American League players on our team, and it was making it tough for him. It was not a round number. It was not five or six. It was 13. So I had him come in the next morning at 8:30 am and told him to write down the 13 players he had in mind. When he was finished, I told him to add a 14th one and to put it on the top of the list…him! In actuality, Cloutier was a great kid; it wasn't fair that he had to be thrust into a position to be a number one goalie on such a young team. He had no chance. He was still just a kid.

Ira Kaufman (Tampa Bay Tribune reporter): Goaltending was terrible. If there was one main problem, it was the goaltending. They went through Puppa, who was a disaster; they traded for Kevin Weekes, who was a backup – he has proven to be a backup. And there was also Cloutier – with him, you never knew what you were getting.

We tried everything and anybody: Puppa, Cloutier, Zack Bierk, and Deiter Kockan. Actually Bierk was all right but he suffered from vertigo. Not a great malady to have if you are a goalie in the NHL.

I knew we didn't have an abundance of talent, but we had a good young nucleus. I also came to the quick conclusion that we would be hard pressed to get many wins with the talent we had.

Ira Kaufman: I will say this about Ludzik, he was the ONLY coach, and I mean the only coach, who I covered on the beat who did not ever say, "Look at this roster, what do you expect me to do?" He knew and I knew, but he never, ever, said it or insinuated it. He always took full responsibility.

One of the most unusual and weird situations I ever encountered, in or out of hockey, occurred when I was approached about a possible reason why the Tampa Bay Lightning were not successful. Somebody suggested our building was built on ancient Seminole burial grounds and there was a curse on it. I heard murmurs of this before. I gotta be truthfully honest with you. I am not a big believer in that kind of crapola. I am just a skeptic, I guess.

I know whenever I see those types of shows on TV, they will inevitably ask the psychic, "Do you know the name of the boy's killer?"

And the psychic will say something like, "I see the name J, yes, I see the killer's name as John."

Well, you know what? If you can see it so well, why don't you just give us the last name while you're at it! I guess my feelings concerning this subject came from my readings of Harry Houdini. During the last few years of his life, he tried to debunk these fraudsters who bilked honest people out of their money. I love watching the TV evangelists, with their two-dollar toupees and their gift for the gab. And sooner or later, the topic of money always sneaks in.

So anyway, they found a famous Florida psychic that was convinced our arena was built on an ancient burial ground. Because of the psychic session that was planned, I was not able to accompany the team to Montreal. It was near the end of a long season, and it didn't matter too much, but there was speculation I had to stay behind because I had some sort of court case I had to go to. Some thought I had to go to a DUI case. But nothing could have been further from the truth.

There was me, my wife, Rick Dudley and his wife, a few team executives, and the team secretary in the dressing room. Well, doesn't this lady come into the dressing room and start throwing what seemed like bags of salt around the room saying that this will keep the spirits away from you. The psychic started putting everyone in a trance, and everyone was holding hands. My wife had put a tape recorder on, and the psychic said we might see and hear some things we didn't want to see. To tell you the truth, I never saw anything. All I kept thinking was if these ghosts and goblins were so feathered up, why were they taking it out on our team. Why don't they take it out on the opposing teams that come into our building? The whole thing didn't make any sense to me.

It kept on. She started to go into some trance and put us all in a hypnotic state. I sat there looking around with everyone with their eyes closed, and thought to myself, "Christ, you think we got better things to worry about than this!"

The funny part was when the lady started to speak in a different voice and cried out in a woman's voice, "Oh no, oh nooo."

As I could best comprehend it, the gist of the story was that some soldiers had mutilated this woman's kids and done some horrific acts to her. The mother was searching for her children to come home or something like that. So the psychic started to talk to the distraught woman, "Come over to the other side, come over to the other side." Doctor Seuss could not have spun a better tale.

And then apparently the old woman replied, "Oh, there's an old man sitting over there and he doesn't want to come."

I quickly piped in, "Hey, this should be a two for one sale, get them both out of there if they're the problem. If they're in there, get 'em out!"

Everyone started laughing – as much as you can at a séance, I guess. I never felt too comfortable with all that stuff. The pathetic part was there was no way I could make up a story like that.

Mary Ann Ludzik: I don't believe in this stuff at all but this medium, Dale, came down to Tampa. I was asked to do a walk around (the arena) with her, and she said she felt 'vibes.' There was a picture near a fountain that she had a bad feeling about. The arena was supposedly built on an Indian burial ground and until it was appropriately claimed, the ghosts would not allow the team to win. She walked around with special salt bags, crystals, and she blessed the place all the time. And then she decided we needed to have a séance to get rid of these demons! She had us sitting around holding hands, and it was all kind of strange. She did predict that the Lightning would one day be champions, however Steve and Rick would not be part of the team.

When I came to Tampa, I encountered some tough guys there, too. One I particularly enjoyed was Kyle Freadrick, a 6'7," 260 pound lad from Edmonton, Alberta. Most likely because of his size, he was drafted in the third round, 64th overall in 1997. He was signed by Tampa Bay as a free agent on July 16, 1999. Kyle did not touch the puck very often, not only because he didn't get much ice time, but also because he was not a grade A skater…actually, come to think of it, he was a god awful skater. But he was one tough cookie.

Freadrick was in one of the best fights I have personally witnessed in my hockey career. It was in Chicago with tough guy Kyle Vanderbush. It was something out of a John Wayne movie. Freadrick with a right, Vanderbush with right, Freadrick with a left hook, Vanderbush with a jab, a left, a right, another left, and so it went for what seemed like an eternity. Finally, Vanderbush caught Freadrick with a shot to the chops that literally propelled one of Freadrick's teeth and part of his gum into the air and somehow landed on the blade of Matt Elich's stick, who was sitting on our bench. Elich could barely speak, he just pointed to the end of his stick with the hunk of flesh and tooth on it.

I said, "What is the matter with him?"

Vinny Lecavalier pointed to the end of Elich's stick. Sure enough, there was Freadrick's tooth. I guess Elich was not used to that sort of violence. He incoherently babbled away. He didn't want to move in case we lost the tooth. We took the tooth, packed it in ice, but I don't think it ever made it back into Kyle's mouth. After that, Freadrick had a smile on his face like a jack-o'-lantern. Considering the magnitude of the fight, it was appropriate that Bob Probert, still associated with the Blackhawks at the time, was in attendance that night.

He came down after the game and commented to me, "What an unbelievable brawl that was!"

That's quite a statement from a man of Probert's pugilistic prowess. We both only had to glance down at the blood on my jacket to see that I concurred with Probert's evaluation.

Freadrick was a nice, quiet kid that could only be used sparingly in the NHL because of his talent. He made the most of his time there but ended up playing only 23 games for the Lightning in 1999-00 and 2000-01. He had to officially announce his retirement on June 30, 2002, after having suffered a head injury during training camp.

During my first year in Tampa Bay, the Lightning made a deal with a little clothing store to provide me with some suits. The tailor was one helluva nice guy and had a small, small shop. I don't think he worked out the greatest deal for himself because if you did the math, I got six high end suits for nothing. Over several weeks, I got to know him quite well. We had some great hockey talks. One day, when I was getting measured up in the back, the owner came running back and asked if I wanted to meet Evel Knievel, who was in the front of the store. Apparently, he frequented this shop quite often.

Evel Knievel was a hero of mine when I was a kid. In my youth, he was larger than life, a human publicity machine, a P.T. Barnum with balls, who reportedly made over 50 million in his lifetime and spent 60 million frolicking and free wheeling along the way. He was the stuntman who performed daring jumps over buses, cars, construction equipment, and even the Snake River Canyon, which was shown on Pay per View in theaters across the nation. The tailor explained that Evel recently had a liver transplant and was pretty much bankrupt, which I found tough to swallow, as a plain golf shirt in this place was $150. Nonetheless, I jumped at the chance to meet a childhood idol.

Evel headed toward the back room where I was and the tailor ran in ahead of him and warned, "Steve, Evel is an old and grouchy man, so if he gives you any trouble, let me know and I will get him out of here."

I was stunned to see how frail he looked. The impression you had of him was a swashbuckling, motorcycle riding, whisky drinking hellion, but that man had totally disappeared and was now a hobbling shell of his former self. He walked with the aid of a diamond studded walking cane, accompanied by a young blonde lady friend, who looked about 22 years old and provided stability for Evel to walk. Evel did not introduce her to me, and I did not ask her name. In the 1970s, Muhammad Ali was the most recognizable name in the sports business but, if you ask anyone of my generation, Evel Knievel would have easily been in the top five. By taking an excruciatingly long time to make his way to the back of the store, I was able to think of something appropriate to talk to him about.

I remembered Evel Knievel best for the time he came to Maple Leaf Gardens and took three breakaways between periods against Les Binkley of the Toronto Toros of the World Hockey Association. I think he scored TWICE! I could never figure out if Binkley was trying or not but it sure looked real and was pure entertainment. Evel didn't skate very well, but it was stellar public relations all the way. He wore his famous red, white, and blue leather outfit and the fans loved it. I think all the money went to charity.

When I brought that up and we started talking hockey, he was very engaging and said he enjoyed the Tampa Bay Lightning. In fact, he was really a frustrated hockey player from Butte, Montana. He always wanted to play hockey for a living but was not good enough. We struck up a quick friendship. I noted to myself that he showed no signs of bankruptcy; he had diamond rings all over his bent fingers and expensive necklaces. I had played with John Bassett's son in minor hockey when Bassett owned the Toronto Toros. I remembered hearing the story years ago that there was a pretty large bet between Knievel and Bassett on the result of the Les Binkley adventure between periods. To try to tip the scales in his favor, Bassett took Evel out the night before and had gotten him quite drunk. Much to my surprise, Evel confirmed that the story was 100 percent true.

Evel kept in touch with me throughout my stint in Tampa Bay. It all stemmed back to the chance meeting that afternoon in the little clothing store. We sat in the back of the store in a small cubicle for about an hour, while his girlfriend had to endure the salty and profane storytelling of both of us. After about 30 minutes, she gave Evel's arm a gentle tug, which was a not so obvious signal that she wanted to leave.

Knievel just turned and blurted out, "Fuck off," and continued to talk about hockey.

Here was yet another example of becoming friends with a larger than life childhood hero that I never dreamed I would ever come in contact with. The last time I saw Knievel was on television, when he was in the Crystal Cathedral with Reverend Robert Schuller. He appeared to be having great trouble breathing and was asking for forgiveness for a life fueled by booze, extravagance, and poor decisions. As I watched him repent, I was sure that at any time, the ultimate ballyhoo artist was going to look into the camera and declare, "I'm just looking for loopholes to get to heaven," but he seemed to be very sincere and at peace with himself. Robert Craig "Evel" Knievel died on November 30, 2007 from lung disease.

Alexandre Daigle was a strange dude. I heard all the stories about him. He dated Pamela Anderson, and although I really didn't care who he went out with, I must admit I was pretty impressed he had the game to go out with her after her marriage to Tommy Lee. He had big shoes to fill, if you know what I mean. But he was a very gifted individual. When I came to Tampa Bay, in my opinion the team had been in disarray for a few years and was full of malcontents. We thought Alex Daigle might be able to come into a situation like that, where there was no clear leader or direction already established, and be able to jump into that role. We thought it might allow him to become the player everyone thought he could become. I guess when I found out he had posed for a hockey card in a nurse's outfit, I knew I was facing an uphill battle, but I was desperate to try to get some offense going on the anemic Lightning. Looking back, I would have had more luck making Soupy Sales into the Heavyweight Champion of the world, but I was desperate to get some offense and leadership going.

He was unusual in that he almost always referred to himself in the third person.

"The Daigle is going to lunch now," he would say.

"The Daigle does not feel well today," he would lament.

John Cullen, one of the assistant coaches in Tampa Bay, passed Daigle in the hall one morning and simply greeted him with, "Good Morning, Alex."

I overheard Daigle reply in his lofty voice, "The Daigle does not wish to speak today!"

I could not believe my ears. I turned to Cullen and deadpanned, "Well, I hope 'The Daigle' wants to skate today, because that's what he's fucking going to do."

As most everyone knows, players have their names on the top of their sticks: "Lecavalier," "Modin," etc. Daigle insisted the name on his stick say "The Daigle." Different.

As we found out with "The Daigle," if the horse is dead, get off. He had no leadership skills nor did he even bluff you into thinking he was a leader. Nor did he have a scintilla of passion for the game. His 'give a shit' meter was on zero.

Dan Kesa is, without doubt, one of my favorite players I have ever coached. I first coached him with the Detroit

Vipers in the IHL. His heritage is Serbian and he was a big strong, husky horse. His first name was "Dragon" and at his best, he was exactly that. His nephew is Milan Lucic of the Boston Bruins. He eventually got a chance to play in the NHL with the Pittsburgh Penguins, and when I came to Tampa Bay, I thought he would be a player that could solidify the offense. I have often been asked if I actually kicked him off of a plane. The answer is yes. We had just played in Ottawa. Rick Dudley and I decided he had to be sent down to the Vipers. I went to bat for Kesa several times, but now he deserved to be reassigned. His play was slipping, and he was not his usual rambunctious self.

We were stuck on the runway while the plane was being de-iced. I called Kesa up to the front of the plane. In retrospect, I should have waited until we got to our destination, but I figured rather than wait until four or five in the morning when we landed, I would give him the news now. Not surprisingly, he did not take the demotion lightly and said he was not going down to the minors. I said "Yes you are," and we had some words. He headed to the back of the plane, and he was not in a pleasant mood. When I looked to the back of the plane a few minutes later, he was pointing his finger at Phil Thibideau's chops. Phil was our traveling secretary at the time. I immediately went to the back of the plane to get Kesa off of Phil's ass.

"Hey, you have a problem with me, not Phil, so don't be pushing him around."

Kesa then made the fatal mistake of saying, "What, Ludzy, you going to kick me off the plane?"

Why he ever made that fatal comment, I will forever wonder.

"Actually, that's a pretty good idea…get off the plane!" I snorted.

"You serious?" Kesa questioned.

"Absolutely," I said and booted him off the plane.

I had Phil make alternate arrangements for Kesa to get to Detroit. I did not want him traveling with the team in that situation.

Dan Kesa: We were already on the plane in Ottawa, and he called me over and told me he's sending me down to the minors. You have to remember everyone was pissed we had just lost, and we were not playing very well. And we were having a tough year. Both Ludzik and I are very competitive and don't like losing. I had known him for three years by then, so I was a bit of his whipping boy. I walked back to my seat, and we kept chirping at each other. Everyone was stressed. Some of the players in my card group like Chris Gratton, Mike Sillinger, and Petr Svoboda were telling me not to go.

There are always certain things you do as a coach that you may regret, but you do not have the privilege of having a remote control in life; you know, fast forward this or reverse that, or even pushing the pause button. No sir! To me, Kesa had now crossed the line and was in uncharted waters as he was calling my bluff in front of 25 guys.

Dan Kesa: But after a while I didn't want to cause any more of a fuss so I reluctantly got off the plane. I really did respect Ludz.

Ira Kaufman (reporter on the plane at the time): Ludzik had no choice but to do what he did. Kesa was his boy. He was one of Ludzik's favorite players. We all knew that. Let's face it. It was not Lecavalier. Now that would have been a story. I did not find it even newsworthy. And I felt anything that happened on the team plane was out of bounds.

When I got back to Tampa and was recounting the story to Dudley, he remained silent until I got to the part where I actually kicked Kesa off the plane. Then he asked calmly, "You didn't kick him off while the plane was in the air, did you?"

The next year Kesa came to camp but he was pretty banged up and did not make the team.

Dan Kesa: Ludzy was the best coach I ever had. I talk to him all the time. Today, I feel sorry that plane incident defines our relationship.

Bobby Taylor was the radio color man for Tampa Bay – a good guy but a bit of a smart ass, especially after he had consumed a few beers. The week after the Kesa incident, Taylor decided to approach me in a hotel bar in Carolina and tell me that, "We, the media, should not have seen that episode concerning Kesa."

His holier than thou attitude curdled my boiler, and I replied, "Hey pal, you travel with us, you eat with us, you fly with us, you talk about us; you've got some balls, and next time you want to talk to me, do yourself a big favor, don't drink beforehand."

Ira Kaufman: I thought Chief (Bobby Taylor) was wrong in his thought process. He thought it was a great story and we in the print media could not have cared less. Ludzik was less than cordial when Bobby spoke about it in a bar in Carolina, and I really don't blame him.

I still speak with Kesa frequently, and he has to be rated as one of the best people I have met in the game.

Taking a walk with Mary Ann at the start of my second season in Tampa Bay, I expressed to her the sinking feeling that I couldn't shake – that if the team got off to a slow start, everything would be blamed on me. Rick Dudley and the rest of management continually claimed they had a four-year plan to build the team up, but I had been around hockey long enough to realize that "four years" in hockey years is an eternity. I just had that feeling in my gut that the big finger would be pointed at me. And so it came to pass. In reality, we just didn't have the budget at the time, or the right mix of characters to move forward quickly enough. We had fellows like Stephane Richer who really didn't care to break a sweat. He had so much talent and just refused to utilize it to its full capacity. That kind of stuff really burns my balls.

Ira Kaufman: Ludzik almost took it as a personal affront when a talented player was lazy. He might have thought that way about Stephane Richer. He had a lot of talent… great skater, tremendous wrist shot…a natural. I think Ludzy was one of those guys who got the most out of what he had as a player, and he would see guys, like a Daigle, and it really bothered him that they weren't cashing in on their God given talent.

Eventually Richer quit when he realized we were beginning to put an emphasis on young guys. Why put Richer and his laissez-faire attitude on the pond when you had youngsters like Lecavalier and Richards busting their ass.

Tampa Bay did have a few up and coming good players when I arrived. I did inherit a young Lecavalier. I remember hearing a lot of negative things about his father, Yvon, and how critical he was of people in the organization, and even Vinny. Yvon was in town early in my first season, and after one of my first practices with the team, I invited him down into the coach's room for a coffee. I heard he was very unhappy with how Vinny was treated under Jacques Demers the previous year. He felt they put undue pressure on Vinny and expected things from him that he was not yet ready to do.

We had a cordial chat and I said, "Look, Mr. Lecavalier, I can't tell you what went on here before, but I can tell you this. I'm going to treat him like he's my kid. If he's out of line, I'm going to give him a kick in the ass, and if he's playing well, I'm going to give him a pat on the back."

Yvon responded, "That's all I've ever wanted to hear from anybody around here. You got my word I will never interfere."

And that was that. I never heard another word from him. Actually, that is not true. He was one of the first to call me when I got fired and simply asked, "Why?" I know one of the reasons Vinny has been successful is because of his father.

Jay Feaster was someone in the organization that I really didn't know. Rick Dudley was asked to keep him as an assistant general manager when he was hired by the Lightning as GM. Feaster continually came down to the coach's office and complained about how bad our product was, about our $16 million budget, and how we were supposed to compete against $70 million budgets. It really didn't bother me because I knew we were in the developmental phase. I knew the 19-year-old Lecavalier would be a totally different player at 22. And we had several young players like that.

Feaster initially came over to Tampa Bay from the Hershey Bears. On one particular flight, he came over to me and said I was wasting my time using number 19 on the point on the power play. I had to almost check my Rolodex. My God, Number 19 was a young Brad Richards. He said we should just send him to the minors. I couldn't believe it. Considering Richard's young age and relative inexperience, he was one of our best players at the time.

One of the rituals I went through before a game was to make sure my roster was correct. The odd time, a coach is negligent and is penalized for an inaccurate starting roster or lineup. So I always did a four-way checklist to ensure that didn't happen. I had our trainer, both assistant coaches, and me review the list to ensure its accuracy.

One night in Anaheim, when I reviewed the lineup, I said to our assistant coach, "Nils Ekman is out tonight."

All of a sudden, I heard Feaster's voice, "What? I thought he was one of our best players the other night."

I calmly got up and went looking for Rick Dudley and told him, "Look, if you want to say something to me, I welcome your input, but I do not want that guy to give me one more opinion before first going through you." Feaster was not my cup of tea.

Duds could tell how pissed I was. Another incident cemented my concern. On a flight from Colorado to Tampa, my assistant coach and pal John Torchetti walked to the front of the airplane and handed me the morning edition of the Colorado newspaper. In the sports section was a small snippet and quote from Jay Feaster. It was something to the effect: "Bob Hartley is the most competitive man I know." Hartley was his coach when they both worked in the Hershey organization.

I felt like feeding Jay the sports section, business section, and front page.

"He has no idea who you are, does he?" asked Torchetti.

In our business, we're traveling all the time, and it never ceased to amaze me the different people you ran in to. We were on a flight going from Boston to Detroit. Many times, we just flew commercial. It was more convenient, and cheaper. The GM and coach usually flew first class as a bit of a perk.

As we boarded the plane, most of the players, especially the older ones whispered, "There's Matt Millen; there's Matt Millen."

I didn't know who Matt Millen was from a hole in the ground. I pride myself on being a bit of a sports historian in general but am not much of an expert on pro football. The boys said he was named as one of the 50 best players of all time. As luck would have it, he ended up sitting beside me in first class. He was a big, rugged, ugly mother.

I sat down and was reading a book on team motivation. He just reached over and grabbed it to look at the cover. We started to talk, and he was a rather nice man. I decided to have some fun with Bobby Jay, one of my assistants, who was a big football fan.

"Hey, Matt, you want to have a little bit of fun?"

Matt agreed. So I had him pretend I had told him that Bobby Jay told me he was a horseshit football player and Matt would go back and confront him. Matt and I slowly sauntered back through the rows pretending to look for Bobby J. Matt was a gruff looking guy. One of the meanest faces I have ever seen. Even the kids were hiding under their mothers' coats as he walked by.

We came upon Bobby Jay, and I said, "Mr. Millen, there's the guy you're looking for," and I pointed at Bobby Jay, "There's the guy who thinks you're a horseshit player."

Poor Bobby Jay looked up with the fear of God in his face and cried, "Luuuddddzzzzyyyy!"

Matt slowly reached over the seat and put out his hand to Bobby. Bobby Jay weakly smiled and shook his hand. That was a great ruse that the whole team appreciated.

Near the end of my time with Tampa Bay, I received a letter from Bill Davidson, the owner, telling me how happy he was with the team and the way our young players were developing. This was sometime in December. At the same time, I couldn't help but notice Dudley wasn't coming to talk to me several times a day like he usually did. You didn't have to be a rocket scientist to figure out something was afoot. To me, it felt like the Roman Empire was crumbling down around me. There were little, and big, signals going off all around. It was not good. My time clock was ticking and I knew it, too.

Ira Kaufman: The Lightning was in Los Angeles, and it was getting near the end (of Ludz's reign), in late December 2000. Things were very tense, and the team was playing terrible. We were in Marina Del Ray. We had an off night and I was sitting in the lobby restaurant with Bobby 'The Chief' Taylor and a couple of other Lightning employees – having some bar food. It was about 6:00 pm on a Saturday night. All of a sudden, Jay Feaster comes out of the elevator. Tortorella was with him, and off they go, arm in arm, through the lobby doors. They were going out to dinner. I figured, under the circumstances, that wasn't a good sign for Ludzik. Ludzik came down about 15 minutes later to go out somewhere, and he caught my eye.

'Kaufman, what's going on? Anything happening?'

I said, 'Well, I just saw Jay Feaster 15 minutes ago; he was going out to dinner.'

'Oh yeah, anybody with him,' Ludzy asks me.

'Yeah, Tortorella,' I answered right back.

And I swear, it was like a scene out of Godfather I. It could have been Michael Corleone. It was like Al Pacino, and all of a sudden, one of the eyebrows went up, one of the Ludzik eyebrows. It might have been the left, it might have been the right, and I watched the whole thing, and it was like a light bulb went off. Tom Jones (Tampa Bay writer) thought that Ludzik bore an eerie likeness to

Robert De Niro, both in speech and in mannerisms. I would concur on that.

'Oh, is that so,' Ludzik deadpanned.

He didn't say anything else; just walked out the door and got a cab someplace. That was the moment I think he knew for sure. He suspected for some time that he was on borrowed time.

The Tampa Bay Tribune published a story soon after with the headline that read something like, "Ludzik's Job on Line Tonight."

Phil Esposito came to the rink and gave the reporter hell for allowing that story to headline that way. The reporter pleaded that he only wrote the story and not the headlines, which is the way it happens with most newspapers. There is almost always an independent headline writer.

That night, we played the New York Islanders. With around 30 seconds to go, we were losing 4-3. Kim Johansson for the Islanders had a wide open net, and Lecavalier hooked him down and drew a penalty. So there's a face off in our end, we're shorthanded, and almost no time left. Somehow one of our defensemen chipped it out and went down the ice and miraculously scored. And then to top it off, we won it in overtime. I looked up at Mary Ann in the stands and she's bawling her eyes out.

I remembered thinking, "This is fucking horseshit. This is fucking horseshit. Is this really fucking worth it?"

Never let 'em see you sweat. This picture was taken just before my beheading in Tampa Bay, with all fingers pointing at me and swords drawn. I had gone from a boy genius coach with a 700 plus winning percentage to an idiot in a year. My past would hold me in good stead.

The Beginning of the End

I was still shocked when my pal Dudley came to our facility to talk to me while I was putting on my skates getting ready for practice. He wouldn't look at me.

"Ludzy, they tell me that if you don't get the team going, I gotta fire you."

I replied, "You gotta be kidding me. You kidding me?"

The long and short of it was I started to get pissed off at him. "Are you firing me?"

Dudley responded, "Ludzy, I knew you would react this way. I didn't come here to get in a big fight with you." I must admit I do not respond to threats very well.

"How would you expect me to react to this," I responded. "I'm not going to coach any different. I'm going to coach to win! Oh, by the way, did you fire me yet?"

"No," Dudley replied.

You have to remember that by this time, Dudley and I had been together for a long, long time. We were as close as any brothers could be.

I continued to do my skates up and said, "The next time you come to me like this, don't threaten me. Do it."

Unfortunately for me, Rick Dudley also did not like to be threatened and he followed my instructions well. The next time we came face to face like that, he fired me!

The following week in Ottawa, we lost a game we should have won. I grabbed Tortorella between periods and got on him for not teaching a delayed breakout properly. We hopped on a plane and headed for Chicago for the next game. It felt kind of eerie because I could feel it all around me. I jumped in a cab and headed by myself to a restaurant I knew, the Vernon Park Tavern. Not surprisingly, even the cab ride was eventful. I really wasn't in any mood to talk to anyone, but the cab driver was some sort of Hindu spiritualist. He started to talk to me. I wasn't listening at first but he just kept talking.

"Let me tell you something. You have dead man's eyes."

"What?" I said incredulously.

"Yes, someone has hurt you very badly, and I must tell you this. The people that have made the decision on you, they have already made it. You can not stop it. It is a force of nature. It will come true. You cannot stop it, no matter how much you worry."

Stranger than fiction, except it happened to me. We arrived at the restaurant, and I tipped and thanked him. Just another eerie coincidence.

For some reason, that night I had the urge to walk back to the hotel. Maybe I was afraid I would get the same cab driver again. But it was a long walk back to the Drake Hotel where we were staying. Sure enough, the next morning, Dudley called at 6:15 am and asked what room I was in.

"707," I said. I still remember.

I went and unlatched the door so it was open and went and sat back on the bed. I was putting Sports Center on, because I wanted to see if my dismissal was already on the news.

He knocked on the door and walked in, then came over to me and solemnly said, "I've gotta make a move. I have to relieve you of your head coaching duties."

I simply replied, "I only have one question. Who are you going to name as coach?"

"John Tortorella," he said quietly.

"Well, I guess that's why I couldn't get him in the foxhole for the past four months, eh Duds."

Ira Kaufman: Ludzy has a creed he lives by. Ludzy said to me one day when we were talking in a hotel lobby, 'Ira, you know how I judge somebody…would I want them in a foxhole. It's black and white. It's either yes or no.' Not only did he say that, which I found fascinating, but he added the second line, which made it even better. He looked at me and said, 'Kaufman, 95 percent of people don't make it. They fail the test – 95 percent!'

The irony of it was that both Dudley and Ludzik both looked at each other and they both passed that test, and that cemented the relationship. Dudley's looking for people like that. Ludzy's looking for people like that, and I think they found a kindred spirit.

And then I just told Dudley, "Good luck."

Ira Kaufman: When the knock came on the door at 6:15 am, Steve Ludzik knew it wasn't room service. That must have been very, very tough for both of those guys. Especially Dudley. These were two great friends who had conquered everything together. It was really tragic because both knew that the team could not go any further without a change, whatever the reason.

I got my stuff together quickly and headed for the airport.

Ira Kaufman: I got Ludzik on the phone. He was gracious enough to talk; a lot of guys would have said 'catching a plane, talk to you later.' But he gave me 20 minutes. I still remember him saying, 'It's not about getting knocked down, it's about getting up. You gotta get up when you get knocked to the canvas.' I asked him what he was going to do now. He simply replied, 'I'm going home. I'm going to sit on my back porch, light up a cigar, and have a beer. I'll be back somewhere in coaching.' He was hurt. It was his first NHL head coaching job. He deserved better. No one was going to win with Robert Petrovicky, Steve Guolla, Jaroslav Svejkovsky, Sergei Gusev, Marek Posmyk, Kristian Kudroc, and add to it no goaltending.

When I was fired from the Tampa Bay Lightning, the third call I got was from Kerry Fraser. He called to simply say that he had done a number of our games and thought the team had made a big turnaround in respectability under my regime and he thought I deserved more time. He finished by wishing me all the best. It was something that most officials would not have done, and I greatly appreciated his gesture.

In the early 1970s and 1980s, you could have fun with officials. A lot of them had distinct personalities that made the games fun for the fans, coaches, and players alike. Referees and linesmen, such as Andy Van Hellemond, Wes McCauley, John D'Amico and Ray Scapinello were all like that. A referee of that ilk today and who seemed to do a lot of my games when I was in the NHL was Kerry Fraser. Fans of different Canadian teams do not like Kerry Fraser for one reason or another; either for his hair, his style, or the fact that he has made some controversial calls concerning their teams. One could argue that it is not the referee's show, and they should not try to be the center of attention. I, for one, enjoy the different personalities in the game. I considered Kerry Fraser a good referee. A lot of officials today, who have no personality and take themselves too seriously, will not admit to making mistakes. It takes a confident official to freely admit his errors. Kerry Fraser was, and is, one such official. He would never hesitate to come over and admit to being out of position on a play, or the fact that he thought he might have missed a call. The game is so fast now that, even with two officials, a lot of fouls go unpunished, so it is refreshing to have some officials who are man enough to admit it.

The change to Tortorella? The hockey club actually got worse. I felt no satisfaction at all. It was a very tough time for me. They do not offer college courses on how to be fired as a coach. The media were extremely nice to me. They actually had a going away lunch for me, and 250 people showed up. They were all given black t-shirts that said, "We are gonna miss you, Ludzy." This was all put on by that 'evil' and 'sick' radio host, Bubba the Love Sponge.

Duds made a key move at the end of the year that I was fired. He made a bold move for a goalie. Tampa received Nikolai Khabibulin in exchange for Paul Mara, but it was not in the cards for my pal Duds to be present when the team he built won the Stanley Cup two years later.

I didn't speak to Dudley for the next year and a half. He left me a few messages, but I felt no need to return his calls. Then I was about to play in a charity game back home when I got a phone call from my good friend's father, Norm Kirk. He told me he had just heard Rick Dudley had just been fired by Tampa Bay. I had no feelings of, "See, I told you so." A little while later, I got a call from Dudley. He was in his car driving back from Tampa Bay. He wanted to get together right away when he returned. He actually came and watched the charity game, which was near Chippewa, a suburb of Niagara Falls. Then we came back to my place. It was a little uncomfortable at first. We had a long chat that night. We spoke about the fact I thought I saw the big picture in that I realized the team had to build around Lecavalier. I played him 23 to 25 minutes a night, even though he was raw. Duds and I talked about a lot of things. Dudley and I had a great night, and he actually ended up spending the night at my house.

By the time the Bolts won the Stanley Cup, they had a legitimate Stanley Cup goalie in Nikolai Khabibulin and a lot of the young kids had matured. Watching them win the Stanley Cup was like a father watching his children's stepdad taking them out on a Sunday afternoon picnic.

When I got fired I told everyone, "Everyone gets fired…even Jackie Gleason got fired, and this will be a great team one day; no one will remember Steve Ludzik then, but this will be a great team, and I will be rooting for all the players."

To top it all off, when Tampa Bay finally won the Stanley Cup, the nucleus of which was germinated with the shrewd dealings of Rick Dudley, Feaster went on my station, The Score, where he certainly knew I would hear him exclaim that the Lightning would never have won the Cup with me as coach. He blasted me and claimed it was too much like a country club when I was there. Country Club? Any athlete I ever worked with probably thought they were hearing things. Steve Ludzik and 'Country Club' do not go together.

The next morning, I immediately called the Palace of Auburn Hills and asked to speak to Tom Wilson, the president of the club for owner Mr. Davidson. When I got him on the line I told him, "A) Congratulations on winning the Stanley Cup; your group deserves it."

He responded that I was a big part of the building process.

Then I added, "And B) Tell that Jay Feaster to shut his mouth, and if he ever mentions me again, I will tell everyone the whole situation."

I told Tom what he had said, and Tom was shocked, "It sure wasn't a country club when you were here in Detroit!"

Ira Kaufman: I was not a fan of the moves Feaster made.

Andy Bezeau: Everyone around the team knew Feaster was second fiddle, and it was Dudley who built that team.

Moving On: Cherry and Me

I decided to take it easy for a while, but as everyone who knows me is aware I can't sit still for long. Going on a cruise or on one of those all inclusive vacations is brutal for me. You're expected to sit and pretty much do nothing for days on end. That drives me crazy, even though you would think I would enjoy a break from the hectic professional sports schedule. So when an old friend Nick Ricci bought the Mississauga Ice Dogs and asked me to be the head coach and general manager of the team, I couldn't resist. I thought it would be a great experience to work with young kids.

Don Cherry was part owner and had coached the team the year before. It would be like going full circle for me so – back to junior, where I had started out.

By taking over the Ice Dogs, I inherited Patrick O'Sullivan. His story has been well documented in television exposés plus newspaper and magazine articles concerning the abusive relationship he had with his father. He was drafted first overall the year before I got to the Ice Dogs, after playing his minor hockey in Carolina.

It definitely was not my first encounter with Donald S. Cherry. Our most recognizable Canadian, most either love him or hate him; there isn't much in between. I am in the former category. It might seem a bit extreme, but I feel Cherry is one of the greatest Canadians of all time. No Canadian, in my eye, has done as much to inflate Canada's ego, attitude, and pride as Donald S. A few years ago, in a national poll, Cherry was named the second most popular Canadian in the history of the nation. If it was an official election, I would have called for a re-count.

I first met Cherry way back in my early playing days with the Blackhawks in the early 1980s. We were in Montreal playing the Habs on a Saturday night. I was on the elevator in the hotel when Don walked on and said hello.

Knowing about Cherry's famous Bull Terrier, Blue, and the fact he was a dog aficionado, before getting off at the lobby, I mentioned to him, "Hey Don, I've got an American Staff Bull Terrier."

"Beauuuutifullll breed. Beautiful breed," Cherry responded.

We briefly discussed the differences between Bull Terriers and American Staffs. He was not yet the icon he would become, but he was well on his way. I think the mutual respect we had for dogs made us kindred spirits of sorts. The next time I saw him was in a pregame warm up in Toronto, when he had come down to talk to Al Secord, a player he previously coached. Just as a joke, I asked him to bless my stick for my game against the Leafs. He grabbed my stick, did a quick sign of the cross and, lo and behold, wouldn't you know it, I got a goal that night.

When I started to coach in Muskegon, I sent him a game worn sweater from the Fury to try to get a little publicity for the team. To my surprise, he pulled out the sweater on a segment of Coach's Corner and labeled me as the next coach in the NHL. Well, it took a while, but in the end, he was prophetic.

Let me state emphatically that the way I dressed while

coaching and the way I dress as a hockey analyst on The Score is not an imitation of Don.

Gary McCarthy (sportswriter for the Mississauga News): Ludzik is an outstanding dresser. To see him stand behind that bench was something.

My apparel is a tip of the hat to the original "Great One," and I don't mean Wayne Gretzky, in this case. I am speaking of the GREAT ONE, Jackie Gleason.

As a small boy, I remember thinking to myself, "Here's a man that weighs close to 300 pounds and he's in a well pressed blue suit, red vest, and a carnation, sipping out of a coffee cup that obviously had some embellishments in it, and bellowing out 'How sweet it is!'"

I marveled at his presence and his attention to detail.

I have always strongly believed there is no way you can win anything, not even a game of marbles or a dart game, without attention to detail. It starts in the dressing room. I want everyone's equipment hung up in the correct fashion. I want the room spotless, and I mean really spotless.

I heard a story that has stayed with me. It concerned the New York Yankees during the career of the great Joe DiMaggio. The trainer meticulously shined and polished every player's cleats before every game. When a rookie asked the "The Yankee Clipper" why the equipment manager went through this tiresome routine game in and game out, DiMaggio was quick to respond something to the effect, "In the back of our minds, deep down somewhere in our thoughts, we know we've taken that extra step that the other team has not."

Lou Saban, the famous football coach, came from the same genre – he came into the dressing room on the day of a game and saw a piece of gum on the floor. He hustled out to get the trainer, showed him the gum on the floor and yelled, "This is why we will never win!" That is the attention to detail I am talking about and believe in.

Don Cherry has a few idiosyncrasies. His cars are always spotless. And I mean spotless. He had a Mercedes Benz convertible, gold in color, and it was in pristine condition. I happened to have the same car, same year. They were not late model cars, but knowing that Don kept his cars immaculate, one day, when I was going to meet him for lunch, I spent a couple of hours washing, cleaning, waxing, and buffing my car inside and outside, knowing that Don's car would be in showroom shape. We finished lunch, and as we walked out to the parking lot, I went over to his car with him and said, "Hey, Don, beautiful car. I have the exact same one parked down a couple of spots."

Don floored me with his matter of fact reply, "Ya, I noticed it as I was coming in. You don't take very good care of it, do ya, eh?"

I could not help but smile. Here was a man you just could not fool.

Don is one of the few people that can comment honestly about OHL draft choices. He literally watches hundreds of games each winter in the cold, dark, and dreary rinks in Ontario with his son Tim, who is with Central Scouting of the OHL, and is a super guy. You would think Don would be mobbed by all the kids around the rinks, but he always stands or sits by himself, or with Tim, with a baseball cap pulled down low over his head, and often wears the best pair of tiger skin track pants I've ever seen. When I coached the Ice Dogs in Mississauga, Don probably watched 200 games in a matter of six months. His scouting reports were always handwritten in the most beautiful penmanship I've ever seen. His handwritten notes gave one the impression that he writes with the old pens you dip ink in. I am sure he has had to do it over the years, but I have never seen him turn away an autograph seeker. I learned Lesson #35 from Grapes and Gordie Howe: Take your bloody time when you are signing an autograph and make sure the person can read the signature on the paper. If someone thinks enough of you to want an autograph…make it legible!

When I think of Don, a few things come to mind: He is in great physical shape. A very broad shouldered man with thick powerful arms that he inherited from his dad, Delmer, who was a massive man and is in the Kingston and District Sports Hall of Fame. He finishes all of his telephone conversations with the old phrase "toodle-oo." A great expression and signature sign off. Great guy to have a beer with when times are good. Great guy to have a beer with when times are tough. Very proud of his Scottish heritage, and rightfully so. A foxhole guy!

At this writing, he now has an American Staff terrier. A big, beautiful dog, also named Blue.

My relationship with Don was not always smooth sailing. Although we've enjoyed a lot of good times together, it would be safe to say he's been miffed with me a few times throughout the years. That's another thing I love about Don. You don't have to guess that he is pissed at something. He is one of the few guys in hockey I can honestly say is a man of his word. What you see is what you get. I can never knock a guy for being like that.

Like I mentioned, Don was part owner and head coach of the Mississauga Ice Dogs the year before Nick Ricci bought the team. Cherry stayed with the team to help with hockey operations. He took a lot of arrows concerning the performance of the Ice Dogs during the first four years of existence. When Don was the coach, I think he knew deep down he was going to get criticism directed his way. With the team they had, that was going to be like getting hit with rock salt. The team was just not ready to roll yet.

Like any good jockey on a lame horse knows, Don knew you could have brought in Punch Imlach, Scotty Bowman, or Fred Shero, and the club was not going to win. Instead of putting a lame duck in as coach, Cherry, forgoing the blindfold before the execution, took it on the chin and went behind the bench himself. He emphatically stated on numerous occasions that he believed the OHL should be for Canadians and refused to take, or draft, any Europeans onto his team. Drafting a couple of skilled Europeans would most likely have stopped the bleeding and improved his record, but Don stayed true to his word. He received a standing ovation from the entire Ice Dogs club when exiting the bus for the last time that season. It was a tough, tough year for him and he was 65 by then.

I vividly recall the Jacques Demers' press conference when he took over from a struggling Tampa Bay Lightning team under Terry Crisp. Jacques, whom I like very much, sent lava spewing at the media conference exclaiming, "The cheating stops now," or something to that effect. He was banging the podium like a frustrated Judge Judy with a gavel.

Did this mean Terry Crisp condoned "cheating" hockey? I always believed that when you take over a ship from another skipper, don't worry about the other guy's navigational skills, just worry about reading your own compass correctly.

Unfortunately, I did not follow my own dictum when I took over the Ice Dogs. I made a reference to the fact that we had a lot of work to do. The next thing I knew, I got a call from Don. He wanted to see me that day. He drove from Mississauga to Niagara Falls, and laid a beating on me concerning that reference. He was right. It was a subtle knock of the performance done before me, and I should not have said it.

Very early in the season, I thought there would be trouble with Don and me. He had his way of doing things before me. Although I was now chief bottle washer, he was still around the team on a regular basis. No ship can navigate through choppy waters with two captains at the helm. We both have strong personalities and strong feelings for the game and the players that play it. There are certain people in this world that when they walk into a room, you know they're something special. Call it charisma, aura, chutzpah, whatever you want. When you've got it, you got it. If you don't know what it is…you don't got it. If you need to explain what it is to someone, they don't have it. Don's got it. I just knew deep inside that I had to talk to Don and make sure that my voice was going to be the one that was listened to, and there was no question who had the ultimate authority.

I took Don to lunch, and it was not good. This was his baby, and I was asking him to let me be my own man and put my mark on the team however I saw fit.

I told him, "I don't know if I can fix this up, but I won't be able to when there's always two voices being heard."

Grapes got up, paid the bill, and said "toodle-oo."

Mistake #243: Don't piss off a legend, especially in a Chinese restaurant. I wasn't sure what was going to happen next between him and me. I stewed about it all the way home. To my utter shock, Cherry called me that night, and called me the alpha wolf. He respected the fact I spoke to him about my concerns. He said he would not interfere in what I was trying to accomplish. His last statement meant a lot.

"You've got the Cherry word," he said.

The words echoed in my ear. I will never forget them. As I already suspected, and would confirm during that season, the Cherry word is better than anything.

Just before a practice at the Hershey Center one day, Don bumped into Paul Henderson, who was there as part of a big 30th anniversary celebration of Team Canada 1972. Don mentioned that Paul would love to speak with the team just before we started practice. I really didn't want it cutting into my practice time but could tell Grapes really thought it was a good idea, so I acquiesced. After a brief warm up, I blew the whistle and brought the players over to the bench. Don introduced Paul and he proceeded to give the guys a bit of a pep talk.

It helps to have the visual here. Don stood there, looking straight ahead, no blinking, no head movement, no eye contact. I think he was looking at the Canadian flag. Henderson's short oration went on for about five minutes. Then Paul suddenly spoke about his days playing junior A in Hamilton. While in Hamilton, Henderson said he invented the "snapshot." This comment jolted me out of my slight daydream, as I wondered what Stan Mikita and Boom Boom Geoffrion would've thought about that statement.

The instant the sentence came out of Paul's mouth, Don moved for the first time in five minutes, and his eyes slowly turned sideways to look at me, and with the slightest, almost indiscernible shrug, to let it be known that he didn't think that was 100 percent true. Paul finished his talk, and Don and I met up at the end of the bench.

I asked Don, "Did he just say what I think he just said?"

Don broke out in laughter and said, "It doesn't really matter, I guess. In 1972, these kids weren't even born yet!"

Don and I don't always see eye to eye on hockey tactics either. He didn't like the way my defense handled two on ones. He didn't like the fact I don't like scrimmaging in practice. I prefer to do game situation drills. I love watching a Coach's Corner segment when he gets miffed about down low coverage in hockey. I always think he's talking directly at me. Once he actually said, "See that Steve!" I loved it.

He got real sour at me when I showed a video on The Score that highlighted seven and eight year olds fighting in a minor hockey league game, and their parents throwing punches at each other. He decided he was not going to air it and called me to suggest that I shouldn't air it either. He thought it would make some people think that happened in minor hockey all the time. On the other hand, I thought it was an important story to tell. Cherry cut me to shreds for showing it and mentioned it on Hockey Night in Canada and his radio show with Brian Williams. Again, I wasn't blindsided by any of this. Don already told me how he felt about the matter.

He couldn't resist rubbing it in again the next day when he called me and stated, "Congratulations, thanks to you, even the people in Poland know what happened in the kid's game!"

The next evening on my show, I countered his blast. Cherry would not have wanted it any other way. He would have been disappointed if I hadn't.

In 2005, Don and I decided, along with my lawyer Ernie Coatzee and good friend Terry O'Malley, that the OHL could prosper again in the Niagara Falls Region. We were not that welcomed by the mayor of Niagara Falls, Ted Salci, who dragged his feet so bad, they left scuff marks on the dance floor. But we found St. Catharines to be more receptive. Our group had to go to Council one night to inform them of our plans to possibly bring a team to St. Catharines. To watch the spectacle of Don Cherry entering the Town Hall was like watching the emperor arrive home after doing battle. Cameras were on. City councilors were passing pieces of paper, agendas, and even napkins for Cherry to sign before, and even during, our presentation. It was really something to see. Unfortunately, things did not work out in our favor, but it would have been fun if it did. And Don Cherry and I were right. The Niagara Region was ready for the OHL again.

But back to the Ice Dogs, Don took me for lunch a couple of weeks before training camp opened at the Hershey Center in Mississauga. For several hours, we went over the entire roster from the previous year from top to bottom. Meticulously, Don jotted down three or four detailed points about every player.

When he got to the name Patrick O'Sullivan, he said, "Ludz, I don't know how you're going to handle this guy. I've coached a long time, and I've never seen anything quite like him. He almost makes you want to strangle him some nights."

He said Patrick was perhaps the least favorite player he ever had in a dressing room. I'd like to say I was nervous hearing this coming from Don, but I think I was so cocksure of my ability to handle the teenager, I fluffed it off.

"No problem, Don. I've handled a lot of difficult players along the way. Patrick will be no problem."

"Well, we'll just see how you handle this guy."

To be naïve can be both blissful and stupid. Don was really trying to give me a heads up concerning Patrick O'Sullivan, and I was too pigheaded to listen. In the first exhibition game, and I mean the *first* game, I could not believe what I saw. Without all the gory details, he was exactly what Don had declared him to be. Cherry saw me after the game and had a sly grin on his face as if to say, "So you think you know everything, kid. What did I tell you?"

O'Sullivan had talent for sure, but he just had a different demeanor about him, and quite frankly, was very selfish. He was only 17 and looked as if he carried the weight of the world on his shoulders.

Don warned me that O'Sullivan would try to con me into thinking he was all for the team and in support of me. Don was right. O'Sullivan would saddle up beside me and put his arm around me and pretend to be my buddy. For anybody who knows me, they would know that is totally against my coaching style. You would think with a new coach coming in, a player would tread lightly to see what kind of style that coach used and where you would fit in. But O'Sullivan just had an overall arrogant attitude about him, and no one could tell him anything because he knew it all. He was a tough nut to crack. He was a riddle to me from the beginning. On the one hand, here was a kid that was reportedly abused by his dad, but on the other, he was himself abusive to his teammates.

We actually had a court order that the father could not be in any arena that his son played in. To this day, I have no idea what Mr. O'Sullivan looked like, nor did I ever talk with him. All of Patrick's mail had to come through me by the order of our owner. His dad would post letters to him and send him money in the form of a check, and I would hand over the whole kit and caboodle to Patrick. He would just take the letter and check and fire it all into the garbage.

Patrick's mother was a very nice woman who was extremely interested in the well being of her son. I would speak to her about him and she would explain to me all the crap that had gone on in his life. Patrick was 185 pounds and carried around 1,000 pounds of crud.

In speaking with his agent, Rick Morris, I explained I knew all about Patrick's past but needed to have a psychology degree to deal with this guy. I was gravely concerned this young man would implode. His antics were a distraction. One of O'Sullivan's most annoying habits was to take liberties with his teammates at practices. He would slash them across the ankles, trip them for no reason, and in general, just play dirty against them. I think some of the players thought that because he was the star of the team, talent-wise, they had to put up with it. All players know you practice hard, but almost all know where to draw the line. In a game, if you see a player with his head down, you give him a good solid hit. In practice, you just yell "Heads up" and don't hit him, or at least you don't paste him. Patrick would paste him.

I continually told him, "Patrick, you just don't act like that with your teammates."

But he continued to do it. He had years of anger built up.

One day in practice, I saw enough and called everyone over to the rink board, including Patrick. I told the whole team that if O'Sullivan ever speared, slashed, or hacked anyone again, they were to turn around and give it right back to him. Don't take any crap from him. It showed the team that Patrick was definitely not bigger than the team. Patrick improved a little bit after that but still did not act like a teammate should.

Midway through the season, there was an incident at a sports store in Mississauga involving a missing stick. Patrick had apparently walked out with it after going to an autograph session that a couple of the players were at. That was the last straw. I called him into my office and told him he was suspended from the team. The police were involved in the incident, and I told him they wanted to speak with him upstairs.

O'Sullivan acted like Edward G. Robinson as we walked up the stairs. When we were halfway there, he began to have a meltdown and said, "I can't believe you're giving up on me, Ludzy!"

"I'm not giving up on you, Patrick," I solemnly replied. "In fact, Patrick, just the opposite."

The police were very good. They knew I was going to suspend him from the team and send him home. I told Patrick, "Go home and stay with your mom. You are suspended indefinitely, and I want you to call me every day at 6:00 pm."

The incident reminded me of something I did when I was a kid that I am not proud of. I had gone to Simpson's, believe it or not, with my good friend, Don Strang, and had $15 with me to buy a hockey stick. While we were perusing the sticks, the one I wanted was $20, so I changed the price sticker on that stick with the stick that was $15! Real smart. Of course, we got caught and the security guards took Don and me into a back room and gave us a tongue lashing and threatened to call in the cops. I'll never forget one of them was C. Hill because I noted his name badge. When Mr. Hill asked me to spell my name, I said it was "L..u..d..z..i..c," thinking that would make all things better.

Don, who was a couple of years older than me, figured they weren't going to make a huge deal for $5.00, so he said, "Whatever you do, don't tell his father. He will *kill* him."

He was just trying to get us out of there. At that, the security guards looked at each other and told us they would let us go, but I had to have my father call them by the end of the day. I would have preferred the cops. A gun would have been cleaner.

Don Strang: Ludz was about 13, and I was a few years older. I told Ludz not to worry; we would get someone's older brother to phone. I knew telling his dad was not a

viable option if Ludzy wished to keep all his extremities intact. When we couldn't find anyone, and were getting a bit desperate, I agreed to make the call. In a voice slightly deeper than my regular one, I said 'This is Mr. Ludzik. Steven has told me all about the stick incident and rest assured, we have already taken steps to make sure this will never happen again.' I started to get louder and louder and continued, 'Thank you for bringing this to my attention. Don't worry, he will be very, very sorry he did this.' By the end, I was just yelling into the phone! The guard actually sounded a little contrite, as if he was afraid of what would happen to Ludz.

So thanks to the quick thinking of Donnie, a crisis was averted.

I felt I had to draw a line in the sand with Patrick because at the time, I couldn't help but remember what happened to the late Bryan Fogarty. As many hockey fans know, Bryan Fogarty was ordained as the next Bobby Orr. He was a kid out of Brantford and a child protégé. Fogarty was big and fast. I never saw a more pure skater. It was as if his skates never touched the ice. He was as gifted as anyone who donned the blades. The problem was he always got what he wanted from being a star player at the get go. In his final year of junior A, he played for the Niagara Falls Thunder. His coach, Bill Laforge, asked me if I knew of any really good billets that Bryan could live with while he was with the Thunder. My former billets, the Mundys, agreed to take him in.

This was the season Fogarty devoured Dennis Potvin's junior A point record for a defenseman. Watching him skate in full flight pulled everyone out of their seats. But behind the brilliant exterior lurked a dark inside that was pleading for help. About two months into the season, Mrs. Mundy called Laforge to discuss her deep concerns about Bryan. The list was long and detailed. Mrs. Mundy explained that Fogarty was not coming home at night, he had alcohol on his breath all the time, and the smell of marijuana permeated his car. She also commented on the slippery, slimy, scummy characters that would take him out on the town in the wee hours. Bryan Fogarty, for all his talent, was a lad led easily astray. Most young men would have quickly realized they were in the company of hooligans. In Fogarty's case, those people created a monster. They have blood on their hands.

Bill Laforge's answer to Mrs. Mundy's concerns was that he would have Fogarty out of her house by the afternoon. Mrs. Mundy was very upset at this and responded quickly.

"I didn't ask you to remove him from our home. But this boy needs some discipline from the team and you need to give it to him now!" Norma "Mum" Mundy was one tough gal.

Bryan Fogarty had so much talent, he was able to surpass the records of Bobby Orr and Dennis Potvin, but that was not enough to get him off his endless downward spiral. Fogarty did not live the last half of the season with the Mundys. The coach and management apparently turned a blind eye to his indiscretions. They were only interested in winning at all costs. Unfortunately, all of Bryan's natural ability went to waste. His career never took off as predicted. Cocaine addiction, alcoholism, and prescription drugs swallowed him up alive. The Quebec Nordiques, with the acumen of a plate of poutine, roomed two recovering addicts, Fogarty and John Kordic, in the same condo. Obviously, it was a recipe for disaster. Unfortunately, someone's going to be going ten toes up.

Brian Fogarty played a handful of games for me in the IHL, and it made you want to cry when you saw that he had nothing left in the tank. Bryan left his game in hundreds of smoky bars along the way. The last time I spoke with him, he had been arrested for breaking into his former high school in Brantford. He was a hell of a guy and died in a hotel room in South Carolina at the age of 32. His life may have been different if someone had been strong enough to pull in the reigns a long, long, time ago.

I know that Patrick never touched drugs at all, but at the same time, I felt he was screaming for help to deal with his own demons. When I suspended O'Sullivan, the American Olympic program was the first to call. They were in a feathered up state. I received a call from the US Olympic coach, Lou Vairo, who told me he thought I was making a huge mistake. He said Patrick O'Sullivan was a very big part of their program and when they had him in a two-week summer camp, they had no problems with him. The conversation was quick and to the point. I got somewhat irked when I realized I was on speaker phone.

"First of all," I said, "take me off the speaker phone; I don't know who else you have in that room."

So he took me off the speaker phone. Then I sternly told him, "Mr. Vairo, with all due respect, you had him for two weeks. I've had him for *four months!* This kid has been pampered and gotten his way everywhere he has been. Well, it's not happening here. I have spoken to his agent and he is being suspended."

Patrick's agent was great during this stretch and fully supportive of my actions. He knew something had to be done. Many people thought I had no contact with Patrick when he was back home in South Carolina with his mom, but we spoke every evening. Like I mentioned, I instructed Patrick to call me every night at six o'clock. And he did. He asked how the team was doing. Actually, the team was doing great now that the constant distraction was gone. After the first week, he asked every night if he could come back to the team. I always said, "Not yet, Patrick," and also told him I had every intention of trading him as soon as possible when he returned. This made huge news across Canada for some reason. I really had no clue why.

It broke my heart to do this to O'Sullivan but I honestly felt something really bad, and I didn't know exactly what was going to happen to him if someone didn't stand up to Patrick and knock him down a notch. He had obviously been the best player wherever he had been, and like it or not, there are different rules for the elite athletes from the time they start organized sports. They are coddled and pampered all the way up through minor hockey, as coaches are afraid to lose them. The reason I loved coaching junior hockey so much is because you can help shape a young man's life, both on and off the ice. You are really working with a blank canvas.

Further, I have always believed in the old adage that nobody knows what a man has been through until you have walked a mile in his shoes. After a couple of weeks, I spoke to the team about the possibility of O'Sullivan coming back and talked about the fact that, although he had been disruptive to the team, everyone deserved a second chance. In a way, we passed judgment by sending him home, but we did not have the right to destroy the kid's potential career. We had no right to be judge and jury. Several players voiced the opinion that we were playing well and didn't need him back. I told them that even from a hockey angle, we could use him down the stretch, either by playing him or trading him. I put it to a ballot on the team, and they voted to have him back. I was happy to welcome Patrick back. I hoped he would accept the punishment that was given and would come back with a new respect for both his teammates but, more importantly, himself.

So Patrick came back to the team, but I did not dress him. I knew that because of what had happened I would not get full value for O'Sullivan in a trade, but I did not realize how bad it would be. I quickly learned that the teams in the OHL, like any hockey league, I suppose, once they see a piece of meat lying in the desert, they're like scavengers – they want it all but were not willing to give you ANYTHING in return. So I was getting offers of a second round draft pick and a utility forward for Patrick.

To one such offer, I replied to a GM, "What the hell, do I look like I just fell off a perogie truck?"

The trade deadline was fast approaching and I kept sitting O'Sullivan. I was still planning on trading him. Even on the last night, I told Patrick I would have him dealt by 10:00 pm.

Ten o'clock came and went, and there was absolutely no deal out there I could make in my right mind. I really wanted to move him and get a couple of decent players. So I spoke with him outside of the bus.

"Patrick, I couldn't trade you. Your stock has fallen so much because of your actions that nobody wants you. So…you have two ways to go now. You can put your head down and work like a warrior for the last two months of the season and help us make the playoffs, or you can just fall into the abyss like a lot of players have over the years, and in spite of all your talent, trust me, you will quickly be forgotten."

The last two months of the year, he did everything we asked of him. He played hard, he blocked shots, and he wasn't selfish on or off the ice. Now, someone can't change overnight but he appeared to be making an honest effort. We were able to make the playoffs and played Ottawa in the first round. If we had won, it would have been an upset, but I thought we had a chance to beat Ottawa in that series. However, one of our young guns, Robbie Schremp went down with a concussion in the first game. His father came up to me and asked if I was going to have him play anymore. It was his second concussion of the year. He was hoping and praying that I would give the response I did.

"No, he is done for the season. His long-term health is more important than a playoff series."

I know his dad had great respect for me after that decision. I was warned by more than one person about Robbie when I came to coach the Ice Dogs. They told me I'd better get on a first name basis with the chief of police in Mississauga because Robbie could get into that type of trouble. But other than being a regular teenage boy getting into the odd mischief here and there, he was a pleasure to have on the team. I admired his determination, feistiness, and of course, high skill level. The only incident I had with Robbie Schremp was in mid-November when he missed a class one day. My wife, Mary Ann, used to phone the school every day to see if any of the players were missing. This one day, they told her Robbie missed a couple of classes. I called him in and told him if he missed even one more class, I would send him back to Syracuse, no questions asked.

"Are you serious, Coach?" He didn't think I was. When he looked at my face and saw I was, he said he would not miss class again.

No other issues with Robbie. He is one of the most talented players I have ever coached. Robbie Schremp was the "nature boy." Without going into explicit details, let's just say he enjoys going "buck ched" wherever he is. He is also one of the favorite players I have ever coached. I actually picked him to be Rookie of the Year in the NHL in his rookie year with the Oilers, but he really didn't get the opportunity to play enough to prove himself in his first year. He would never give you the conservative answer. By that I mean, he would always say what he thought when he might have been better off being more guarded in his speech. But that is not his style.

With respect to O'Sullivan, I keep in touch with Patrick whenever I can. At a recent conditioning camp, he told me it took him 1.5 years of junior before he finally got it. Playing junior was a great adventure for Patrick. He turned the corner in his life and career. His talent was always unquestioned. He is a natural goal scorer who needs one shot to score when others need five or six. He is a great player who should score 25 goals in the NHL. O'Sullivan's story is one about a boy who has beaten the odds and battled back. Fogarty could not. There would be no requiem for the tragic figure that was Bryan Fogarty.

No matter how gruff someone's exterior is, you can truly tell a man's soul by how he treats kids. When a friend of mine had his son, Scott, who was 10, work as an occasional stick boy for the Ice Dogs, he always said Patrick was one of the players who spent the most time with him. O'Sullivan would let Scott tape his stick (he probably re-taped it later), let him help with torching his stick into the curve he wanted, and always ruffled his hair when they passed.

Scott Wilson (Mississauga Ice Dog Stick Boy): Patrick was always great with me. All the guys were great, but I remember Patrick always said hello to me and made me feel important.

So for all the demons that were inside O'Sullivan, which probably made him act the way he did to his peers, when push came to shove, perhaps the way he treated a 10-year-old boy sadly illustrated how he wished he had been treated when *he* was 10. The small 10 year old was no threat to Patrick. He could act like himself. Patrick has gone on to a solid NHL career with the undying love and support from his mother, who still lives in South Carolina.

A couple of times when we played Sudbury, Bert Templeton would come around before the game and visit me for a coffee. Bert really didn't associate with many people, so I felt privileged he would come and visit. We really wouldn't say too much. We just enjoyed being in each other's presence. Wayne Crawford, who played on the Flyer team under Bert in the late 1970s, was my assistant coach in Mississauga.

Bert would leave and Crawford would say he was still petrified of Bert.

Wayne Crawford: I was scared to death of the guy when I was 17, and I was scared of the man when I was 40 years old. Really. He'd come around to see Ludz before the game and sit and have a coffee. I had to leave the office. My fucking legs were shaking, literally trembling.

Here was Crawford, a 40-year-old man, and he couldn't even speak in his presence. That's how badly Templeton intimidated almost everyone he met.

I had to go to an OHL sponsored general managers' meeting one day while with the Ice Dogs. They brought in this motivational speaker for one segment, and she asked us all to draw a picture of a pig on a piece of paper. So I drew my pig and looked at Bert beside me and he said, "I'm not drawing a fucking pig," and for good measure blurted out so all could hear, "What is this? An art class?"

The leader asked Templeton if he would show his pig, and Bert just said he was a hockey coach, and under no circumstances was he drawing a pig.

Perhaps one of the funniest on-ice incidents I ever witnessed occurred when I coached the Mississauga Ice Dogs. Our team was awarded a penalty shot. Our player Danny Revelle was struggling a bit, so I figured this might be a great opportunity to give him a goal to boost his confidence. What transpired in the next 20 seconds left me in complete shock. The coaching staff, players, and in fact, all the fans at the Hershey Center couldn't believe their eyes. I'm sure the tape has been destroyed by now. At least I hope it has. As poor Danny started his voyage to the net, he almost lost the puck at the center line as he stutter stepped as soon as he touched the puck. Then the puck jumped ahead of him, but he caught up to it, and then proceeded to almost lose it at the blue line again. Then he did lose it as he swerved towards the face-off circle and it started to go into the corner. He tracked it down and brought it around to the front of the net, but then he slipped as he was cutting to the net, fell down, took a swing at the puck, missed it, and then hit it on the backswing, and the puck miraculously ended up in the neutral zone, where he began this whimsical venture. It was unbelievable.

Assistant Coach Wayne "Red" Crawford: That penalty shot…you could not get it to happen again. The puck started at center, and fittingly, ended almost in the same spot at center ice. Here we were on the verge of making the playoffs. It was an important penalty shot. We were speechless.

My only year in Mississauga, we ended up making the playoffs and losing out to Brian Kilrea's Ottawa 67's in the first round.

Gary McCarthy (Mississauga sports reporter): Ludzik took them from a team that had won 27 games in three years to a team that won 23 in one year and made the playoffs for the first time.

After the first year, Ricci decided the OHL racket was not for him and sold the team. I could not make a deal with the new owners to continue to coach, so we parted company.

Back to the Sunny South

There were a few offers from other teams in the OHL during the summer. The Windsor Spitfires and Sudbury Wolves contacted me, and we had some discussions. Then Dudley, now with the Florida Panthers, called me and asked if I would be interested in coaching their American League farm team, the San Antonio Rampage. After much consideration, I figured that was a good option for me. I also looked forward to working with Rick Dudley again.

Dudley was brought in as general manager, and the head coach was Mike Keenan. Now, Mike and Rick did not get along that well. Keenan was summarily dismissed. So, after 10 games in San Antonio, Dudley called me up to be an assistant coach to him and to take over the power play and penalty killing responsibilities. That arrangement worked out well, but at the end of the year, owner Alan Cohen had a falling out with Rick Dudley and fired him.

Surprisingly, Cohen brought back none other than Mike Keenan as general manager. I figured that was it for me. He was the one who didn't want me as a player in Chicago anymore, even though I had another year left on my Florida Panther contract. Keenan brought in Jacques Martin as head coach of the Panthers, and somewhat unexpectedly, asked if I would like to go back to coach the Rampage in San Antonio. I said that would be fine. That was the year of the NHL lockout, so it was kind of a messed up year from a player perspective.

I got to know a most interesting man when I went to coach San Antonio. Most hockey fans remember Clint Malarchuk as the Buffalo Sabres goalie who almost died on the ice in Buffalo when a skate blade cut his jugular vein and blood spewed all over the ice. Only the quick actions of Jim Pizzatelli, the Sabres' trainer, saved his life. Anyone who saw the video will not soon forget it.

While Clint was lying on the ice during that incident, he calmly said, "Get me off the ice…I don't want my mom to see me die on the ice."

Clint was my assistant coach and goalie coach with the Rampage in 2003. He and I also worked with the Florida Panthers. He is a misunderstood individual and a good friend – extremely funny. If you had a choice to go out with one guy for one night to have a good time, Clint would be your man. He is one of the most honest people I know, he talks the talk and walks the walk. Clint has never hidden from anything in his life and has battled, and still battles, from deep bouts of depression.

People often ask me about the big cowboy belts I like to wear. They are because of Clint Malarchuk. I was hitching up my pants in San Antonio one day, and Clint told me, "If you would wear a cowboy belt, you would never have to hitch up your pants again, and would never wear another kind of belt again."

He was right. To this day, I rarely go out of the house without one on. Down in San Antonio, Clint clipped his chin in his garage when he was cleaning up and cut himself pretty badly. Clint, being a trained horse doctor, figured he would just go and get a needle and thread and sew himself up using the paraphernalia from a sewing kit! When I saw his face, I asked Mary Ann to go get our next door neighbor, who was a real doctor, to come over and take a look at it. When the doctor looked at it, he said he could not have done a better job himself. And it was the equivalent of 15 stitches!

Clint, Guy Charron, and I took our wives once to a restaurant in San Antonio that had one of those mechanical bulls. Clint, a cowboy through and through, decided to get on the bull. The attendant, who could tell Clint was an expert, decided to be a bit of a prick, and set the bull to maximum speed. The bull was able to dump Clint pretty quickly. It made Clint sour for the rest of the night. Against my better judgment, I decided to make my first, and as it turned out, last attempt at being a real cowboy. I got on the bull and actually lasted five or six seconds before being tossed off like a rag doll. I was kind of sore the next day and found out I had broken my pubic bone. Thanks Clint!

Another memorable time was at the end of the Florida season. We went out for a few pops in a bar and ran into none other than Michael Moorer. Being a boxing fan, I was well aware of the fact that on May 15, 1992, Moorer got knocked down in the first and third rounds, but rebounded to beat Bert Cooper on a knockout to win the HBO Heavyweight Championship of the world. He was a solid man, 6'2" and about 225 pounds, but not overly large for a heavyweight champion – but massively built. He joined us. We were standing at the bar and I recognized him right away, but it was apparent he was not a big hockey fan. He didn't know much about the game. But he certainly seemed friendly enough. He was wearing one of those skull caps people wear. As we were having a drink, a lady walked by and recognized Moorer and planted a big kiss on the top of his head.

Clint looked at the both of us and joked, "Hey, what's he got that I don't!"

Moorer looked at him funny and his big frame slowly rose off his stool, kicked over a bar stool, and glared at Malarchuk, "What did you say motherfucker?"

Clint just kept casually sipping his beer and replied, "Hey, I'm just joking with ya."

I noticed Clint was keeping one eye open. He now knew who Moorer was. Moorer wouldn't let it go.

He stood even closer to Clint and kept saying, "What do you mean by that comment? You're being an ignoramus!"

Clint just kept sipping his beer, which is pretty hard to do when you are chewing tobacco at the same time, like Clint always did. Moorer kept causing a scene, and I kind of stuck my hand out to diffuse the situation.

Moorer threw it back saying, "Get your hand off of me."

You have to remember, we had just met this guy and were not familiar with his character at all. Moorer started to take his jacket off, and I could hear Clint under his breath, "Here we go, here we go," and then Clint took his cowboy hat off to prepare to do battle with the heavyweight champ right then and there.

As they both got up, Michael Moorer leaned over and kissed Clint on the forehead and said, "Punked ya, got ya!"

Malarchuk almost sank to his knees. He didn't want to go, but that was the type of man Malarchuk was, and is. If challenged, he will NEVER back down when it means standing up for himself or his friends.

Clint and I stayed in a hotel when we were coaches with the Florida Panthers. We were in the bar having a few drinks when I got a call around 10 o'clock telling me that Bert Templeton had passed away. After our drink, I excused myself and went back to my room. I made a call to Don Cherry to let him know about Bert. I mentioned that I had been with Clint and we were having a few pops. I phoned Don because I wanted to make sure he would do a little tribute to Bert on his Coach's Corner segment that weekend. He heard about Bert, but he said he was hesitant to mention him on his show. He felt Bert was always a pretty cantankerous guy, he kept to himself, and only beat to his own drummer.

I quickly pointed out, "Yeah, Don, sounds an awful lot like you."

I told Don three or four stories about Bert. Don didn't need much prodding actually, but he concluded, "You're absolutely right. Get someone to tape that show for you. I will do a segment on Bert on Saturday night."

I got the TV station in Florida to tape it for me. There was Don in a red crushed velvet jacket, I will never forget that. He began something like, "I was talking to my buddy Steve Ludzik the other night, down in Florida with the Panthers, having a few beers in his hotel room by himself…"

Clint was sitting beside me watching. "Did he just say what I think he said?" he asked.

So we ran it back, and sure enough, that's what he said. Don went on to do an awesome tribute to Bert, something that I was very proud of.

Later on that night, I saw on my cell phone that my mom had called about four or five times and hadn't left a message. I called her back.

"Hey, Mom, what's up?"

She didn't even say hello. She just started right in, "I heard Don Cherry on Hockey Night in Canada tonight say that you were drinking in your hotel by yourself. Your dad got into a lot of trouble doing that, you know?"

Of course, Don didn't mean anything by it but I had "some 'splaining to do" to my mom.

Clint Malarchuk is an amazing individual and not afraid to push the envelope. Alan Cohen, one of the owners of the Panthers, came down to have a serious discussion with Rick Dudley one morning. I happened to be in the office at the time and the door was open. You have to picture this. Clint was in an office right across the hall, and it could be seen clearly from where Dudley was sitting but not from where Cohen was standing.

Inexplicably, Malarchuk stripped down bare ass and laid across his desk with one leg up. Dudley could not believe his eyes and had difficulty keeping a straight face. I could also see Clint from my angle. Clint just lay there like a stripper on his desk. He looked like a big hairy playboy pinup. If Cohen had taken a few steps and looked into the hall, he would have seen it all. Dudley just couldn't comprehend why Clint would do that. Clint was just like that. You never knew what he would do next. He would do things no one else would ever think of doing. He would do them without a second thought.

Malarchuk is an excellent goalie coach and worked closely with Roberto Luongo during his time in Florida. He was excellent at explaining the mental side of the game to young goalies. Clint is a strong, strong man, and perhaps the best compliment I can give him is that he is a definite foxhole guy. You would want Clint Malarchuk in the foxhole right beside you, because he would be with you to the end.

Most expected Mike Keenan and me not to get along, but in actuality, for the most part, he let me run the Rampage as I saw fit. I really didn't know what to expect, but I gained respect for Mike on a drive back from Houston after an exhibition game with the Rampage. I told him and Director of Scouting Jack Birch that I wanted to ride back with them in their car rather than the team bus. I wanted to inject my two cents worth into the molding of the club. So Mike, Jack Birch, and I drove back from Houston. Jack wanted me to keep a player named Lou Dickenson instead of the player I wanted to keep, Greg Jacina. Jacina played for me in Mississauga. There was no way I was going to keep Dickenson. I didn't think he was any good. Jack said the Ice Dogs had drafted him too high and that they had messed him up. Well, maybe the Ice Dogs were bad because they drafted him. The coup de grace was when Jack said we should keep Dickenson because his dad was an all-star in the Canadian Football League. What the hell does that have to do with anything? I didn't want him, and the fact he was being pushed on me made me not want him even more. I said I thought Jacina was one of the best guys in camp that year. Keenan was in the front seat and was kind of quiet. I think he liked the fact I was sticking up for a player that I liked.

Then Keenan said, "Okay, Ludzy, will you *sponsor* this Jacina?"

I had never heard that terminology before. He was obviously asking me to personally stand behind, and put my stamp on, Jacina's selection.

"Absolutely, without a doubt," I quickly replied.

And Jacina was one of our better players that year. I greatly respected the fact that Keenan let me make the call on players.

It was a difficult situation towards the end of the year because we were running out of players. Between having to move players for money and our own injuries, we were a little thin on talent. We had to use several East Coast League players, who would normally not make an American Hockey League team.

With about three games left, we lost a game at home. Keenan was down to watch, and right at the end of the game, a young kid we had called up from the junior ranks, Jeremy Swanson from the Barrie Colts, got tangled up with a big broth of a guy from Houston and was going to get pummeled. It was Swanson's very first game as a pro. Even though he was 6'0," 208 pounds, he was extremely overmatched. He also made the mistake of telling his opponent he did not want to fight. The Houston tough guy started to take his gloves off, and I could tell the call up was going to get roughed up pretty good. He had already raised the white flag. So I figured I had two ways to go with this one. I could watch this young kid get the shit kicked out of him for no reason, or I could send one of our resident tough guys in there to break it up. I quickly decided on the latter.

"Get in there and break that up," I ordered.

After the game Mike, Clint Malarchuk, and I were discussing the game. Keenan observed, "Hey, you gotta love that kid for jumping in and breaking up that fight."

Malarchuk, trying to be helpful, added, "Thank God Ludzy sent him, or Swanson would have got the beating of his life!"

Everyone's nerves were shot because it was near the end of a long season. Keenan then changed his opinion of the interjection, "You didn't send that fucking kid in there, did you Ludzy?"

"Yeah, I did."

"Oh shit. Great! Now we're in line for a suspension, and we don't have enough fucking players as it is. What were you thinking?"

We started going at it. At one point, Keenan yelled right in my face, "Fuck you!"

Now, I have a funny thing about that comment. I don't mind someone telling me to "fuck off," but when someone says "fuck you," I take it a little more personal.

We ended up having a "fuck you" screaming match for five minutes until Keenan finally walked out the door. Well, Malarchuk was just busting a gut. He couldn't stop laughing at the two of us and the whole situation.

About five minutes later, I was sitting at my desk when Keenan came back in and walked over to me, and tapped me on the shoulder, and said something like, "I know, it's been a tough stretch and your nerves are a little on edge."

"MY NERVES are a little on edge?" I responded.

And sure enough, we went at it again. Clint had tears streaming down his face now. Mike left the room again. A little while later, he came back.

"I want to see the tape of that fight. I don't think it was as bad as you say."

So we got out the tape, and you could tell the incident would have had an unhappy ending. I couldn't resist and yelled at Keenan.

"There, you happy now!"

Keenan stomped out again. Five minutes later, he stuck his head in the door again and said, "Hey Ludzy, you wanna go out for Chinese food tonight?"

That was Mike Keenan. He was always a great guy to go out with. He was a lot of fun and was quick to pick up the check. Teammates always joked that I threw my nickels around like manhole covers, so I was most appreciative of that side of his character.

There were always two Mike Keenans. There was the one you saw on the bench and the one you saw away from the arena. I can't say that I really knew Mike Keenan. He's a complicated guy. All I know is that I enjoyed going out and having a beer with him after a game. I don't think he was as much of a hard ass as everyone said he was, and I think he found it difficult to keep up that persona constantly. I think Mike tried to emulate the style of Scotty Bowman but he could never quite pull it off. Keenan has had a very long, successful, coaching career, however.

The next season, San Antonio was no longer a farm team of the Florida Panthers. It had been a pretty lonely year there, being so far away from my family. My boys were tied up with school and hockey in Niagara Falls, so the family did not come down with me for those two years.

So I headed back to Niagara Falls and got hooked up with The Score television show again. I had first been contacted by the show back when I was fired by Tampa Bay. Producer Brian Spear called and asked if I wanted to work on a segment. Apparently Steve Kouleas remembered seeing me during a game at Maple Leaf Gardens when I was coaching Tampa. There was a goal we scored that had been called back that I thought was a brutal call. I made some disparaging gesture to the referee to indicate my displeasure, and Kouleas thought that I would be funny if he could ever get me on his show. So that was the genesis of it.

Steve Kouleas: We had Rick Vaive and Gord Stellick set up for the show, and Brian said we needed another guy. From the time he said we need a guy 'til the time I got back to my desk, I came up with the name Steve Ludzik. I had never met him, talked to him, or even been

in the same room. I didn't even know where he lived. We phoned the Lightning, found out he lived in Niagara Falls, and just dialed 411 and got his number. I just knew he would be good.

I went down for the first show and Gord Stellick was there. I figured it was like a local TV cable show. For the first episode, I had done no preparation whatsoever, as I did not know exactly what was involved.

Just as we were about to go on the air, they handed me an earpiece, and I asked Stellick, "Hey Gordy, where does this show go anyways? Etobicoke? Mississauga? Oakville?"

"Ludzy, this goes across Canada," he replied, surprised I didn't know.

That kind of threw me for a loop. I didn't know what I was doing to begin with. Well, I was just brutal. Brutal.

Ryan Ludzik (my son): My mom, brother, and me were watching the show, and Dad was awful. Mom just told us to tell Dad he did fine.

Steve Kouleas: The first time he was on the air, he would start a topic, and let it fizzle a little bit, and then jump on to something else. Something an old man would do in his 80s. And I thought, oh no, did I make a mistake here?

The next day, I drove around doing some errands and was listening to Gord Stellick's afternoon radio show. I will never forget that "Malcolm from Mississauga" called in and said to Gord, "*WHO* was the guy on your right last night?"

Gord replied, "He was the coach of Tampa Bay, and that was his first show." Malcolm screamed, "Well, heeeee STINKS!"

So I did a few shows after that and then went back to coaching. After finishing in San Antonio, they called me up again and asked if I wanted to do the show, this time on a more regular basis. I really enjoyed it and felt I slowly got a little more relaxed and began to be a little more like myself. We would get the game highlights from that night and recap everything from 11:00 pm to midnight several times a week.

I have done a lot of TV and radio since and really enjoy both. I especially liked doing the highlight package show several times a week with Steve Kouleas. I think the show is very professional, and I have improved a lot.

<u>Steve Kouleas</u>: Ludzy quickly got it, and he just took off from there. We have great chemistry on the air together.

I do not know where my broadcasting future will go. I have not ruled out getting back into coaching or ownership. My attempt at getting an OHL team back to the Niagara Region really got my juices going, and I have not ruled out another attempt of some sort.

For the time being, I am keeping all of my options open, and enjoy the fact that I am home a lot more than I used to be.

The Score: Al Strachan, Steve Ludzik, Erin Peterson, Steve Kouleas

It's Getting Late

Any book that I would write must include the infamous Markland Marauders, the self proclaimed ball hockey kings of street hockey. From the age of 10, we challenged all comers: streets, schools, and neighborhoods of Etobicoke. We played on streets, tennis courts, school parking lots, and in back of abandoned factories. As we grew older we took on teams from all over the Niagara Region, and in fact, North America, including Boston, Pittsburgh, Detroit, and Chicago. Every game was a battle as we looked at each other as brothers.

Steve Willie Wilson, our argumentative captain; Donny Strang, the levelheaded one; Johnny Kirk, the game breaker; and me "Lucky Ludz" in net. And I was always the goalie. "Lucky Ludz" was the nickname handed to me by my buddies for my penchant for playing net like Gerry Cheevers or Bruce Gamble. I have been called that ever since. I bounced around the net like a jitterbug, making stupendous save after stupendous save, at least in my mind. We also had Patty Graham, Mark Osborne, and Daryl Evans. Rounding out the squad were the Moon brothers, who were both 6'6" and 230 pounds of controlled mayhem. Both brothers were Canadian heavyweight wrestling champs. Over the years, we gained a reputation as the uncrowned champs of ball hockey. We belonged to no league, no organization, no governing body.

We would play after school *every* day and from 8:00 am until dark on the weekends.

Don Strang: Ludz was always up at 7:00 am and would be banging on your door at 7:30 am to play hockey. This did not endear him to everyone's parents. One word to describe Ludz is competitive. This is classic Ludz.

Everyone would take turns going in for lunch so the game could continue. We made random teams, changing them frequently, playing up to five goals, 10 goals, and rarely playing with any time limit involved. The others would laugh at me because I spent the week at school trying to organize other streets to play us.

Don Strang: Ludz would get a game at any cost; we were like a traveling side show. Never got us a home game on Burnt Log Cresent; he did crazy stuff like have a mini training camp in the summer. "If you don't run, you can't play," he would lament. And he would find opposing guys to play us that would scare the shit out of you. We'd walk six miles to play a ball hockey game at the West Mall, and the guy Ludz had engaged us to play against was a complete lunatic named Joe Dyminsk. He apparently punched out teachers, wore a dog collar to school, just a sick mother. We looked at Ludz and said, "Nice work Ludz, we're not getting out of here alive." And then he pointed to an old, beat up Volkswagen entering the parking lot and out popped the Moon brothers. We knew a little about the Moon brothers, but Ludz thought they would be a great addition. "There's our equalizer," Ludz proclaimed.

I would indeed learn a very valuable lesson that afternoon. The Moons swabbed the decks with Joe Dyminsk, a kid who petrified everybody when we were 14 years old. They ran him from stem to stern, intimidating the muscle bound thug, and slapping him around like a human piñata. When finally unveiled as a three-dollar phony, he did what all bullies do when exposed: he quit.

We decided on our team name, the Markland Marauders, because "Markland" was the name of the big community we lived in, and we figured we were the best. Like other communities throughout the country, we had some classic battles against other streets, which, in our case, included the likes of the Winsdale Warriors, Burnt Log Crashers, and the Golf Valley Greats. My sister, Karen, even came out the odd time to take pictures and sell popcorn.

One day, I organized a road game and the other guys refused to come.

<u>John Kirk</u>: Ludz surprised us one Saturday morning about a game against another street. It was another "road" game we had to play.

The other guys stood pat and said they didn't want to play. So I told everyone, "I'll take 'em on myself."

So off I went to play. I guess after about 15 minutes, when I had not returned, the rest of the guys thought they'd better come and bail me out. They finally reached me. I was running all over like a madman – hacking, slashing, shooting, diving in front of shots.

Willie yelled, "Hey Ludzy, we've come to play…what's the score?"

"3-1," I turned and yelled at them.

"No problem," Kirky said, "we'll tie it up in no time."

"What do you mean?" I said as I shot the ball into the bush to get a delay, "I'm up 3-1!"

My best friend was always the sniper on those teams. You will not find the name John William Kirk in the Hockey Hall of Fame, but everyone knows somebody who has his story.

John Kirk: Hey, my name is on the Memorial Cup, inside the Hockey Hall of Fame. Let's get that straight, big boy!

In fact, if you Google his name, you will find world explorers and sausage salesmen on your beloved computer. John Kirk was my next door neighbor and my best friend since the age of three. As I have already told you, we were line-mates all through minor hockey, and incredibly, were both drafted to the Niagara Falls Flyers Junior A team. The first year with the Flyers, along with Steve Larmer, we formed the Kid line. Kirky was, and still is, my "brother." He is the funniest person I know by a country mile and the most naturally gifted athlete I have ever known. Put a toothpick in a pool and watch him log roll it for 20 minutes.

John Kirk is also a foxhole guy. Before you say, "who the hell is John Kirk and who cares about his story," take a listen to this and you will learn a lot. His story is not uncommon in the hockey world. The great Doug Gilmour was quoted as saying the odds of getting hit by lightning are greater than making it to the National Hockey League. I'm not sure what the odds are of being belted by a bolt from above, but I think you get the point. Hall of Famer Dale Hawerchuk and the aforementioned Gilmour both echoed similar thoughts at a recent gathering. They both said John Kirk was maybe the most dominant player on their team that won the Memorial Cup in 1981. Why, or how, did my best buddy get hoodwinked out of a chance to play in the apple? He was a strong skater, had a great nose for the net, was big and strong, and simply a natural. His rocky road was unique.

I read a story about Bobby Orr running at night in the dark with old work boots on to strengthen his legs and cardio. If it was good enough for Bobby Orr, it was good enough for Steve Ludzik. And here's the difference of why some just make it and some just miss. I would always try to get Kirky to come along but he was never really interested. We would always joke about the three B's that Kirky excelled at: booze, broads, and buffoonery. My good friend was not going to get cheated in any of those departments. He was always the life of the party.

Paul Coffey's dad, Jack, once said he knew his son would make the NHL when he missed a high school dance to attend an optional practice. I think this is a keen observation by a very smart man. If you wanna dance, you gotta pay the fiddler. In Kirky's case, he just left a big tip. Kirky and I have closed down many a watering hole over the years, and we would always come back to that old "what happened" scenario. John Kirk is also one of the most honest men I know. He does not shy away from the question and knows the answer.

I have often said on my TV gig that great hockey players are born, they are not made, but one trait that must be in their DNA is the ability to have discipline and to drive themselves individually. Kirky was traded twice in his junior career: once from Niagara Falls to Sudbury, and then from Sudbury to Cornwall, where he won that Memorial Cup. He played two seasons in Muskegon in the old IHL. In his second year, he scored 46 goals and dominated. That summer, I ran into his coach, Doug McKay Sr. and was mystified why my best friend could not get a sniff in the Show. Mr. McKay said that Kirky was a character for sure, and he knew he could score a lot of goals, but he could not score on breakaways, and he would get three or four a game. Boy, that sounds like a reason not to give a guy a shot. He was not going to get a chance.

This would not be a tragic story. John Kirk would not look back in anger. He was stick handling in the dark and knew nobody was watching. He was fed up to the gills with the life altering decisions the suits would make. Yeah, his hair was long, longer than most. Yeah, he liked a good time and was always the most popular guy on his team, but at 23 years of age, he had seen enough. Like a man with a stomach ulcer gobbling down a spicy jalapeño laced burrito, he knew it was gonna hurt, but he stopped playing the game he loved, and with courage, he went back to school at Guelph University. He did not play hockey the first year while attending class full time but was enticed to play for the university squad in his second year. He found the competition a joke and not stimulating enough and decided to put all of his energy towards school.

My best friend is not going to go insane over the fact he did not make it. He was probably more talented than 80 percent of the guys who played in the NHL or AHL. Kirky is content, as I would be, to know he was a top end guy who never got a break. All of his close friends would concur. So all the stars have to align for you to make it to the Show. You have to have ability, luck, courage, determination, dedication and attitude. I am happy to report that John William Kirk has been in the sports distributing business for several years, and at this writing, is an executive with a major sports manufacturer.

I look back at all the players I coached and see that they had a lot more pressures on them than in my era. I don't think that can be underestimated. I take great pride in the fact I usually get three or four calls a week from former players that I coached in Muskegon, Detroit, Tampa Bay, San Antonio, and Mississauga. Most of them are now in various walks of life, but still phone me to tell me how they are doing, or to ask advice on a variety of matters. I took a lot of passion to the game of hockey and did not take losing lightly. That made me be extremely hard on some of my players but deep down, most of them knew that when push came to shove, I would push back for them and help them. The greatest thing about coaching, especially in the younger ranks, is the fact you can mold young men into being a benefit to society. There could be no greater honor. If you are just there for simply running the practices and winning the games, you are in the wrong business.

I treasure all the great people I encountered in this great game and look forward to continuing the journey in whatever facet of the game I am involved in.

Steve Ludzik, Steve Wilson, John Kirk, Don Strang

Okay, Last Call

It was Grade Six and my teacher, Miss Ansara, had just posed a question to her class. "What do you want to be when you grow up?"

There were two days left until summer vacation, and looking back, she was probably just killing time. As each student sprung from their chair like an uncoiling Jack in the Box, they delivered the standard answers one by one.

"Police officer," "banker," "fireman," "nurse" (we always wondered about that guy afterwards).

One chiseler even said "millionaire," which I thought was pretty lame. I was always in the back of the class, if I was not already brandished to the hall where my high jinks would be quarantined from the scholars of the class. I had no reservations about what I was going say. The teacher pointed to me. I stood up, cleared my throat, and announced to all my ambition.

"I want to play in the National Hockey League," I boldly declared.

The class broke into hyena-like laughter, and for a brief second, I thought my zipper was down. My teacher, who was wonderful, quickly silenced the masses.

"Everyone should have a dream," she wisely spoke.

Everybody should have a dream, and my friend, there are dream makers and dream breakers. The dream makers are the people you meet who balance the scales and are in the foxhole with you. The dream breakers are the takers who kick you when you are down, and not only are they not in the foxhole with you, but they will lob a grenade in there when you are not looking. I've made a lot of friends along the way and some enemies, too. I'm not Switzerland. I'm not neutral. Silence gives consent, and I have never been accused of

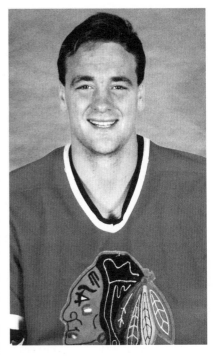

being silent. I have been blessed with great friends from an early age, and we rarely, if ever, talk about my hockey exploits. To my lifelong pals Kirky, Willie, the Strangler, and the Moon brothers, I'm just "Lucky Ludz," the ball hockey goaltender for the legendary Markland Marauders.

John Kirk: Ludzy is a love him or leave him guy, there's no middle ground. His dad, 'the Bear,' my dad, Bert Templeton, Don Cherry, Orval Tessier, and Rick Dudley – all very strong personalities. The man's my brother. We laugh at the same things, talk the same, and finish each other's thoughts.

My favorite singer is Frank Sinatra, "Old Blue Eyes," because every song he ever sang, you could hear him tell a story. He could tell it because he had lived it; the ups and downs, the good and the bad, and he had the beautiful ability to get up when he was knocked down. If you listened closely to him singing, you could tell that this was a man who had a lot of laughs, a few close friends, and some heartache. Come to think of it, kind of like a lot of us, I guess.

I've regaled you with lots of stories and took you from a hospital bed in Toronto to the roar of Niagara Falls. We've traveled from a barroom battle in Moncton, New Brunswick to the rabble rousing confines of old Chicago Stadium. I've let you feel the adulation of being wanted as a player and exalted as a NHL coach, and also shared with you the inevitable decline of athletic talent and the execution like experience in Tampa Bay. I promised you that you would meet the good, the bad, and the ugly, the tough and the talented, and the devoted and the demented. I think I kept my word.

My friends, the fridge is bare, the bar is empty, and my wife is giving me the "let's go" nudge; she's heard all these stories before. I hope you enjoyed yourself...the best is yet to come.

About the Authors

Steve Ludzik played for the National Hockey League Chicago Blackhawks for nine years from 1981-1989. Before that, from 1977-80, he had a distinguished junior career with the Niagara Falls Flyers of the Ontario Hockey League, amassing an incredible 125 goals, 233 assists, and 358 points, breaking the career point total record for the Flyers, which still stands today. He was named to the Five Man All Star Flyer team of All Time. He then turned to coaching where he first coached the Muskegon Fury of the IHL for two years before moving on to the IHL and the Detroit Vipers for four years, where he won a Turner Cup with General Manager Rick Dudley.

Ludzik and Dudley teamed up again when Steve was named the head coach of the Tampa Bay Lightning of the NHL in 1999. He was fired a year and a half later and was promptly hired to coach the Mississauga Ice Dogs of the OHL, leading them the next year to the first playoff appearance of the team's existence. He then joined the Florida Panthers organization, where he served as head coach for their American Hockey League affiliate, the San Antonio Rampage, and then as an assistant coach with the Panthers.

For the past several years, he has been on The Score television station, usually doing highlight packages with Steve Kouleas. In 2009, he was inducted into the Etobicoke Sports Hall of Fame. He lives in Niagara Falls with his wife Mary Ann, and two boys, Stephen (23), Ryan (21), and American Bull Dog Derby.

Steve Wilson is a lifelong friend of Steve Ludzik and has enjoyed his stories for years. He resides in Oakville with his wife Cathy, son Scott (17), daughter Kendyl (15), and dog Macie.

Visit www.ludzy.com for more information on this book and other hockey items.

Sponsors